Jonny Bealby wa[...] [...]tland and
Canada, he developed [...] [...]g college
journeyed exten[...] [...]en he has
earned a crust [...] [...]rse rider,
circus roustabout, motorcycle courier and photo-journalist to name but a
few. As a writer and traveller he has visited more than seventy countries
and has had features in a variety of publications including the *Daily
Telegraph, Observer, Elle, Global* and *Traveller Magazine*. He is also the author
of *Running with the Moon* and *Silk Dreams, Troubled Road* and now runs the
adventure travel company Wild Frontiers (www.wildfrontiers.co.uk).
While not travelling, he lives in London.

Praise for Jonny Bealby

For a Pagan Song

'Entrancing... compelling... completely engaging... The very best of the
summer's travel books.' – *Daily Mail*

'A rollicking tale... No one has written a better travel book about the
region since Eric Newby came down from the Hindu Kush.' – *Daily
Telegraph*

'Rudyard Kipling's *The Man Who Would Be King* is a classic tale from the
golden age of Victorian adventure. By following in the footsteps of
Peachey Carnehan and Daniel Dravot, Jonny Bealby courageously echoes
the spirit of those daring times.' – *Michael Caine*

Silk Dreams, Troubled Road

'A truly enthralling book.' – *Daily Mail*

'Reads like a cross between Ray Mears' *Extreme Survival* and *Streetmate*. An
incredible adventure.' – *OK! Magazine*

Running with the Moon

'Honest and passionate, one of the best travel books I've read.' – *GQ*

'Bealby handles this tragic tale with endearing honesty and tenderness. It
is the romantic's naivety, not to mention his irrepressible energy, optimism
and courage, which charm the reader.' – *Daily Telegraph*

FOR A PAGAN SONG

In the Footsteps of the Man Who Would Be King: Travels in India, Pakistan and Afghanistan

Jonny Bealby

Published by Arrow Books in 2004

3 5 7 9 10 8 6 4 2

The author would like to thank A.P. Watt on behalf of the National Trust for
permission to quote from Rudyard Kipling's *The Man Who Would Be King* and *If*.

First published in the United Kingdom in 1998 by William Heinemann
First paperback edition published in 1999 by Arrow Books

Arrow Books
The Random House Group Limited
20 Vauxhall Bridge Road, London, SW1V 2SA

Random House Australia (Pty) Limited
20 Alfred Street, Milsons Point, Sydney,
New South Wales 2061, Australia

Random House New Zealand Limited ·
18 Poland Road, Glenfield
Auckland 10, New Zealand

Random House (Pty) Limited
Endulini, 5a Jubilee Road, Parktown 2193, South Africa

The Random House Group Limited Reg. No. 954009

www.randomhouse.co.uk

A CIP catalogue record for this book
is available from the British Library

Papers used by Random House are natural, recyclable products made from wood
grown in sustainable forests. The manufacturing processes conform to the envi-
ronmental regulations of the country of origin

ISBN 0 09 943673 6

Printed and bound in Great Britain by
Bookmarque Ltd, Croydon, Surrey

For my parents, with love and thanks.

Contents

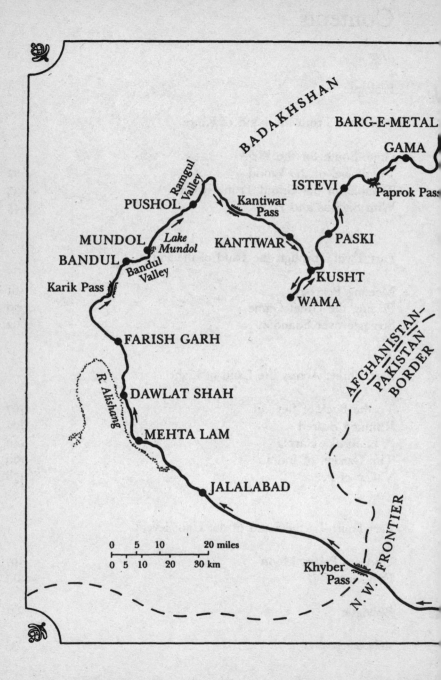

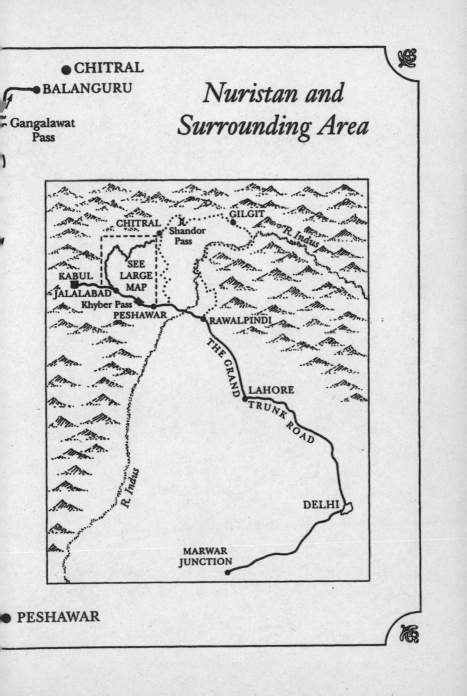

CHITRAL

BALANGURU

Gangalawat
Pass

*Nuristan and
Surrounding Area*

CHITRAL

GILGIT

Shandor
Pass

R. Indus

KABUL

SEE
LARGE
MAP

JALALABAD

Khyber Pass

PESHAWAR

RAWALPINDI

THE GRAND

LAHORE

TRUNK ROAD

R. Indus

DELHI

MARWAR
JUNCTION

PESHAWAR

The dolphins are jumping again. From the veranda of my hut I sit and watch as they gambol through the clear water just beyond the surf. They jump in pairs, glistening silver beneath the Indian sun. When I arrived last week the beach was deserted. Thick black clouds rumbled overhead, palms swayed and a warm rain drove hard against the sand. The fishermen said it would be the last of the storms. It looks as if they were right.

It's almost a month since I saw the mountains, the snow, the trembling rivers and the giant pines; almost a month since I felt the chill edge of winter's hand. But if I close my eyes I'm there again, on the ridge above the valley, beneath the pale moon, listening to the haunting song.

Prologue

*'Tell me all you can recollect of everything,
from the beginning to the end.'*

By the age of twenty-one I had never read a book. And though I'm
now ashamed to say it, I was actually rather proud of the fact.
'Reading's boring,' I confidently told my new girlfriend, Melanie,
who seemed to devour books by the dozen. My world appeared
new and enthralling, bursting with all manner of experiences. I
didn't have time to read, there was too much else going on.

But the excitements of life were not the real reason I'd never read
a book. I had plenty of friends playing just as hard as I who still
managed to waltz through a couple of novels a month. No, I had
the concentration span of an Andrex puppy and to make matters
worse I was dyslexic, which made reading a chore. This caused my
school days to be something of a pain – both for my teachers and
for me.

'Bealby,' Mr Bolan, my English master, would say, pushing a
hand through his greasy hair, 'you read the part of Coriolanus . . .
Come on, boy, stand up.' Page after page of Shakespearean
monologue? I would rather have pushed pins into my eyes. The
thought was preposterous, and well the seemingly sadistic Mr Bolan
knew it. How could I stand up in front of my class, most of whom I
was keen to impress, and mumble in a pathetically disjointed and
unintelligible way? I tried, believe me, but the humiliation was
excruciating. So instead I made fun, somehow playing the fool in
order to get the class laughing; it was all I could think of to save
face. The outcome was usually the same. A low flying blackboard
rubber would whiz past my ear with a reddening Mr Bolan
bellowing, 'You useless boy, you'll never go anywhere . . . Now get
out, get out!' Regrettably, in retrospect, I spent as much time

outside his classroom as I did in it. In all I took my English language O level five times and never attained higher than a grade 'E'.

It was when I arrived home one evening, a couple of months after my twenty-first birthday and a few weeks after meeting Melanie, that things changed. She was sitting on the sofa, a slightly strained smile on her face. 'I've bought you a present,' she announced as I sat down beside her. And from her bag she withdrew a neatly wrapped rectangular object – obviously a book.

I could tell she was nervous, so was I. For all my bravado about reading, the real reason for my aversion was, as I've said, more complicated than that I found it 'boring'. The last thing I wanted was this wonderful girl, who was already particularly special to me, thinking that I was incapable of enjoying something that obviously meant so much to her. She might not understand and think me stupid. I could see in her eyes and by the expression on her face that a boyfriend who never read – especially one as apparently indifferent to the concept as me – was of little use to her. This was no simple present. It was a gesture, even a challenge, that might well decide our future: read the book or take a hike. To hell with exams, for the first time in my life I was really going to be forced to read.

With trepidation I removed the paper.

The cover showed two magisterial elephants, draped in golden cloth, with painted heads and bejewelled tusks, royalty on their backs and guards at their sides, parading past an ornate Indian palace. Colourful crowds in silk robes, turbans and saris lined the street, gazed through arches and watched from the balconies above. It was an evocative picture, foreign and exotic, and it made me smile. At the top was written 'World Classics'. It was Rudyard Kipling's *The Man Who Would Be King*.

Selected because of Melanie's passion for anything Indian, it was an inspired choice: the short stories were not too taxing for my fragile concentration and appealed to my love of travel. But it was the title story that really drew me in, catapulting my imagination to an entirely new realm. Following the journey of two loveable rogues, Peachy Carnehan and Daniel Dravot, from northern India, through what is now Pakistan and Afghanistan to become Kings of

Kafiristan, it transported me into a pagan world of fierce tribesmen and strange customs, of fighting mountains and marching plains, searing heat and deathly cold.

The name of the land itself was instantly fascinating to me: the hard attack of 'Ka', followed by a threatening 'fear', closing with the hissing 'issstaaan' ... it sounded as if it must be the most mysterious, far off, impossible to reach travel destination on the planet. A place that couldn't really survive in the modern world, and was sure to exist only in history or fiction: uncharted, outlandish and dangerously exciting. Even the origins of its people were steeped in romantic adventure, descended, Kipling maintained, from the armies of Alexander the Great, who, while still only in his thirties, was one of the greatest, most heroic warriors the world has ever seen.

Much more than a captivating tale, *The Man Who Would Be King* struck a powerful chord within me. The setting was a bygone age where adventure was a trade and courage, honour and daring were its qualifications. 'If you can keep your head when those about you are losing theirs ...', as Kipling later wrote. I sensed a powerful affinity with this intrepid pair of vagabond misfits who had shaped their destinies and made their dreams come true. Their education and careers hadn't amounted to much. Neither had mine. They dreamed of adventure. So did I. We seemed kindred spirits and I felt foolishly inspired. Amazing myself, I read the story twice in a week, struggling at first, but with Melanie's help sailing through by the end. From that day to this I can honestly say I have never been without a book.

Melanie died some years ago while we were travelling in Kashmir. In the five years we spent together we shared many wonderful times and an extraordinary understanding and trust. I was a small man when I met Melanie; through her love and wisdom I was shown the world. But of all the legacies she left me, one that I am now particularly thankful to her for is introducing me to the joy of reading.

In the aftermath of Melanie's death, attempting to deal with the havoc it wreaked upon my life, I set off around Africa on a motor bike with a notebook and camera to record my travels. The unexpected result of this was *Running with the Moon*, a book I wrote about the cathartic, life-changing experience of driving a grieving heart across that wild continent. And so Melanie ultimately enabled me to call myself something I'd never dreamed I could be: a published author.

The problem this fantastic, completely unforeseeable career development threw up was: where did that leave me now? Into my thirties I still hadn't a clue. Did *Running with the Moon* really make me a writer, or, given the personal nature of the tale, was it just a one-off? Should I remember Mr Bolan's damning words, leave literature in more gifted hands and return to being a musician or photographer, a sound engineer, strawberry farmer, motor cycle courier, waiter, stunt horse rider or any of the umpteen occupations with which I seem to have dallied at one time or another? Or should I say, what the hell, though Mr Bolan might well be right he also might be wrong.

After the first rush of euphoria at being published had faded, the answer was clear, if daunting: I wanted to write and I wanted to travel — what better job could there be? It had been more than three years since the African adventure. How I longed to feel that freedom again. To live life in that exaggerated form where everything you see and do is new and exciting; to witness life closer to the edge, treating each day as though it may be your last. To escape one's own reality and live for a while in some other world.

I had spent time in the bush, jungle, mountains and deserts, and London had a job to compete. I wasn't unhappy, just bored, treading water. There were few commitments burdening my life. Hoping a new soul-mate could fill the void left by Melanie, I'd married Amel, an amazing spirit I had met on my African travels. Whether because of my own personal demons, or just a basic incompatibility between us, the marriage had floundered for a while before finally crashing fatally against the rocks. The flat I was renting was soon to be sold. And I was painfully aware that if I didn't act fast the slender thread I'd managed to weave on to the edge of English literature's colourful carpet would be lost in the shadows and forgotten. Wherever I was heading I needed direction and it came at the flick of a switch.

Back at my flat after a weekend away, I turned on the television and settled down with a glass of Glenlivet, expecting to be bored to sleep by some Sunday night twaddle. How wrong I was. *'And whose loss is it anyway? Why England's of course. If such as you and me were given our heads it isn't 70 millions they'd be making but 700 millions . . . Right?'* Before the picture cleared on the screen I knew what I was watching and happily put my feet up on the coffee table and lit myself a cigarette. In a dusty Indian railway carriage, on the to Marwar Junction, Peachey Carnehan was berating the colonial government for stifling commercial opportunism. Looking into his impassioned face Kipling, to whom the comment had been addressed, felt disposed to agree.

As I watched John Huston's excellent film adaptation of *The Man Who Would Be King*, with Michael Caine and Sean Connery superbly cast as Carnehan and Dravot, and Christopher Plumber as the erudite writer, I was struck by the thought I had originally entertained all those years ago when I'd first fallen under Kipling's spell: how I'd love to follow Peachey and Danny on their quest to become Kings of Kafiristan. Back then I was just a kid, buzzing around London, happy and in love, thinking more about cars, bars and electric guitars, and the dream had remained fantasy. But now I was free and looking for a challenge. From India and Pakistan, through the Northwest Frontier, over the Khyber Pass and into Afghanistan, to cross the Hindu Kush and find a pagan tribe, possibly descended from Alexander the Great: if ever there was another journey for me to undertake I knew in an instant that this was it. To break free from reality once more and escape into fiction in the redoubtable footsteps of my greatest friends from English literature – why, they would be my guides and companions on a real adventure, Victorian style. A journey to, well . . . Shangri-La. *Romantic loon!*

For a time, Peachey and Danny had fulfilled their quest. They became Kings of Kafiristan – complete with an army, law courts, revenue and policy. If this renegade pair could become rulers of a nation, why couldn't this ill-qualified bum become a real author and write a second book? It was just the inspiration I needed.

When the film finished I went over to the cluttered bookshelf above the hi-fi and pulled down Kipling's tale. The cover had faded, the spine was split and the corners were bent and creased, but just holding it in my hand revived memories and brought a thoughtful grin to my face. I wiped the dust off on my jeans and turned to the first page. In Melanie's rounded hand was written: 'From the reader to the traveller, I hope the two combine . . .'

PART ONE

From the Land of Kings

1 Gone South for the Week

'A wanderer and vagabond like myself,
with an educated taste for whisky.'

There had been a commotion.

The regional stopper to Jodhpur had ground to a halt two hours short of Marwar Junction. Beyond the iron-barred window a landscape bleached and rough shimmered silver through the morning haze. Dried out river beds lined by wilting acacias and parched neems stretched like wrinkles across the pale land to where the Khamli Ghats rose purple in the distance. On a stone track, running parallel to the railway, camels wandered and goats foraged. The air moved by thermals. Dust climbed.

It didn't take long for the passengers to begin to fidget, look anxiously around, exude restless sighs. Getting to their feet some leaned out of the open doorways and peered back towards the rear of the train, the more inquisitive among them jumping down on to the hard yellow chippings to discuss the situation in uneasy groups. From my hard bench seat I could just see the guard and ticket inspector standing by a telegraph pole deep in conversation. They too were looking concerned.

The troubled faces surprised me. An unscheduled stop on one of India's numerous branch lines was hardly a cause for great concern. On this graceful form of transport delays are normal; the timetable is only a rough guide, engines are old – still steam in places – and frequently break down and maintenance work or gauge conversions can often leave you kicking your heels in the siding of some dusty backwater for hours on end. Over the past ten years major improvements have been made to the mainline services, with trains that travel the entire length of the country regularly arriving on time. But this advancement in efficiency has passed the branch lines by. That's how it is, the people know it and usually no one cares. You sit and wait, reading the papers, listening to cricket, eating from your tiffin carrier or just staring vacantly into the middle distance happy with the knowledge that if you aren't at your destination today you probably will be tomorrow, and that's just fine.

The train shuddered as though shivering from cold. The haunting wh*oooh* from the engine's whistle sounded way off down the line, then one by one the carriages clanked together to take the strain and the train began to move . . . backwards. I looked at my turbaned neighbour and asked for an explanation but he just shrugged, tweaked the tips of his buffalo horn moustache, spat a great jet of paan across the floor and returned to scratching his genitals. He wasn't much of a conversationalist.

After a minute or so the train stopped again. This time I rose with the others and followed them out of the carriage to the rear of the train. Lying in a heap at the foot of a shallow embankment, just beyond the guard's van, were the crumpled and twisted remains of a young man. By his head the ground was stained dark with blood. A crowd of curiosity-seekers had gathered, forming a semi-circle around the poor wretch. Neither especially frightened nor wholly at ease, they murmured quietly to each other, shifting their weight from one foot to the other, or pointed vaguely at the dead man's remains. Apparently he'd fallen asleep while sitting next to an open doorway. As the train rattled over a particularly bumpy set of points he had lost his balance, fallen from the carriage and dashed his brains out on the rocky ground below. By the time the train had stopped, reversed and reached him, he had died – or expired as the Indians like to say.

The problem was what to do with him now. The guard and ticket inspector pushed to the front, full of self-importance, and started the debate. Some, it seemed, were not overly keen on carrying the corpse on the train, citing it as inauspicious. One old dark man whose white dhoti and grey stubble gave him the appearance of a photographic negative, began gesticulating madly. Reciting something or other from the Vedas – the divine knowledge of Hindu philosophy – he claimed the gods would be angry and bring calamity to us all. But most agreed that we could hardly leave the unfortunate man there. With the train on the edge of the Great Indian Desert, the corpse would be at the mercy of the vultures and jackals – a terrible situation for the man's rebirth. There were no buildings close by and with the sun high, precious little shade. Besides, as the ticket inspector pointed out, having rummaged through the dead man's pockets, he had a valid ticket to Jodhpur and should be entitled to use it. The man might have a wife waiting for him there, he pondered. The decision taken, the corpse was scooped up, thrust through the carriage door and plonked on to a seat. And once a blanket had been placed over the battered skull and the old man had been calmed, the train rolled on.

I resumed my position by the open window, looked out across the barren land and smiled to myself. It had been an eventful twenty-four hours. I'd left Udaipur late the previous afternoon on a bus driven by the devil incarnate. Relying on the fact that he was the biggest lump of metal on the tarmac he'd torn down the centre of the road, horn blasting, lights flashing, driving for all the world as if his cargo was the president of some world super-power late for a summit rather than a few peasants and a lone backpacker. Everything that didn't want to risk a head-on collision was forced off the road and into the scrub. Oblivious to my profuse sweating, dilated pupils and intermittent cries of 'Fuuuuuck!' he threw the vehicle around, leaning from one side to the other more in the manner of a motor cyclist than a coach driver. Either the man had a profound belief in reincarnation and had come to the conclusion that a Rajasthani bus driver was about as low as you can get on life's great wheel or his supper had consisted of a couple of bottles of whisky. None of us had been disappointed when the gear box seized. A night sleeping rough under the sheltering arms of a peepal tree had been a blessed relief.

Then in the morning, while wandering the bazaar, much to the joy of all who'd seen, I had been knocked to the ground by a cow trying to avoid the copulatory advances of a large red bull, in the process cutting my big toe in an open sewer. The doctor I'd found to disinfect my shit-smeared foot had told me I was lucky. A Canadian girl he'd heard about had fallen through a manhole cover and been completely submerged in effluence. She had survived, just, but had subsequently become a little loopy in the head. I didn't doubt it.

And now this death. Not knowing the man I couldn't feel too sad. In fact, to be brutally honest, I found the drama rather enthralling. A man falling from a train, dying, a debate between hundreds – India is after all the world's largest democracy – a corpse being sat back in his seat because his ticket was still valid, all in the vain hope of delivering him to his imaginary wife. It was just so Indian. A situation common enough to be practically normal here you wouldn't witness in the UK if you lived for a thousand years. Some may say, thank God for that, and it certainly would be a pain if people regularly tumbled from the 8.15 Brighton to Victoria. Imagine the delays! But that's India – anything can happen and usually does.

As one fellow traveller put it to me: 'It's the only place on the planet where everything that has ever happened in the history of the world is happening every minute of every day, right under your nose.' He's right. I mean where else could I have watched a cow casually give birth in the middle of a three-lane inner-city ring road or seen vultures swoop to pick the flesh of recently deceased humans? Where else could I have observed a camel wandering the streets under a mountain of straw while being shaved by a blind man on the pavement? And where indeed at three in the morning after a riotous midnight dinner could I have abandoned my dangerously drunk taxi driver in favour of an enormous elephant called Rubkali with 'STOP – HORN PLEASE!' painted across her arse? Though not always pleasant, travelling here is about ten times more intense than anywhere else I've been; a vitality unmatchable.

Of course there are also days of hair-pulling frustration. Days when those trains just don't run on time, leaving you stranded at some tiny, fly-infested village station for fourteen hours. When the only rickshaw driver around demands an extortionate fee. Times when the exasperation of ordering a meal from a menu . . . hell, just ordering the menu, will leave you feeling capable of sadism that Joseph Mengele never even thought of. But these days are rare and, though usually for different reasons, can happen anywhere.

India was a land I had longed to explore since childhood. My grandfather was a colonel and surgeon in the British Army Medical

Corps stationed in India during the dying days of the Raj and ever since I can remember India has loomed large within my psyche. As a child, my grandmother would show me old black and white photos of their homes in Bangalore and Cochin, or of their holidays in the north. She'd tell me stories about the bazaars, riding the tongas and about people she had known with strange sounding names. Even my mother, who spent only the first five years of her life in the country, could remember some things: her dog Bonzo, cobras under the bath and having to drink some foul gunk to remove the tapeworm that had found a home in her gut.

Of course, I had been to India before. But Melanie and I had decided to go straight to Kashmir, with a view to travelling the rest of the country later. Only that never happened. Melanie died in Kashmir. For three weeks we'd floated on the lakes, walked in the hills and watched the eagles fly. We'd both gone to paradise but only I'd returned.

So you see, in my mind India owed me. It had claimed Melanie's life, thus, in a way, ending the first stage of my own, and also deprived me of the opportunity to see a country I longed to experience. My mother had been born here and the girl who was to have become my wife had died here. The ghosts of Hindustan had been with me for an age and I was eager to set them free.

With a sudden jolt the train slowed. Forcing my face against the window bars I could see the beginnings of a small town. A black water tower stood on stilts above faded buildings surrounded by hard waste ground. A group of kids played a game of cricket, kicking up dust as they scampered to and fro, and a herd of buffalo wallowed in a weed-covered pond. The battered old train was finally pulling into Marwar Junction and something in my stomach was spinning like a top.

I stood up and pushed towards the open door, forcing my way past a family of four seated on the floor. Like Kipling before me, I was to change trains here on to the mainline heading north. A mass of mud shacks with iron roofs, many draped in plastic tarpaulins, was sucked in by the track, some so close I could have leaned out and touched them. Women, their brilliant saris dazzling against the pale walls, squatted beside piles of dung cakes, crushing chillies and rolling out bread. Their children shrieked and began to wave. Then the platform disdainfully forced them away behind white iron railings. The train slowed further, then shuddered to a stop.

Grabbing my bag, I climbed down on to the platform. What had been a quiet place exploded into a riot of life. Those of us disembarking were suddenly swamped by a mass of hawkers, beggars and dogged porters. The piercing cries of the refreshment wallahs sliced through the air, easily drowning out the station announcer and the train's hissing brakes. A pack of stray dogs howled at the commotion and chased a boar under a carriage. Even the sadhus – Hindu holy men – momentarily took to their feet, looking confused, wondering to which destination the train was heading. Passengers filled water bottles, lit beedies, bought food, relieved themselves against the nearest wall, and officials ran about like startled cockerels, blowing whistles, waving flags and ignoring questions. So timeless seemed the station I half expected to see Kipling's short sinewy figure rushing along the carriages, looking for Danny so he could deliver Peachey's message. But there was only one Englishman there today. Then the engine's whistle blew again and all who were leaving clambered aboard. The train moved on, clattering north through the rest of the town to head out into the desert once more.

On the platform, kiosks and refreshment wallahs offered chai, samosas, curry and parothas, fruit, newspapers and a mobile mini-mart wheel barrow was selling everything from babies' botty powder to screwdrivers, batteries and pink plastic ray-guns. Just opposite the waiting room a fat man was making omelettes on a contraption that more closely resembled a pram than a stove. Having some time to wait for my connection, I bought one and sat in the shade on the steps to the iron walkway that crossed the tracks.

With the train gone, peace had been restored. The ancient porters who might well have been doing the same job during the Raj, sat on their trolleys, re-lit their beedies, and hacked happily as they let out the smoke. The stray dogs left the boar alone to chew on a plastic cup and settled in the shade to scratch their fleas. A young girl with one leg severed just above the knee begged a rupee, her mother telling me she'd lost it to the Ahmadabad Mail while playing last March. The near-naked sadhus returned to their haunches and a cow lowered herself on the vacated line. Even the large brown rat that crawled out next to me to consume the crust of my discarded bread seemed so at ease that I didn't flinch. I just let him carry on with his business, as calmly and quietly as everyone else. Taking my battered copy of *The Man Who Would Be King* from my bag, I leaned back against the railings and began to read ...

'We have been most things in our time,' said Dravot. 'Soldier, sailor, compositor, photographer, proof-reader, street-preacher, and correspondents ... We have been all over India, mostly on foot ... and we have decided that she isn't big enough for such as us. The country isn't half worked out because they that governs it won't let you touch it. Therefore we shall let it alone, and go away to some other place where a man can come into his own ... we're going away to be Kings ... Kings of Kafiristan.'

I was filled with an overwhelming sense of kinship for my fictional friends as I reread Danny's words to Kipling – I could practically hear his gruff voice in my ear. Sitting in Marwar Junction, where Kipling's tale takes shape, my imagination was fired as it had been ten years earlier. Here I was, like Peachey and Danny, with many 'professions' behind me, preparing once again to play by my own rules and embark on a hazardous journey to an uncertain destination. Riding their coat-tails all the way to Kafiristan I would throw myself backwards in time to an era of opportunism, diplomacy, tactics and disguise. From now on rent, careers, relationships, even football results, would mean little.

Though I felt a strong connection with Peachey, it was with Danny, the leader of the pair, that my heart really lay. *'I won't make a nation,' says he. 'I'll make an empire ... Oh it's big! It's big, I tell you!'* For him fate and fortune were wrapped up in this desperate roll of the dice: a challenge and a chance to break the bonds of the world he knew and become something greater. A king. A god even. While my ambitions were not quite so lofty, deep down I felt sure that I too was now set on a path that would lead me further than Kafiristan; to other revelations, other discoveries.

After a while I picked up my bag and ambled along the platform to the ticket office where a group of uniformed men was gathered around a television.

'Excuse me,' I said to no one in particular, 'what time does the Delhi Mail come through?'

'Thirty-nine for two in the twelfth,' came a voice in reply. It was as well I was an Englishman or I might have thought the bloke mad. I couldn't see the screen and had no idea what they were watching. Of course I should have been able to guess. There's nothing but cricket on Indian television that would have the same effect – well, except *Baywatch*.

'That's great,' I tried again,'but what time does the Delhi Mail pass through Marwar Junction and can I have a ticket?'

This time the station master turned and reluctantly got to his feet. His uniform had seen better days. A pocket peeled away from the main body of the jacket and the collar was frayed. A long and crooked nose carried a thick pair of plastic-rimmed glasses and pinned to his breast pocket was a name tag. It read, VK Patel.

'Actually speaking, you will not be getting a sleeper berth,' he said in a clipped, sing-song voice. 'All tickets have been sold in Ahmadabad. Second Class General only now. And it vill be coming through Marvar at 6.15.' He looked at his watch. 'One hour and thirty minutes pre*eee*cisely.'

I'd known securing a sleeper berth on a train half way through its journey would be a problem. Second Class General was really just a polite way of saying Third Class Crap: open carriages with slatted bench seats, packed to the gills. Still, there was little option.

When the train arrived, on time, an hour and a half later, I found a section where I could at least sit down. There were twelve of us – fourteen if you include the two babies that lay in makeshift hammocks strung between the luggage racks – occupying a space designed for eight. No one spoke English and everyone chewed betel, its strange bittersweet odour hanging in the air like cheap perfume. What space wasn't occupied by the living was crammed with luggage of various sizes and forms.

I knew it wouldn't be long before the food came out. Placed on top of a central suitcase, there would be vegetable curry, raw chillies, a pile of chapatis, chopped onions and poppadams. It would be shared amongst all; in this class it always is. After that there would be much farting and belching, spitting and smoking. The men would drink cheap whisky with exotic sounding names –

Officers' Choice, Ambassador, Secret Agent – and start playing cards, the women would chatter and the babies would cry. By midnight I would be cold, hideously uncomfortable and with eight hours of the journey still remaining, ready to sell my soul to be anywhere else.

But right then as the train pulled out of Marwar Junction, I have to say I was very contented. I opened my book again to have another read but soon, distracted by my own adventure, my eyes slipped up from the page and stared out at the evening sky. Would I, like Peachey and Danny, really find Kafiristan? Geographically, I knew that things did not look hopeful.

Since that night in my flat watching Peachey and Danny struggling over the mountains to find their hidden land and become the pagans' kings, I'd learned a fair bit more about this magical land – and the risks involved in getting there. 'Don't go! You'd be lucky to make it back alive,' a worried professor and expert on the region had exclaimed, echoing Kipling's words of warning to Peachey and Danny. But he introduced me to two books on the subject and through them I had discovered a great deal. Located in north-eastern Afghanistan, Kafiristan remained barely touched by the outside world. Curiously though, its name had been changed.

In 1893, some years after Peachey and Danny's escapade and towards the end of the Great Game – the epic, century-long game of attrition fought out by Imperial Britain and Tsarist Russia for control of Central Asia – the Durrant Line, defining Afghanistan's eastern border, had been established by the British. Designed primarily to create a buffer between the two great powers, it placed Kafiristan on the Afghan side of the border. The Afghan Amir, Abdul Rahman – known by his subjects as the 'Iron Amir' – siezed this as the opportunity to invade the country, convert the unruly infidels to Islam and annexe their land. One hundred years ago, in what was probably the last forced mass conversion in history, Kafiristan, meaning land of the unbelievers, was wiped out and renamed Nuristan, the land of light.

Situated towards the southern end of the mighty Hindu Kush mountain range, Nuristan is surrounded on all sides by steep and jagged 5000-metre peaks. It consists of three main valleys, the rivers of which all flow into the Kabul and eventually the Indus, is partly wooded, in places lush and, as it breaks the subcontinent's monsoon, has a relatively high rainfall. It was also said to be stunning; so beautiful in fact that mullahs had been known to stop travellers from imparting their tales of the land for fear that those listening would think they had been to paradise.

But it's the people who make the region so interesting and their roots have had anthropologists baffled for years. As Peachey and Danny were to discover on their journey, many are fair skinned with blond hair and blue eyes . . . 'as pale as any Englishman'. They sit on chairs or stools rather than on the floor as others in the region and their languages, of which there are many, are varied and hard to define. Some say the Kafirs – as they were known – came from Syria, others that they formed part of the Aryan migrations between the fourth and second millennia BC. And there are yet others, my fictional friends included, who claim that the Kafirs are in fact descendants of the armies of Alexander the Great, who marched through the area more than 2000 years ago.

As pagans, the Kafir tribesmen worshipped a plethora of ancestral gods, placed effigies over the graves of their dead, imbibed vast amounts of wine – even venerated the drink – and judged a man by the size of the parties he gave. They were known for their strong sense of independence, their prowess as warriors and their talent for intrigue. As Muslims, Nuristanis, bar a little less indulgence on the wine front, seemed pretty similar. The books painted a picture of a wild place with ferocious tribes living an existence rather like the one they had in Kafir times. They farmed maize, raised goats and chopped timber but thieving and murder were still the order of the day. Families fought families, villages fought villages and valleys fought valleys. They stole each other's goats, seduced each other's women and killed each other as a consequence. Praising a different god was the only change; Kafiristan or Nuristan, as far as I could tell, life remained the same. The land appeared as mysterious and foreboding in reality as it had in fiction.

As the train rattled north, however, I still found myself thinking about the pagan past, the land Peachey and Danny had known, and wondering whether there could still be any pockets of the old polytheistic ways left. It is after all an isolated region, packed with steep ravines and narrow valleys, cut off for much of the year by the heavy snow falls and divided by a hard, uncompromising race. Could a pagan tribe have survived, unaffected by the Amir's jihad and still be hidden in the Hindu Kush?

It seemed unlikely, yet somehow it also felt possible. Aboye the western horizon the new moon lay silently on its back, floating across the sunset like a ship without a sail. It was an auspicious time to be sure. For the Muslims it marked the religious festival of Id el Fatr and the end of the holy month of Ramadan; for the Hindus it signified a time of rebirth, a new beginning; and according to the horoscope in that morning's English language newspaper, with the earth moving from Aquarius to Pisces, for me as a Libran it meant 'a particularly good time for travel . . . and young authors'.

In my mind's eye I saw myself as a king in front of a great orange fire on which meat roasted. A gnarled old chief sat beside me and offered up his cup of wine. The eerie wail of a pagan song rose into the velvet night. My quest to find the mythical land of Kafiristan, a land of forged destinies where dreams come true, flickered before me like a dusty reel of cine-film.

I smiled to myself, offered cigarettes to my fellow passengers and happily lit up. I had no idea what lay ahead and I really didn't care. I was young and free at the beginning of a great adventure. What more tremendous feeling could there be? A man, a mission, a land of kings: Kafiristan.

I was on my way.

2 The Navel of the World

*'I will sell thee a charm —
an amulet that shall make thee King of Kafiristan.'*

Soon after dawn the hessian sack and corrugated iron world of Delhi's north-eastern squatter camps closed in around us, spilling over the railway's perimeter fence and tumbling down to the track. Beneath graffitied bridges, against crumbling walls, under ripped tarpaulins or simply in the open beside black stagnant pools, some of India's 400 million poor did their best to survive. Some stood in buckets next to stand pipes, naked save for their underpants, lathered in soap, taking a bath; others, dressed in cheap nylon suits, teetered on planks that crossed open sewers, carrying cardboard briefcases or sewing machines; still more stood silently in grimy clothes watching the train as they pulled at half-smoked beedies; and rows and rows of blank-faced people squatted by the track, going about their morning ablutions with water jugs in hand. A yellow smoke rose from countless dung fires around which women cooked and sleepy-eyed children sat and stared.

The station was crowded. I jumped down on to the platform, thankful to be finally out of the train, stretched and pushed towards the exit gate. It wasn't easy. A battered commuter train, licensed for a thousand but carrying ten times that number, had arrived at just the same moment and people poured from the carriages like grain through a chute. All around me commuters hurried. The musty smell of cheap hair tonic and a curried body odour hung in the air, warm and thick.

A hundred years ago Sarai Rohilla Station had been on the edge of town — a quiet place dealing with, among others, passengers of the Bombay Mail, heading, via Marwar, to Rajputana and the coast. Now the heaving station was deep within the ever expanding city.

I finally reached the exit, struggled through and found a rickshaw wallah. He was a fat man with a bald head and a mouth so full of blood-red paan you might have thought he'd been punched in the face. Other drivers, eager for a tourist's business, pushed in around us. 'Where going?' they yelled. 'Best price!'

'Aurangzeb Road,' I said, giving the address of an old friend who was working as a lawyer in town.

'Aurangzeb Road?' They shook their heads in unison, as if I'd just asked to be taken to the moon. 'Veeery far, 150 rupees.'

I didn't know the usual fare but was sure that was too much. Too tired to argue I stood in silence. My fat friend suggested 100 rupees and, agreeing, I climbed aboard. Leaving one scene of chaos behind, the suspensionless machine crunched out of the station forecourt, crashing through holes in the broken asphalt and plunged headlong into another.

The streets were narrow, lined with shabby wooden stalls. A few were open, chai and fat-fried parothas being prepared on kerosene stoves, but most were still boarded up. There were people though, great hordes of them, walking, running, pushing, shoving. The traffic was dense too and the fumes choking. Clapped-out buses, trucks, taxis and cars spewed their hideous black discharge into the air, throwing up a pall of fumes thick enough to suspend the day and return the night. Only motor bikes, bicycles and the more courageous of the rickshaws managed to make headway, wriggling though the mayhem like moles in a bog. Horns blasted, drivers shouted and engines thumped and whined. I poked my head out from under the yellow plastic roof and tried to find a landmark I might recognise – the minarets of the Jama Majid or the sprawling mass of the Red Fort – for I was sure I was somewhere in the old town but I could see no further than the next brick wall.

Then the road broadened slightly. Now there were shops, mottled and crumbling. Above them a mass of spaghetti twisted cables hung next to gaudy banners and faded signs. And higher still, stretching towards the heavens like modern messiahs, climbed the giant billboards of the bollywood heroes. To my right a maze of alleyways led invitingly into the quieter heart of Shahjahanabad, where the traffic couldn't reach and to the left, beyond a row of dingy workshops, ran the Yamana river.

In an instant, the world changed. Passing Delhi Gate, the bottlenecked traffic suddenly burst free and disappeared on to the wide tree-lined avenues that dissect the new town. The sun, framed by the mighty arch of India Gate, rose soft and red over the imperial city.

We turned down Rajpath, the broad avenue boarded by eucalyptus and casuarinas, canals and lawns, and approached the Secretariat Buildings and Rashtrapati Bhavan – in earlier times, Viceroy House, and home of the British Raj. Built in a mixture of Moghul and western styles from two gentle shades of Agra sandstone – dark pink beneath, mellow yellow above – topped with domes, towers, cupolas and chhatris, the whole complex is stunning and easily comparable to any of the great parliamentary buildings of Europe or America. I was struck by the immense cost and effort that Lutyens and Baker went to in creating this extravagant imperial citadel when providence would decree that British rule in India had but a few years to run. Britain, in one form or another, effectively held power here for the best part of 200 years and yet when the last brick of Viceroy House was laid in 1929, they had less than eighteen years to govern. Did they really have no inkling that the imperial age was drawing to a close? Judging by the magnitude of Rajpath and its treasures it wasn't another eighteen years the British thought they'd rule India, but 180.

The rickshaw turned south down Janpath and a few minutes later pulled up outside 6 Aurangzeb Road.

'What's that rat doing stuck to your face,' said Jeremy, tugging at my new goatee. For the past month, I had not shaved my chin. 'You're supposed to kill them, not eat them.'

I grinned and gave him a hug. 'Yeah, well sorry, but they'd run out of napkins in Second Class General.' It was good to see my old friend again. I kicked off my boots and threw down my bag.

He led me through the dark hall and into the living room where it was bright and cool. The morning sun reflecting off the pale walls and marble floor filled the room with a clear light. The french windows leading to the balcony were open wide but the sounds of the city seemed far away, only the pigeons' coos distinct.

'You do realise you're completely mad?' Jeremy picked that morning's *Asian Age* off the table, thrust it towards me and took a large gulp of his orange juice. 'With your wanderings down in Rajasthan, I guess you've been a little out of touch. Things ain't too good in Afghanistan.'

The headline was about a recent Taliban attack on Kabul with a grizzly picture of corpses strewn among the rubble. Fighter jets had strafed the city, killing ten and injuring scores more. I had hoped that by some miracle a peace deal might have been on the cards. It certainly didn't look that way. 'Ah well,' I said, showing a good deal more indifference than I felt, 'Kabul's a long way from where I'll be going.'

'It's not just Kabul.' Jeremy finished his drink and regarded me strangely. 'Look inside.'

I turned to the second page and saw the article immediately. Under the headline 'Afghan War: Ready to Explode', the piece argued adamantly that the fighting was likely to get worse before it got better. Reporting from frontlines in five Afghan provinces – from all over the country – it concluded that an all-out offensive by either the Taliban or the government looked imminent. It was not the news I had hoped to receive. I threw the paper on to the table and shrugged uneasily.

Jeremy turned towards a desk. 'A fax came through for you yesterday. You might find that better reading.' From the top drawer he removed the correspondence and handed it to me. I scanned the first page and, much enthused, turned to the second.

'That's fantastic,' I whispered, still reading the last of the words printed lightly on the shiny paper. I looked up and Jeremy was grinning.

'I thought that might cheer you up,' he said. 'It would be good if you could get him to go, hey?'

It had occurred to me pretty soon after hatching the plan to travel to Kafiristan, or Nuristan, that I was heading for the middle of a war zone. Journeying through a vicious civil war is never easy at the best of times – I'd gathered that much on my journey through Africa – and is, as you might expect, usually fairly dangerous; naïve as I was about local ways, travelling safely would indeed be tricky. I had tried to glean as much information as I could on the endless conflict – reading articles, listening to the news – but, to be honest, without being there and seeing the situation with my own eyes, it was all a little baffling: Hezb-i-Islami this and Hezb-i-Wahdat that, Jamiat and Jumbush-i-Melli, Rabbani, Masood, Dostum, Hekma-tyar and the Taliban, some faction holding this city, another taking that province, making alliances and breaking them.

Being a traveller though, the foreign section of my morning paper is always the first to be scoured – once I've checked the footy results. I knew therefore that the Russians had invaded the country at the end of the seventies, stayed ten years and then pulled out, leaving a puppet government led by a man named Najibullah. I had read about his fall from power as the various armed factions had closed in on Kabul and the consequences this vacuum had caused – all the warring groups craving dominance for themselves, the reason for the current civil war. And recently I'd read an article in *Newsweek* about a group of religious students called the Taliban, or the seekers of truth. Extraordinarily, in six months some 200 youths, strengthened by little more than the Koran and an absolute belief in divine assistance for their new-found cause, had swollen to a formidable fighting force of over 25,000 heavily armed men. Having swept through a large part of the country barely firing a gun, they were now camped on the hills around Kabul, waiting for their moment to capture the capital. I had even managed to persuade Tim McGirk, the *Independent*'s man on the subcontinent, to sit down with me and explain just who all the players in this confusing game were, good guys and bad. He'd been friendly and patient in the extreme, describing which groups held which provinces, who they were allied to at the moment and a little about the current fighting and how it might unfold. He'd even explained the best way across the Afghan frontier – in disguise, smuggled over the Khyber Pass and through the border on a flying coach! But without seeing and talking to the people, taking in the sights, smells and atmosphere of the country, it still all felt just a little unreal, even meaningless.

And how it all affected Nuristan and my chances of getting there, I hadn't a clue. Was that province today up in flames like so much of the country or had this conflict, like many before, passed it by?

Tim wasn't sure, neither was I. As ignorant as I was about Afghanistan and its ways, what I really needed was someone with knowledge of the country and its problems to go on the journey with me. But who? Amazingly, the fax held the answer. Sent by a friend who worked for MERLIN, a small but extremely efficient Non Governmental Organisation (NGO) who deal in emergency relief aid to Afghanistan, it gave me a huge list of contacts, all based in the Pakistani frontier town of Peshawar, one of whom was singled out and was the cause for my delight. 'John Hayward,' ran the fax, 'is a great guy working for the Swedish Committee, been in Afghanistan for five years, speaks the lingo, knows the customs. I've had a word with him and he might even want to go with you. Send him a fax.' It didn't take me a moment to see what an advantage it would be to have someone as experienced as this guy with me. The spirit of Peachey and Danny burned bright within my chest and here was my chance to pull fantasy and reality together – a real-life Peachey to accompany my Danny, a commander-in-chief for the king! It might make all the difference. I scribbled out a fax introducing myself and telling John roughly of my plan, asking whether he really was interested in accompanying me on a journey to Nuristan. Once written, it did seem more than just a little absurd. I sent it anyway.

In the heart of Old Delhi, Chandi Chowk was buzzing. The street itself was wide but blocked by a mass of cycle rickshaws, cars, Harley Davidson tricycle taxis, an elephant, some cows and a dead pariah dog. The pavement was a wall of humanity. Blocking the way, a family of albinos was creating a stir. Having laid out a rug they sat – Mum, Dad and three young kids – wailing, flailing their heads, arms and naked torsos wildly. A fascinated crowd stood watching close by, many throwing down rupees. Shop touts and salesmen, beggars and police, pilgrims, hawkers, shoppers and cripples squeezed past. Though this part of town is predominantly Islamic every part of society patronises Chandi Chowk; rich and poor, Muslim, Hindu, Sikh and Christian: a microcosm of Indian life.

'Meeester, come buy jeans,' cried a hawker shrilly into my ear. 'Theese yellow, very tight, very sexy. Or rucksack, Babu, ees very nice, 100 per cent nylon, perfume, belt.' I smiled patiently and told him no. Walking on through the crowded thoroughfare, a familiar voice echoed in my ears. It was Peachey:

'*Stone the crows, I ain't surprised you're hassled so. If you dress like a foreigner, you'll be treated like one – same today as it was always. It's time you got out of those . . . "things" you wear and into something a little more in keeping with the road. Ain't that so, Danny?*'

Maybe Peachey was right. According to Tim McGirk, I'd need a disguise simply to cross the Khyber Pass, and one would surely remain useful beyond it. But it wasn't simply for Afghanistan that less intrusive clothing would be helpful; it would be good to blend in more in India as well and try – however naïve the notion was – to see her as Indians did. Over the past couple of months I'd thought about this a great deal, hence the goatee. More often than not if you look like a tourist you are treated like one. The assumption is made that you have mountains of cash, you wish to visit each and every temple, museum and, most importantly, craft emporium in the area and are a productive target to beg from. You can't walk unhindered in any major town for more than a few minutes, and I was becoming bored of it. Besides, there was certainly garb more in keeping with Victorian adventure than jeans and a Ryan Giggs T-shirt. I stopped outside an open-fronted restaurant where gulab jamuns floated in a bowl of dark syrup. I bought one of the delicious soft sponge balls and stuffed it into my mouth before walking on.

'Hey, Coco.' An unctuous man thrust his face into mine. He wore purple slacks above white patent sandals. 'You want sil'uk sari, good price, bestest quality?'

'No, but I do want a shalwar kameez.' Having observed people on the street I had decided the baggy trousers and long, loose shirt would be a good starting point to convert the tourist into a local.

'You come.' He took me by the arm, looked around guiltily as though it were drugs we were about to deal in, and directed me down a narrow alleyway. All along its route traders shouted to me, holding up their wares – flowers, strange tin cups, pieces of cheap silver, clothes, a food blender, a suitcase, a brace of fighting cocks – in the hope of enticing me away from the tout. But he wasn't about to let his commission slip and kept a firm grip on my arm. He led me up some stairs, away from the noise of the street, to where fat cloth traders surrounded by rows of fabric lounged on cushions in their stalls. Some were doing business with women, others were eating or simply idle. Though there was little natural light, the hall was bright, lit by fluorescent strips.

My tout's boss jumped up, an ingratiating smile beaming across his face. He had a round pug nose, pitted and flat, like a squashed strawberry, and tiny eyes. His mouth was packed with paan. Two top teeth were missing, the rest were stained red. Rubbing his hands together and trying unsuccessfully not to spit, the merchant asked what it was I was looking for. They brought me shalwar kameez of black, white, mustard, ochre, brown and sky blue, all with delicate trimming and embroidered collars and cuffs.

'*Not like that,*' Peachey's voice returned. "'*Tis for the road you're dressin', not a bleedin' durbar. That's too damn fancy by half. Plain you want. Plain and tough.*'

I had to agree, they didn't look very 'street' and I told the merchant so.

'This, no problem,' said the man urgently, seeing a possible sale slipping away. 'We make for you, is better this way. Plain, plain. Buy material, tailor will make.' He turned and waddled to the back of the stall where rows of rolled material covered the wall. He pulled a dark blue fabric down and let a few metres fall free.

'See, thees plain but claaasic. One hundred percent *ees* the cotton and polyester. Is good for the all times; for the indoors and for the out, for the social and for the marketing.' He beamed again like some freakish gargoyle. The material looked strong and I agreed it would do. He took my measurements and I arranged to pick up the garments the following morning. To his almost delirious joy, before departing, I also purchased a pale Nehru-collared waistcoat, a brown shawl and smart black cap embroidered with silver thread. A vast improvement, I thought it would make, and in my head Peachey agreed.

To the casual observer looking north from the steps of the Jama Masjid – the Friday Mosque – the following morning, the scene would have appeared no different to that of the morning before or the one before that. Muslims, Hindus and Sikhs merged in a multicultural sea, some moving towards Chandi Chowk, others to the Chawri Bazaar. But in the midst of that crowd there was a newcomer. None of the touts pressed him to buy a silk sari, none of the rickshaw wallahs asked if he wanted a guided tour. He ambled along, head down, minding his own business and everyone left him alone. The transformation was fantastic, it was as though I had disappeared.

At least it was until a policeman spoke to me in Hindi; then the illusion vanished and I was a tourist again. Without the lingo I would have problems. But my clothes were definitely a vast improvement on T-shirt and jeans for inconspicuously loafing up the Grand Trunk Road – a journey I did not intend to hurry.

As I reached the steps of the famous mosque – a great place from which to sit and observe the Old Town – a group of young schoolboys passed by. In pairs, holding hands, they formed a neat crocodile descending the steps towards the busy street. Some were talking, others laughing but at the back, a few metres behind the rest, a boy meandered in a world of his own. As he came level with me he stopped and regarded me with open curiosity. His gaze met my blue eyes and his mouth dropped open.

'Aadhe jaat wallah!' he shrieked as his face broke into a grin. Then he stuck out his tongue and, delighted with his cheek, skipped down the last steps and raced to join his schoolmates. To call me a half-caste was hardly polite but his impish manner made me smile too. Looking down at myself I quickly burst out laughing and as I sat on the worn steps, the morning sun glancing warmly across my back, I found myself wondering with great amusement what on earth I thought I was doing. Had I gone mad? Finally cracked? Was it really normal behaviour to go dressing up as an itinerant Muslim and heading off into the back of beyond? To imitate your storybook heroes and charge recklessly into their world?

But deep down I knew that I was on the right track. This journey, I had already discovered, was about far more than plotted lines on a map; I was marching into a different period of history. Many a time I have fantasised about having been born into an earlier age. I should have loved to have had the chance to explore or play the Great Game; to have lived in a golden age of adventure. This was my chance. Travelling the road with Peachey and Danny, it was important I looked the part. I wasn't about to stain my skin with walnut juice and caustic soda, as they might have done – that seemed a little excessive just to ward off a few unwelcome hawkers – but the disguise, I realised, was a crucial part of the game I was now playing.

As I looked up I caught a glimpse of the young schoolboy as he disappeared into the crowd.

———— ◆ ————

Aware of the quiet I looked around and was surprised to find myself alone. The top deck was completely empty. Where was Ashley? I stood up and, putting my satchel over my shoulder, walked down the aisle.

'Jesus!' exclaimed the bus conductor, standing at the bottom of the spiral stairs. 'What the hell are you still doing here?' His hair was the greasiest I'd ever seen. 'Didn't your brother take you with him?' As he spoke the cigarette he held in the corner of his mouth bobbed up and down, causing the ash to fall. It exploded against his ticket machine. I shook my head and watched as he pulled a cord which rang a bell. A moment later the bus pulled into the curb.

Taking my hand, the conductor lead me across the road. 'You just walk straight down this pavement here. Don't turn left or right. After about ten minutes you'll come to the school. Can't miss it, got big iron gates and a giant sign outside. You can read, can't you?'

I studied my shoes. They were new, Clarks Attackers, with a compass in the heel.

'Right then,' said the conductor, 'off you go.'

I walked on down the pavement, alone. Jumping as high as I could, I tried to look over the railway bridge wall to see the trains on the Great Northern Line, but I was too small. There were some houses made of red bricks, all packed very close together with no grass between, then a church and graveyard. A tombstone, shaped like an angel, faced the road. I searched the ground intently for the right stick. Having found it, I upped and charged. 'Arrrgh!' I screamed, thrashing wildly at the metal railings. Images of gleaming armour, panting steeds and the glorious deeds of Sir Lancelot raced through my head. A wrinkled woman looked up startled from beside a grave and stared at the five-year-old fighting the railings to save Guinevere. The fence snapped the stick and I hurried on.

It would have been impossible to have missed the school such was the rumpus at the entrance. A frantic ginger-headed man, tall and thin with windmill arms.

A teacher, old and fat with blue hair and white bandages wrapped around her legs. And my brother, bawling his eyes out and red in the face.

The fat woman gripped me firmly by the hand and pulled me up the steps into the grey school house. 'We were so worried — your brother, the whole school, everyone — and on your first day, my goodness.' Down the corridor we walked, she and I, with the smell of stale milk in the air. Then we were through a door and into her classroom.

'Class 1B,' said Mrs Thomas, puffing triumphantly and looking around at the assembled children, 'this is Jonny. He's been for a bit of a wander.'

———— ◆ ————

That evening a fax came through from Pakistan. Rather amusingly it read: 'Received your fax and yes interested in principle but as I could only make out, Peachey Carnehan . . . Nuristan . . . summer . . . Jonny Bealby, it might be a good idea if you come up and see me when you reach Pakistan.' It was signed John Hayward.

Later Jeremy took me out for a farewell drink.

'I've got something for you,' he said thoughtfully, once we were seated and the whiskys had been poured. From his pocket he withdrew a little silver elephant: Ganesh, the Hindu god of protection. Looped through the trunk was a leather cord. 'I was given this last year by a holy man in Jaiphur. He'd blessed it, said whoever wears it will come to no harm, make their dreams come true. You know, the usual nonsense, but I guess you never know. Here.' He handed it to me. 'I figure where you're going you'll need it more than me.' He picked up his glass and thumped it into mine. 'Make sure you come back,' he said. 'I'm sure you'll have a story I shall want to hear.'

I slipped the amulet over my head, kissed it flamboyantly and tucked it in behind my shirt.

3 Trouble on the Grand Trunk Road

*'I shall depart upon my winged camel
and be at Peshawar within a day.'*

Just after four a rickety bus of the Haryana State Transport Corporation put us down in a hot and dusty Sonipat, some fifty kilometres north of Delhi. Crowds of people thronged through the open streets between shacks and shops all squashed together beneath three- and four-storey pale concrete structures, forlorn and nondescript. It was noisy too, with the cries of hawkers and the din of the motor bikes and tempos – strange, elongated, snub-nosed rickshaws, powered by blabbering single-cylinder engines – filling the dry air. Cows lay amongst the rubbish, contentedly chewing on whatever was convenient, kids played impromptu cricket and mangy dogs ambled by. It was a scene that could be seen in thousands of towns across the land.

After a glass of chai, Zahoor led the way back out of town towards the main road where we intended to stay the night in one of the many dhabas, or truck stops, that line the Grand Trunk Road. Walking, hitch-hiking and travelling on local buses, we'd begun our journey towards Amritsar in the Punjab near the Indian border with Pakistan just before noon. On an express coach I could have reached the Sikh's holy city in eight hours, crossed the frontier and made Peshawar within a couple of days. But with the summer still young I was in no hurry. I wanted to see the subcontinent's great thoroughfare that stretches over 2500 kilometres from the Bay of Bengal to the Northwest Frontier. It was the way Peachey and Danny would have come. I wondered how much it had changed.

It felt good to be on the road with someone else – a pleasant variation for a lone traveller. That morning as I was picking up some last-minute provisions from New Delhi's Palika Bazaar, Zahoor had suddenly appeared at my side. Eighteen years old, he was a Kashmiri from Srinagar who had been staying with his uncle in the capital but, with the summer coming, wanted to return home. As he spoke Hindi, Urdu and English, I agreed to give him 100 rupees a day as well as pay for his keep and a bus ticket home if he would act as my translator. When we met at the bus station at Kashmiri Gate a little while later, however, I had realised that my idea of blending in, looking like a local, had been shot to pieces. With his baseball cap turned the wrong way round, his fake Raybans, Stone Roses T-shirt and faded jeans Zahoor would have looked more at home on the Kings Road than on the Grand Trunk Road. Ironically, we had reversed roles.

As we picked our way through the outskirts of Sonipat, a tempo came past packed with people inside and out. Zahoor looked nervous, reluctant to climb aboard. Previous experience has taught me that such opportunities are best taken. I clambered up on to the running boards and held on tight to a metal bar that ran across the roof. When I looked over my shoulder, to check that Zahoor was aboard, his face carried the expression of a child on a fair ground ride . . . 'Like soldiers!' he exclaimed.

The locals clinging to the side of the strange looking contraption told us that there were no dhabas in the immediate vicinity. They advised us to stay the night at a local ashram, situated a couple of miles off the main road. I had never been to an ashram before and was inquisitive to see what they were all about. A few minutes later, at a junction with a narrow track, the tempo stopped and set us down.

It was a heavenly afternoon. A light sky scratched with wispy clouds stretched far and wide above endless fields of emerald wheat. Yellow-hooded mynas, blue jays and parakeets bobbed through the air or rested on telephone lines, while a particularly beautiful, tiny green bird, with a long beak and gold head, rose and fell at remarkable angles catching insects. Tethered buffalo chewed the cud, a farmer lovingly washed his tractor and outside a small, mud-brick home a group of old men lazily passed an ancient hookah. Teenage schoolgirls in pale-blue Punjabi suits with thin silk veils, called dupattas, cast around their necks and down their backs drifted like angels, some smiling shyly to us, as they made their way home. A young boy pushed a bicycle wheel rim and others rolled in the dirt. The sun was falling, the heat subsiding. A bullock cart stopped and gave us a ride.

In the shade of an expansive mango tree the cart idled to a stop. Next to a double steel gate on a prosperous-looking white stone wall, was a sign that read: 'SHRI SIDDHESHWAR ASHRAM – The Third Eye Foundation of India.' We took our bags and wandered inside.

All was quiet. Around a quadrangle of grass and young fruit trees a series of whitewashed buildings formed three sides of a square. To the left was a row of bungalow huts, stretching away towards fields of wheat and sugar cane, and opposite the huts a grand two-storey structure with imperious towers and fake battlements. Behind us was another large construction that appeared to be a canteen.

A friendly man who looked Indian but sounded American directed us up some stairs to a hall where Shri Baba was having 'afternoon discussions'.

We followed his directions and quietly entered the room, sitting on the floor at the back.

In front of us sat about fifty people, some on chairs, others cross-legged on the floor, all wearing identical white cotton smocks and trousers, rather like hospital orderlies. On a stage at the front, lounging on a wooden throne behind a microphone, was the man I presumed to be Shri Siddheshwar Baba. With his dark glasses, saffron robe and wiry mass of silver hair, he looked like an elderly Jimi Hendrix. A huge picture of him, garlanded with petals of marigolds, hung above his head, dwarfing smaller portraits of Jesus and the much worshipped guru, Sia Baba. Around his neck was a white band with claret and blue stripes at its end; did they have any spiritual significance or was he a West Ham fan? I wondered irreverently. Though this was some sort of question and answer session, I didn't like to ask.

The few questions we heard revolved around the deciphering of dreams, feelings over a soured relationship and the nature of mankind's spirit. The guru answered in long, slow sentences.

'At what stage does the spirit enter the body?' asked a man with a strong North American accent, sitting somewhere near the front.

Leaning back, Shri Baba answered, 'Oh, you English and

Americans always talk from the inside, you will have to ask again.' Evidently I then missed something because everyone guffawed with laughter. When the merriment had died down Shri Baba explained that the spirit is present from conception. He talked about 'karma' and how all that we do is related to it, so we should always treat our fellow humans as we would wish to be treated ourselves, and if we do wrong we will pay for it in the end. To illustrate this he told a story of a young child who had come to the Baba in a dream asking him to tell the child's parents not to grieve his death – he had apparently taken a load of pills from his father's medical bag – because he had had to do it to make amends for wrongs in past lives.

It was all very peaceful and friendly but didn't seem to amount to a whole lot more than the old Sunday school lesson to be a good boy. Which has always seemed the main thing to me.

They finished the session by chanting 'Om', followed by a song which sounded a touch South African, like Soweto singers, and was rather beautiful.

Outside the hall in the rich evening sun, a thin man in his late thirties, with a narrow face and an Adam's apple that stuck out as far as his nose, asked what we wanted. We told him a bed for the night, possibly two. Having shown us to a room in one of the bungalows, he told me to go and register at the office. He didn't smile or talk with any animation, his face was blank. When I asked him where he was from, he just sighed 'Czech Republic,' and walked away.

Nobody spoke. As I strolled across the central courtyard I passed an elderly couple, a woman and two men. I said, 'Hi, good evening,' but they all looked vaguely embarrassed, smiled inanely or cast their eyes down and passed without a word. I was beginning to feel a little unnerved.

In the office I found a young American who was quite obviously gaining little in the way of spiritual tranquillity. 'Why won't the goddamn phone work?' He slammed the handpiece back in the cradle. 'How the hell can I book a fuckin' air ticket home if the goddamn phone don't work?' Uttering more expletives, of which I doubt Shri Baba would have wholly approved, he stormed out.

At the side of the desk sat the lugubrious Czech, tapping away on an Apple Mac Power Book. He didn't look up at the American's tantrum or my entrance. I pulled up a chair on the opposite side of the desk.

After a couple of quiet minutes during which I glanced at the covers of some of the guru's books – *Psycho-analysis and Meditation; A Psychological Commentary for Spiritual Seekers and Psychic Sufferers* and *An Experiential Account of a Journey from Dust to Divinity*, among others – a middle-aged woman with a moustache and sideburns of which Engelbert Humperdinck would have been proud, entered and took a seat behind the desk.

'What name?' she demanded, studying me through narrow eyes in the same way a seasoned cop might regard some piece of low life just hauled in on a child rape charge. 'Where are you going? Where have you been? Why did you come here? Name of your friend? Name of your father? Political affiliations?' It went on for twenty minutes and though I answered in as charming a manner as I was able, not once did the Neanderthal woman show a flicker of pleasant emotion. At one point she stopped to bellow at someone outside; the office shook. She spent more than five minutes going through every stamp in my passport. It was not at all what I had been expecting from an ashram. When I was finally released I felt drained, as through I had been through a police interrogation.

The Czech followed me to my room and told Zahoor to go and register while I lay down on the bed. On a shelf beside the tiny window was a time-table and list of rules: 4.30 – 1st Meditation (compulsory); 5.30 – Om chant; 6.00 – tea; 6.30 – Yoga and spiritual expansion; 10.00 – discussions; 12.00 – lunch . . . Conversation is not encouraged and there will be no smoking or sexual relations . . . The list of regulations was three pages long. Just as I was taking out my pen to copy it down, in burst the dreary Czech and told me in that officious but slightly nervous way of people who have some power but are inexperienced at using it, to pack my bag immediately; we had to leave. Oh shit, I thought, what has Zahoor told them.

I climbed off the bed and made for the door.

'Take your bags!'

'Not until I've found out what's going on . . . You can't kick us out into the night. It'll be dark soon.'

Outside the office there was a bit of a to-do. The great Shri Baba was standing imperiously by another helper and the dragon with mutton chops, his orange robes now appearing like a maternity dress, shaking a bony finger at Zahoor. He greeted me with little in the way of calm or kindness in his voice. 'You must go now or I call the police.'

'The police, what on earth for?'

'This man he is very suspicious.' He gestured towards Zahoor. 'He say he is travelling with you but you have given different name.' I hadn't in fact, it was just that the woman had misheard me and written down, Roul rather than Zahoor. I tried to explain this but it made little difference.

'He has no proper ID and he is Kashmiri . . . ' He spat the last word in the same way that I might have said, shit. 'Why you dressed like this?' he then asked, looking me up and down with ill-disguised contempt, which I have to say I thought a mite rich coming from an old man in an orange dress. 'And,' he took a step back and tilted his head regally towards the sky, 'why you have Pakistan visa in your passport?' He folded his arms as he said it. This was the big one, answer that if you can.

'Urr . . . because I'm going to Pakistan.' Failing abysmally to keep the insolence out of my voice, I took the same pose. 'You have no right or reason to suspect Zahoor or me of anything. I am a law-abiding tourist simply travelling up the Grand Trunk Road on my way to Amritsar, then, if I feel like it, on to Pakistan. Zahoor is acting as my translator. Honestly, what was all that about karma I've just heard you preaching upstairs, treating others as you would like to be treated yourself?'

This flustered him for a moment but he still wouldn't soften. Having explained rather vaguely that this had nothing to do with karma – hadn't he just say *every*thing was to do with karma? – he pointed again at Zahoor, 'He say you are writing, but you put in register that your occupation is artist. Why you lie?'

Now it was my turn to be flustered. I had no official permission to be writing in or about India, for that you needed a journalist's visa and I was travelling on one given to tourists. I had foolishly told Zahoor I hoped to write a book about my travels; he had obviously been impressed. I suddenly thought about the press card I'd managed to elicit out of the NUJ and my letters of affiliation from the *Observer* and the *Independent* to help me in Afghanistan. Though they were given more as favours from friends with access to letter-headed paper than editors with any serious hope of attaining a story, they looked genuine. I had a dictaphone and note books already beginning to fill, two cameras and a healthy stock of film. I would have a hard time explaining them all to the police. Moreover, the authorities would be perfectly within their rights to deport me for having lied on my visa application. They had done it in the past, they could do it again. I berated myself for not agreeing a different story with Zahoor.

Again Shri Baba said, 'You must leave now or I call the police.'

Like common criminals we were marched back to our room by the Czech, collected our belongings and were unceremoniously escorted to the gates. With a final word of warning we were told never to return.

Back on the lane with dusk thickening, the reality of the situation began to dawn on me. Here I was, travelling incognito with a Kashmiri lad, who, though I was sure was as far from being a terrorist as myself, I hardly knew, in a disguise that I now realised was pitiful. Unlike outside Delhi's Jama Masjid, here on the dusty roads of Haryana I looked no more like a local than hip Zahoor did. Less, probably. No one had goatees, no one wore shalwar kameez, or waistcoats or little caps. I was dressed as a Muslim in a land that since partition held but a handful. The farmers, their wives and the children, everyone, now seemed to be watching us with suspicious eyes. The walk that had been so magical only a couple of hours earlier now felt like a retreat through enemy territory. If Shri Baba did call the police, which I figured was a distinct possibility, we would be easy to spot and have a hard time explaining ourselves.

As Zahoor, head down, strode out ahead, I stopped and, having removed my cap and waistcoat, pictured my old friends. '*Last time we was bound along the road,*' Peachey was saying, '*there was plenty a' Mohammedans here abouts. All the way to Kabul . . . and beyond.*'

'*Aye,*' answered Danny angrily, '*and a good deal more accommodating they*' *were than that damn fakir. Gord's holy trousers, you should've broken his neck across your knee as I'd have done.'*

Dressed in old shawls, faded cotton pants and shirts, Danny in his dirty turban and Peachey in his frontier hat, they were as rough and ready as any who'd ever tramped along the Grand Trunk Road. In their disguise I didn't doubt that there had been a time when they could have passed unnoticed all the way from the Qutb Minah to the Bala Hasar. But not today. Their India no longer existed and their Kafiristan was gone. There was a border to cross they wouldn't have known and laws and ideas they couldn't have understood. Again a large part of me wished I was back in their day, striking out on the edge of Empire to find a new land, a new people and – and yes, why not – create a new kingdom. But regardless of the wild imaginings dancing around my head, it was important I faced reality. I was standing on the edge of the twenty-first century, a more 'enlightened' age, and if I didn't play this game by the current set of rules I wouldn't get far.

Apart from highlighting the foolishness of my disguise, the encounter at the ashram had revealed another cause for concern. The Pakistan visa in my passport, though not a direct problem – foreigners are perfectly entitled to cross the border between Amritsar and Lahore – did seem to make people jumpy. The two countries have been at loggerheads for practically all of their fifty years of independent history and even though India has come out on top on each of the three occasions these animosities have resulted in war, she still retains a wholesale paranoia about her neighbour. India has an army ten times the size of Pakistan's and a nuclear capability in advance of her rival. Yet she remains constantly wary of anything Pakistani – even a visa in a tourist's passport. And at this time tension was particularly high. Only a few weeks earlier a shell had exploded in a mosque on the Pakistani side of the Kashmir cease-fire line, killing twenty-two Muslim worshippers. The Pakistanis blamed the Indians and sent a few rockets back, while the Indians said that the Pakistanis did it to themselves to gain support for their Kashmiri policy.

But that was not all. Foreigners were also being seen more as the bad guys. The mysterious Purulia arms drop was still fresh in everyone's mind. On a remote hillside in West Bengal the army had uncovered large amounts of weapons dropped by parachute. The authorities were at a loss to know for whom the arms were intended or from where they came but they did know that it was Westerners who were behind it – mug-shots of a Caucasian man, with looks not dissimilar to my own, wanted in connection with the incident, were stuck to the walls of every public building in the country. A Swede had been caught with a large amount of arms and a Swiss couple had been busted carrying 382 guns of various calibres into the country across the Pakistan border.

And here I was, kicked out of an ashram, wandering around at dusk, dressed in a pathetic disguise with a Muslim Kashmiri, loaded with cameras, note books and a tape recorder en route to India's mortal enemy. And I was hoping to get into Afghanistan!

Zahoor turned and grinned. 'Jonny, don't look so worried. You told to me we would have an adventure, so this is where it starts. Maybe police, maybe not, maybe trouble, maybe not – it's exciting, yes?' He skipped a step. 'And it is no real problem, there are plenty of places to sleep along the road.'

'Aye, the lad's right,' said Peachey. 'Adventure's what you wanted, I thought you've always liked it so . . .'

———— ◆ ————

'So we were out on the moor, Dartmoor, you know, and in the middle of the night and everything – well, it had gone nine o'clock – and it was starting to get dark and it was cold and spooky because we were next to the big forest and it was really getting very dark . . . ' I sat on my hands on the little stool and rocked excitedly to and fro.

'What on earth did they think they were doing sending a group of young boys off like that?' Nan picked up her cup and tutted into her tea. 'Summer camping trip, my word. You might—'

'But it was fine, we—'

'Don't interupt.'

'Sorry.' I looked down at my jumper and picked a thread. When I saw she intended to say no more I carried on hurriedly. 'The others, they were all scared. I mean I was scared too, a bit. But not really, not really scared. I kept on thinking about that book Miss Johns read us last term, The Lion, The Witch and the Wardrobe. It was very like that really, like being in Narnia with the Snow Queen and Aslan and things. I wasn't scared, not like Matthew. He started to cry. Matthew always cries . . . '

'I'm not surprised,' said Nan, indignantly.

'Anyway, I took the map, well, me and Steve—'

'Steve and I.'

'—and we led the way, pretending we were soldiers and everything and in the end we came to a farm house and the farmer was angry and he called the police and they came and drove us back to camp in a police car.' I jumped from my seat and charged round the room wailing like a siren. As I stopped in front of Nan she took hold of my arms and smiled.

'Now then,' she said, 'on my bed you'll find your birthday present. As we won't be seeing each other for the next few days, if you bring it in here I'll let you open it early.'

I was back in a flash with a large, brightly coloured, square box. Feverishly, I tore off the wrapping – Nan muttering something about wasting good paper – and found the most amazing, wonderful-looking object. A metal sphere the size of a football, all pink and blue and yellow and green, suspended on a stand. A globe. I sat transfixed, quite unable to utter a word.

'Now that you're nearly ten years old,' I heard Nan say, 'it's time you learnt about the world. Now, bring it over here and let me show you where I used to live and where your mother was born.'

———— ◆ ————

By the time we reached the main road it was fully dark. Traffic thundered fast in either direction. A police jeep went past, heading back towards town with its red light flashing. I turned my face away. The choices were stark. Either we had to return to Sonipat and check into a hotel, sleep rough or try to travel on and make it to a dhaba. The problem with a hotel was that all people checking in had to fill out a registration form which would almost certainly be taken to the police, as was the law. Since the rise of the Sikh separatist movement, security in this part of the country was tight. A Kashmiri and foreigner would be bound to arouse interest, regardless of whether the ashram rang the police or not. We decided to carry on up the road. Having flagged down a tempo, we jumped aboard and headed north.

*

Around a central television, a handful of men sat on chairs and rope beds, known as charpoys, watching a Sikh musician rattle out some sitar ditty. The rear wall and pillars of the open-sided construction were all painted with Pepsi logos. Above, a blazing strip light hung from the rickety corrugated iron roof. On either side of the shelter were workshops where men mended punctures by lamp light and beside them stretched rows of trucks. This was a dhaba like countless others. Four soldiers sat nonchalantly around a rough wooden table sipping chai but none took any notice of us. Under a water pump a Sikh showered. We sat and ordered some food.

Zahoor didn't talk much. Despite his earlier enthusiasm to grasp adventure by the balls the prospect of sleeping in such a spartan establishment now didn't seem to appeal. 'I don't think police be a problem,' he said, looking dolefully around at our new surroundings. 'I think is better we go back and find hotel.' He was a bit of a curious character; up for the challenge of the road but still a kid at heart. It would soon be time for a good kip and he wanted a proper bed. I refused and he went into a childish sulk. Having eaten, we drank and smoked in silence.

The evening turned to night and more trucks arrived. Worried that we might not get even a charpoy to sleep on, we moved in under the roof. Within minutes the wind whipped up and rain began to fall, clattering like marbles against the hard tin roof. Zahoor took a cot stuck away in a corner and pulled a blanket over his head.

A man with a deep scar running vertically down his cheek came and sat on the charpoy opposite me. His teeth were brown, filed into points, and his eyes as black as tar. 'Hey, friend,' he leered, 'you need lift north in morning?' In the stark light I could see his face was smeared with dirt; dust from the road, oil from his hands. To my surprise, I answered in the affirmative. 'OK, then I take you. First thing.' From his grimy jacket pocket he withdrew a bottle of Officer's Choice. 'You like whisky?' he asked, holding the bottle up for me to see. Does Dolly Parton sleep on her back? The rain was falling and the wind howling. A night cap seemed like a grand idea.

He filled the glass to the brim with cheap yellow spirit and handed it to me, a crooked grin upon his larcenous face. Even with my wholesome appreciation of the drink this measure seemed faintly ridiculous. I smiled, remembering a time when I was a child. The bank manager had come over to our house and Dad asked me to get him a whisky. I had no idea about measures and filled a half pint glass up to the top. 'Christ,' Dad had said, 'we don't need the loan that badly.' Still, I took the glass now. The man's expression seemed to give me little choice. The whisky tasted sharp, metallic and burnt like a bastard. 'I come back later, we leave at five.' And with that he was gone, out into the rain.

'What you doing?' Sat Paul Grover, the dhaba owner, came over and crouched where Scarface had been. 'This man very bad.' Looking concerned, he took the whisky and lifted it to his nose. 'You must not drink this, maybe drug.' Checking the rogue had not returned, he poured it on to the earth floor. 'This man very bad,' he repeated. 'He see your camera.'

'I've said we'll catch a lift with him in the morning.' Again, I felt rather foolish.

'No problem, he will be drunk and go late, we put you in other truck early. I know driver go to Panipat early. I keep eye on you tonight and wake you for lift.' He took my bag into the kitchen for safe keeping and returned with two extra blankets. A few minutes later Scarface appeared again and seeing my empty glass tried to give me some more. When I politely refused, he wandered away and luckily, I never saw him again.

Just before dawn the following morning a sleepy Zahoor and I climbed into the orange cab of a Tata truck carrying watermelons north. As we left Sonipat district I breathed a sigh of relief.

4 With Sadhus and Police

*'Then the camels passed away along the dusty road
and I was left alone to wonder.'*

At Panipat, some fifty kilometres further north, the truck dropped us off. Before too long the sun was up, hammering rays through a pale sky. They reflected off the road, off the buildings and off the hard ground between, smothering all in a menacing heat. With no breath of wind, the air burned. We sat in the shade of a chai shack, eating parothas, watching the massed transport moving along the Grand Trunk Road.

In Haryana and the Punjab, India's agricultural heartland, the Grand Trunk Road is at its busiest. A continuous procession of Tata trucks sped through the town, some bulging with cotton, others laden with sugar cane, fruit, onions, chillies or cabbages. Most were old and tired, with chipped paint and dented wings, though some were pristine, without cargo or trailers or even cabs, just an engine, a chassis and wheels. The drivers of these skeleton trucks wore goggles and scarves and had oil-stained faces, like Fangio at the wheel of some giant Lagonda. There were cars and minibuses, tractors and motor bikes; but there were bullock carts, too, and others pulled by camels, ambling sedately along, forced from the road to struggle on the uneven verge. It was a river of life, flooding its banks as surely as the Ganges after the rains.

I'd never known a place with so many flies. Like a couple of madmen, Zahoor and I sat swatting continuously while trying to sip our chai. A Muslim saint who is buried in the town is said to have rid Panipat of all its flies but when the locals complained that the job he had done was too good, he gave them all back, multiplied by a thousand. We were both pleased when two Punjabis from Chandigarh asked if we wanted a lift.

They didn't talk much. They told us they were brothers on their way home from doing some business in Delhi, and that if we had the time we should stop at Kurukshetra, the scene of a great battle from the Hindi epic, *The Mahabhrata*. There we would find an excellent museum and a large holy tank. We asked them to drop us there.

Zahoor had brightened considerably. Once again he was excited to be seeing an India he'd not witnessed before. 'This is amazing,' he exclaimed, looking happily out of the window, watching a new world flash by. 'I have never seen so much. You know I was only ten when problems begin at home in Kashmir. Since then there have been the curfews, the soldiers, violence and things. I have never seen even my home state, never mind all this.' Spending the winter with his uncle in Delhi, he said, had been the best three months of his life, but now he was experiencing a freedom the like of which he'd never had. But to be honest, as the Punjabi's minibus trundled along the dappled road what he wanted to discuss mostly was an Italian girl named Angie. He had slept with her the week before. 'Are all Italian girls like that?' he asked, salivating over the memory.

At Kurukshetra we found the lake, about four or five acres in size and surrounded on three sides by neatly cut grass. All along the length of the fourth side, bathing ghats descended in shallow steps into the water. Behind them was a wide walkway lined with alcoves where long-term pilgrims made makeshift homes. Some stayed for months, others years. It was a peaceful place. There were a few Indian tourists present. While their wives looked on, the men stripped to their underpants and walked down into the water to cleanse their spirit and offer poojas – gifts and prayers – to the gods.

As soon as we had reached the water's edge, five sadhus, brimming with curiosity, came over and asked us to sit with them. They were a ragtag crew. Dressed in orange robes, they all had long rat's tail hair and scruffy beards, beads around their necks and religious thread wrapped tight around their wrists. One had scaly skin like a leper and no nose, just a large hole that continued from his upper lip almost to his eyes, another proudly carried an umbrella cane that had no material, while a third hung a large wireless round his neck, which I never heard play. The man with no nose had a pink plastic satchel. It was stuffed full of marijuana.

Zahoor seemed nervous. Never having met anyone quite like them before, I think he expected, as a Muslim, to receive a hostile reception. Sitting at the edge of the group, he translated reluctantly. They told us that they had met at Haridwar, in Uttar Pradesh, during the festival of Kumbh Mela. According to them more than a crore of pilgrims – ten million – had gathered over the month of celebration.

'And here as well,' said one called Yem Kumar, while packing an elegantly carved chillum with grass. 'When the moon pass in front of the sun October before, many people come to the tank. Maybe five lakh.' Half a million people, seven or eight cup final crowds, in an area only marginally bigger than a football pitch: it was a scary thought. Having passed the chillum in a circle over the rest of the weed and solemnly incanted something that sounded like 'bum shaver', he set fire to the mixture and disappeared behind a large cloud of smoke. When the fog cleared he said, 'Oh yes, many come and many die. They all go under water for moment of eclipse so the demons can't get them. When the sun comes back twenty, thirty are dead.' He then shrugged his shoulders as if to say that that was a perfectly acceptable statistic for such an event.

Yem Kumar passed the chillum to the man with no nose who had a hard time dragging on it. He had to hold his hands over most of his face to create the vacuum needed to make the thing fire. He was obviously used to the arrangement though and after a few seconds the grass burned brightly. Having inhaled copious amounts of smoke he handed it on to me.

Though once extremely partial to a smoke of the old charas, my days of participating are now pretty much in the past; and a good thing it is too, especially when travelling. As a backpacker on my early travels my first job in practically every new place I visited had been to find some dope. Then, it was really just a hassle, eyeing out a likely looking dealer and spending an hour or two in his company securing a small deal. Now it's dangerous as well. These days foreigners caught carrying an ounce or even less by the police without ready cash to bribe themselves out of the situation are regularly given ten-year jail sentences. But that's not the only problem. As a lone traveller, getting wrecked with strangers, either intentionally or otherwise, can mean getting ripped off – and the reputation of the ascetics in these situations is not very good. Many times I had heard of tourists being duped into smoking sessions with purported holy men only to wake two days later with a crunching headache, only their underpants left to their name, and the slow realisation that the stuff they had smoked had been laced with something a whole lot stronger than hashish. In one bizarre incident which I read in the paper a young man invited a Buddhist monk into his room and accepted an invitation to eat the man's biscuits. The next morning he woke in agony to find a blood-stained gauze stuck to the small of his back. On being examined by a doctor he was informed that he'd had a kidney stolen! And then there was the well publicised case of a young American woman who, looking for spiritual guidance, had agreed to be taken by her new guru up to the hills where her lessons would begin. Once there she was drugged and held by a gang as a sex slave for three weeks. After she managed to escape she agreed that it had perhaps been a mite unwise to trust a sadhu wearing brand new Adidas running shoes.

None of these guys wore shoes and the friendliness that flowed from them was so patently real, I didn't worry for a moment. I took the chillum and, being sure it didn't actually touch my lips – it was the guy with the flaking skin handing it over – cupped it in my fist and had a good long pull. Well, when in Rome . . .

As the sun went down, one by one they told their stories. CKT Nair, perhaps the kindest looking of them all, with warm dark eyes and a benign grin that rested permanently on his angled face, had worked for the government as an engineer. While building a lift shaft in a factory in his native Tamil Nadu he had fallen seventy feet and broken his back. For his injuries he had received 18,000 rupees – a king's ransom in 1972. Not being able to work, he'd taken to drinking and womanising, generally getting up to no good, and ended up being accused of a murder that happened in his village. Even though he was acquitted in court his community still believed him guilty so, having spent all his money and finding no happiness, he decided to leave his family to go to find God. In 1978 he took to the road and has been wandering Hindustan ever since.

'And have you found Him?' I asked.

'Oh yes,' he answered quietly, 'I see him many times. He was in Haridwar at the Kumbh Mela.' He looked at the others for support. They all nodded and mumbled agreement. He looked back at me and smiled and as I gazed into his serene eyes, I was inclined to believed that he had.

Karuna Karan, the man with no nose and crumbling face, had left home in Bombay twenty years before in search of a cure for his skin problem. To my surprise he assured me he had found it – the poor man must have been in a hell of a state before. On his travels he'd met an ascetic, had become his chela, or disciple, and followed him on the road. His guru had died of malaria on the way to Haridwar and Karuna Karan had joined this group of holy men. Yen Kumar, who at sixty-four years of age was the oldest, had been a sadhu ever since he could remember. He claimed to have been on a pilgrimage to Pakistan before partition.

It didn't take long for Zahoor to mellow and well before the last of the stories had been told he was gaping with wonder at these men. It was as much as I could do to make him translate their words into English before he was bounding on with another question of his own. He kept laughing, amazed by their words, by the life they lived, surprised and delighted that they didn't deride him for his Islamic beliefs. 'All are one,' said CKT Nair, when Zahoor told them he was a Muslim. 'Religion is unimportant. How you live is what counts.'

With the sun setting behind the tank Karuna Karan took some of the orange religious thread from his satchel, thread he said had been blessed by a venerated holy man in Ajmer. He showed me the guru's card. There was a full-colour photo of the Baba, resplendent in his bright orange robes with a sparkling halo above his head, complete with web site and e-mail address. Karuna Karan cut the cord with his long thumb nail and wrapped one length around my wrist and another around Zahoor's.

'Nam bhia hey,' he said in earnest.

Zahoor, barely able to control his delight, translated, 'Now we are brothers.'

I smiled proudly and patted Zahoor on the back. It felt oddly satisfying to be the accidental catalyst for his taste of a new kind of life.

The sadhus fed us on rice and vegetable curry at the free kitchen in the Krishna temple across the way and then suggested that we stay the night. We had told them about some of the hassles we had been having – they did not know of Shri Siddheshwar Baba and his Third Eye Foundation, but thought the whole episode strange – and pointed out that there would be no hotel registers or police at the holy site. Zahoor didn't seem too pleased by the idea of sleeping rough for a second night, this time on a cold stone floor, but when I pointed out that the alternative might easily be a night in the can, he agreed. This time without a sulk.

By nine thirty most of the lamps had been extinguished; the only lights that remained were the fire-flies that bobbed up and down above the water. Spreading our blankets in a row we lay down. Yen Kumar passed me the chillum for a final toke and with my mellow head cushioned gently on a cloud of tranquillity, I drifted off towards a peaceful sleep.

———— ◆ ————

She was even more beautiful when she was angry. Blonde hair falling forward to frame those perfect lips, with a slash of crimson lipstick, and her flashing green eyes. The gun lay casually in my hand, resting across my lap. I raised my eyebrows sympathetically, then grinned as I reached past her and poured us both another drink . . .

'Bealby. Beeealbyyy!' Startled, I turned from the window and faced the front, feeling the eyes of the class burning into me. 'It's not surprising your English is so bad,' snapped Mr Bolan, eyes bulging. 'If you think things really are more interesting outside why don't you go and view them from closer quarters.*'*

I felt my face colour and studied the book on the desk before me. He had a point, and I knew it. But the effort of trawling for meaning in an inky black sea of type made simple distractions outside the window highly attractive. A tractor mowing the lawn, the wind moving through the trees, a girl wandering along the path. Daydreams were sure to follow. Outside, under the sky, there was sun, there was rain, there was life.

'Sorry, sir,' I said, taking the pen from my mouth. 'No, thank you, I'd rather stay.' I wouldn't have, of course. Truth was I would much rather have been

*almost anywhere, even standing outside the classroom. I did enjoy school – the
sport, activities, friends; I enjoyed life – but English lessons, indeed most
classwork, tended to bore me rigid. The sooner I was away from them the better.
I knew there was a big old world out there waiting to be discovered. I was
impatient to get on with it.*

'Have you read the book – any of it?'

'Umm, in places, sir.'

*'Don't lie, boy. You haven't, of course you haven't.' An exasperated Mr Bolan
exhaled slowly and then continued in a marginally calmer voice. 'The Grapes
of Wrath is a classic of the twentieth century. If you tried a little harder you
might actually find it worthwhile. What on earth do you think you're going to
achieve if you don't read? You'll fail all your O levels and what then, what do
you think you'll become?'*

*'I don't know sir, err, perhaps a teacher, like you, sir.' The class laughed. My
face began to cool.*

*'Yes, Bealby, and my great dane might become Prime Minister. Now kindly
desist from looking out of that window and pay attention. One more lapse and
you're out, and in detention.'*

'Sorry, sir. Yes, sir.'

*But my mind was already beginning to drift. O levels? Careers? What was I
going to be? Hell, I didn't know. A film star? A footballer? Rock singer? Secret
agent . . . A faint shuffle of approaching footsteps. The unmistakable sound of a
key being cautiously turned. I was on my feet in one swift movement, scooping the
girl into one arm and taking aim.*

Inside the carriage it was warm and quiet. Zahoor and I shared the
compartment with a fat Sikh couple, an elderly lady and a soldier
from the Punjab Rifles. Beyond the window fields of wheat,
mustard, sunflowers and rice lay dissected by neat irrigation canals.
There were small mud houses on either side of the track with great
piles of dung cakes looking like neatly stacked frisbees on the roofs
and walls. Away to the right an avenue of eucalyptus defined the
Grand Trunk Road, running parallel to the line. It was a lazy
afternoon, and with the rocking motion of the train, accompanied
by the lullaby of the wheels on the tracks, diddle-i-dee, diddle-i-dah,
I felt my eyelids grow heavy and my mind drift.

'I a rel'teeve leeve en saddle bags!'

'I'm sorry? What?' I sat up blinking and rubbed my eyes.

'Yez, yez, rel'teeves y'know, leeve en saddle bags.' The soldier addressing me had an enormous grin which revealed snow white teeth. He nodded his head in encouragement, making the thin green tassels hanging from his army turban swish in front of his eyes. His sten-gun was lying across his lap, pointing disconcertingly at my gut. Registering my look of incomprehension he added, 'Y'fron Lenden propa?'

'Yes,' I replied, starting to comprehend the gist of the man's strange accent. 'Yes, I live in London proper ... Battersea, just south of the river.'

'Ah, yez ... my rel'teeves fron saddle backs.'

The penny dropped. 'Ah, Southall, Bucks.' We both smiled, then he turned away. The conversation at an end, he pulled a well used neem stick from his breast pocket and proceeded to scrub his teeth.

A little while later a young Sikh man in a yellow pakta – the small turban with a bun at the front – with wispy beard and bad complexion, entered our carriage and asked myself and the soldier to come with him.

We followed him up the carriage, through the adjoining doors and into the next compartment, where there was a nasty scene. Two women aged around thirty crouched on the floor wailing like wounded animals, slapping their heads and burying their faces in the lap of a person I presumed to be their mother who was lying along a bench seat. Two men knelt next to the women trying to console them, while three children sat opposite, two crying and rubbing their eyes, the other gazing silently out of the window. Five or six other passengers had gathered and watched solemnly. They all looked at me, even the soldier, as if simply by being foreign I might be able to redeem the situation, which was quite obviously hopeless. The old woman's eyes stared vacantly at the ceiling, her cheeks were sunk deep into her face and when I went to feel for a pulse I discovered the body had already started to cool. She was dead, no question. I pulled her eyelids closed.

At Amballa station the soldier and three other men carried the dead body down on to the platform and placed it in a bizarre-looking cycle rickshaw hearse. Out in the open the corpse excited more curiosity and soon there was quite a crowd. Once more the daughters started wailing, which made the kids cry and the husbands look flustered. With nothing more that we could do I grabbed Zahoor and headed for the exit. Two deaths on two train journeys. From now on I'd take the bus.

With the evening sun forming lengthy shadows we found a hotel that had a room; after two nights spent sleeping rough, Zahoor had convinced me it was worth taking the risk. The room backed on to the railway track next to a busy shunting line. Dirty black engines were working hard pushing great chains of fuel bowsers, grain trucks and flat-topped carriers, some ferrying tanks and other military hardware, up and down the track. For what reason it was hard to tell. Even with the windows closed the noise inside the room was intrusive. I unpacked the few possessions I had from my bag and lay down on the bed. Almost immediately there was a knock at the door.

'Yes?'

One of the hotel boys stood next to a thin, middle-aged man with a narrow moustache – the type shaved both above and below – and dyed black hair with a grey parting. There was no smile on either of their faces.

'This CID,' said the boy. 'He want talk with you.' I was impressed; we had only signed in ten minutes earlier.

The policeman did not look particularly charming. Short, barely five foot tall, he had a sharp, angled face with a forehead cast in a perpetual frown. As always when faced with authority, I immediately felt guilty.

'Ah, hello,' I said in as carefree a way as possible. 'Come in.'

'I'm Chief Inspector Gupta, Amballa CID.' He barged past me, flashing a card so quickly it could have been the three of clubs for all I saw of it. 'Who are you? Where you going? Who is he?' As the inspector plonked himself on Zahoor's bed I suddenly wondered if he had somehow got news of us through the ashram – he was certainly acting as if we were highly suspicious. But it seemed unlikely as we were well out of that police jurisdiction. Though Zahoor and I did not know it, Amballa was a hot bed of terrorism and subversion. In a few weeks' time a bomb – blamed on Sikh separatists – would explode in the station, killing eight and injuring many more. The police in this town were tetchy as hell and on their toes. I answered politely and asked whether there was a problem.

'That's what I will find out,' said Inspector Gupta ominously. 'What name? Passport.' He held out his hand.

For once I was happy that I hadn't bothered to get a new passport. Being three quarters full with stamps from some fairly out of the way places it always generates a ridiculous amount of interest with customs, police, ashram secretaries and the like, ending with me answering a whole barrage of totally irrelevant and inane questions, usually about Africa. But now, as the inspector placed a pair of scratched, gold-rimmed spectacles on his nose and became absorbed, I was thankful for them. I had unpacked everything on to my bed, so while he was slowly turning pages, I surreptitiously slipped my dictaphone and note book under the pillow. My press card and letters were in an ingenious money belt I had had made in Delhi, wrapped around my ankles.

After a few minutes he turned and asked, 'Why you travel so much? What is your occupation?' That old chestnut.

'Artist. I travel a lot because I'm an artist,' I replied, as if no further explanation was needed and, as in the past, it worked like a charm. Inspector Gupta looked at me with a confused expression, shrugged and handed back my passport. He had missed the Pakistan visa.

'You, sit here.' The inspector gestured to Zahoor to sit at the end of my bed. He took off his glasses and rubbed the lens on the corner of his shirt before replacing them. 'Give me ID.' It didn't take long for the fireworks to begin.

'What is this?' The inspector regarded the 'Houseboat Owners Association' card as though it were a piece of canine excrement. It was the only form of ID Zahoor had.

'My father has a houseboat on Dal Lake, in Srinagar,' answered Zahoor, rubbing his hands together nervously. 'Look here, it is approved of by the Jammu and Kashmir government.' Zahoor pointed to the laminated card where beneath the title was written: Opp. J&K Govt. Srinagar.

'What you mean, "approved of"?' the inspector shouted, partly out of anger and partly to be heard over the noise of another goods train shunting down the track, blowing its whistle. He had a grating, high-pitched voice that seemed to reach a more acute level the more animated he became. Leaning forward, he jabbed an accusatory finger hard into Zahoor's chest. 'Why you lie to me? What do you hide? This mean "opposite government buildings", not "approved of". Why you lying?'

'But surely, Inspector,' I interjected in as soft a voice as I could muster, 'this is still an official card and explains who Zahoor is.'

'Official?' he spat, turning on me, still ranting loudly. 'This not official, he could have this made anywhere . . . it mean nothing. I have seen much better fake ID cards than this.' He scoffed and threw it back at Zahoor. I really thought he was going to take us down to the station. 'You know while travel you should have proper identification. Where your things? Your wallet? Give them to me.' He was starting to sweat, as was I. It was stuffy in the little room. Particles of dust, disturbed by Zahoor's movement, were lit up by the evening sun that cast a long beam of yellow light through the window. I contemplated opening it but decided the noise would be too great. I took a drink of water from a bottle that sat on the cracked formica table by the bed and wiped my forehead.

Zahoor handed over his wallet.

Pedantically the inspector removed each piece of paper and studied it thoroughly – taking a particular interest in a letter from Angie – all the while questioning Zahoor, now in the vernacular.

Closed to the grilling I began to think and it didn't take long to realise that travelling this way simply wasn't working. I had thought briefly about sending Zahoor on to Kashmir after the episode at the ashram but I had hoped that that might have proved to be a one-off. It was now patently obvious that every time we checked into a hotel the same situation would occur. An Englishman and a Kashmiri travelling together was unusual at the best of times, but up here on the Punjab plains where Muslims were often mistrusted and there were hardly any foreign tourists, it was unheard of. We would always be viewed with suspicion. When we left Delhi I had hoped that there would be invitations to spend nights with families we met along the road, as there were in the south, but this had not happened. The sadhus had warned us the police often check the dhabas and sleeping rough was not as easy as it may seem – there were just too many people around. Besides, I was becoming increasingly impatient to meet John Hayward and find out what he thought of the real journey to Nuristan. Since receiving his fax I'd thought of little else but trying to persuade him to accompany me. I needed to reach Peshawar and see him, the sooner the better. It was time to move on.

'So where you going next?' asked the inspector calmly, having written down Zahoor's uncle's address and telephone number in Delhi and his parents' details in Srinagar.

'We'll continue north tomorrow morning,' I said. 'To Amritsar.'

'Tomorrow morning?' A thin flicker of a smile crossed his lips. He was undoubtedly pleased to learn that we would soon be out of his jurisdiction and no longer his responsibility. He wrote down the information. 'Amritsar is very beautiful place. Tourists there, is better you go.'

'So I've heard.' I stood up and held out my hand. 'Sorry to have caused you so much inconvenience.'

A cloud of suspicion momentarily shaded his eyes, then was gone. 'Be sure you do go tomorrow, I will check. And you,' he looked at Zahoor, 'get proper ID.' He shook my hand and left.

The following morning Inspector Gupta was waiting outside the hotel in his green Mahindra jeep.

'Amritsar?' he asked, eyes narrowing, as we passed the open window.

'Amritsar,' I replied.

At the bus station, by the Srinagar-bound coach, Zahoor and I said goodbye. He wasn't too upset, after all he was going home. We clasped arms and hugged playfully but Zahoor clung to me just a little harder and longer than I'd been expecting. We hadn't known each other long but still we'd had some adventures and it seemed we'd formed a bond; a curious older–younger brother relationship maybe. It felt as though I was packing him off after the holidays while I went back to work.

'*Salaam*, Jonny,' he said from the open window, and as the bus pulled away he waved smiling broadly. An hour later I boarded my own bus heading towards the border.

The bus pulled into Amritsar late in the afternoon and I headed straight for the Golden Temple. The moment I descended the marble steps, saw the dazzling sanctuary that stood at the end of a promontory in the centre of the square tank and heard the songs of the priests that echoed from within, I was overcome by a peace and tranquillity I'd found at no other religious site across India. I followed the procession of pilgrims walking clockwise around the calm water and let my mind unwind.

I was leaving India. In her cities, on her beaches, her mountains and plains, I had found the land I had hoped to discover with Melanie all those years ago. It had been everything and more I had imagined it to be – a place I knew I'd visit many times again. I stopped and sat on the shallow ghats.

But the adventurer in me was on the edge of his seat. Though always surprising, India now felt familiar; tomorrow would once again be the unknown. I picked up my bag and found the foreigners' dormitory. The moment I entered, a deranged Lithuanian woman beat me with a broom for not removing my shoes quickly enough. A Dutch Sikh convert called Cornelius was sitting in the corner reading from an English translation of the *Granth Sahib*. He was wearing a navy turban, or pagri, and white robes, with a small ceremonial dagger hanging from a yellow sash. He looked up and smiled.

'Don't worry,' he said, 'she does this to everyone.' He closed the holy book, pulled on his wispy beard and indicated that I should sit down. 'So which way are you heading?'

I grinned. 'Tomorrow I'm going to Pakistan.'

PART TWO
Through the Land of the Pure

5 Meeting Peachey

*'He's a big man with a red beard,
and a great swell he is.'*

I sat, without concern for municipal orders, on a low wall, leaning against the iron railings that surround the famous Ajaib Gher – the Wonder House, as the Lahore museum has come to be known. With my bus north to Peshawar not due to leave for a couple of hours, Pakistan's most famous museum had seemed like a sensible place to kill a little time. Not today, it seemed. A sign, just inside the bolted gates, made the situation clear: *'Museum closed for cleaning first Wednesday of every month.'* I hauled myself reluctantly to my feet and wandered back up the street.

Lahore was instantly appealing. Like Old Delhi, it was crowded and noisy, dirty and hot and like its great Moghul brother it was also alive with scenes from many different times. Turning south towards the station, horse-drawn tongas carrying cargoes of women and children, crated chickens, combustion engines, fat-bottomed sheep, huge tractor wheels and much else besides competed for space with the Mercedes flying coaches and horn-blasting Maruti minibuses. Wizened old men in dirty turbans, with flame-red beards and woollen shawls, stood beside suited business men using mobile phones; youths traded knives and homemade kites next to others selling calculators and nylon wallets; women in burqas – the all-enveloping head-to-toe Islamic cloak – walked along roads where others, wearing make-up and sunglasses, drove small Suzuki mopeds. Yet at the same time it was clear that I had crossed the border, for there were no sadhus, no cows, no incense and no beggars. Much of the colour seemed to have been left behind on the other side of the border as well. Gone were the brilliant shades of the Sikh's pagris, the gaudy Western shirts and jumpers, and the bright pinks and yellows of the women's saris. The colours of the almost ever-present shalwar kameez were generally dour – all shades of brown and grey, with the occasional jade green or sapphire blue to add a sparkle to the crowd. Back in a Muslim world, as outside Delhi's Jama Majid, in my local attire I blended in again.

In front of the red-brick station a busy roundabout fielded three main roads with a large expanse of grass at its centre. A hundred years ago this area was known as the Lahore caravanserai. People from all over Central Asia would mass here to trade their goods. Some came from the north bringing the famous Afghan horses, or furs, carpets and guns, while others travelled from the south, carrying spices and cloth. In those days it was a noisy mass of stabling, brothels, opium dens, eating houses and sleeping shacks. Now it's a concrete horde of dingy hotels, cheap restaurants and coach depots surrounded by honking traffic. It was from here that Peachey and Danny set off north on camels with the summer caravan, disguised as a mad priest and his servant.

'Gord's holy trousers, so it was,' said Danny, 'though I'd scarce believe it now. Going to sell charms to the Amir. Penny whirligigs as I recall.'

'Taa!' scoffed Peachey, 'Penny whirligigs? It was them Martini rifles packed beneath the saddles that was the ticket. Without them we wouldn't a' got far.'

I bought a copy of the *Frontier Post* and, at an open-sided café, ordered a chai. These were troubled times for Pakistan too. The front page was dominated by reports of urban bombings, general strikes and widespread disorder. But it wasn't any of those stories that gave me cause for alarm. Hidden away in the bottom corner of an inside page was an article that put in question the continuation of my journey. Over the past few days there had been more reports in the papers that various diplomatic missions trying to broker a cease-fire and establish talks between the Afghan government and the Taliban militia, were close to a breakthrough. The Iranian foreign minister had been frantically criss-crossing the country in a bid to iron out some of their differences as had the UN peace envoy. The previous morning the *Times of India* had reported that the two sides were finally ready to talk. Now, under the headline 'Taliban Declare Holy War', the article explained that far from talking peace the student army had launched an official jihad, asserting that under no circumstances would it negotiate a peace deal with the government. They vowed anew to fight on and topple the Rabbani regime which they claimed was both corrupt and un-Islamic, stating once more their desire to impose strict shar'ia law over the whole country. An all-out offensive was now looking likely. Eager to find out what John thought of this new development, I stood up and made my way towards the bus.

As I crossed the side road a lad on a lithe bay horse came trotting round the corner. Tassels fell in front of the animals eyes and a long mane tumbled from its neck. It was obviously agitated and white sweat lathered its sides. Riding bare-back the lad wrapped his legs fast around the horse's belly, clinging tightly to the reins and mane. As it passed by a row of minibuses one of the drivers stabbed at his horn, blasting a deafening tune straight at the horse's ears. Startled, the animal swung sharply round, throwing its front legs into the air. Nostrils flaring, eyes wide with fear, it came down with a judder, narrowly missing a barrow laden with fruit. With such swift and violent movement the lad did well to stay aboard. I climbed on to the bus, found an empty seat and sat down.

———— ◆ ————

'OK now Jaarrrny,' I heard the director's booming voice, 'let's just have that one more time.'

Which bit would that be? I thought as I slumped forward hoping the wide brimmed Stetson would hide my humiliation. The part where I gallop down Main Street in a plume of dust, rearing the horse dramatically towards the sky . . . or the intense embarrassment when the saddle slips off and I end up on my arse, in front of the whole crew, still pointing my guns to the heavens?'

Sitting in the dust, I cursed. As far as first jobs go it had looked pretty damn good: three months working as a runner on a cowboy film in Spain. Living up to all academic expectations I had ended up with precious few qualifications to my name so I was deliriously happy to have been picked for the shoot. I was hungry for the chance to experience something more of the world and besides, this was the movie business!

We had barely been filming a week when the stunt man broke his leg. Although I hadn't sat on a horse for at least five years I heard myself confidently volunteering for the post. The extra money would cut out a good few weeks of saving for the Australian trip I was planning towards the end of the year and it sounded like more fun than making tea, positioning microphones and carrying messages.

An hour ago I'd rolled out of make-up with my meanest tombstone sneer: Clint Eastwood in High Plains Drifter. *And what a buzz it had been. Suddenly, I was the star, with everyone pampering me. 'Yo OK, Jarrnny? Need a drink? OK let's go do it then. Ya the man.'*

As I'd always known it would, my new life dazzled with extraordinary excitement. At least it had done. Now I wasn't quite so sure. Clint Eastwood? I felt more like Buster Keaton.

I stood up and slapped the dust off my trousers with my hat. I took the reins of the horse and climbed back on board. Looking around me at the wild landscape, the crew, the wooden façades of the mock cowboy town and up at the sun. I smiled to myself. Come on Jonny, stunt riding may not be your vocation, but life's a circus, so tighten that girth and let's do it again.

———— ◆ ————

As the door to the sprawling Canal Road bungalow swung open, the first thing I noticed was a great red beard. Thick on the cheeks, rather than following the curve on the underside of the chin, the whiskers pointed straight out horizontally, forming an extremely noble wedge. In the style of the Afghans, the moustache was clipped back to a short stubble and above was a broad nose, a pair of piercing blue eyes and a solid mop of auburn hair.

'Daniel Dravot, I presume,' John Hayward said and grinned.

I smiled back and shook his hand, replying in my best Sean Connery accent, 'Peachey Carnehan, how the devil are you?'

'Sorry the place is such a mess.' He turned and led me down a narrow corridor cluttered with bags, boots and what looked like rolled up maps. 'I've only just got back from Mazar-i-Sharif on the Red Cross flight. I'll show you where you can dump your stuff and then if you'll bear with me I've just got to put a few things away. I'll only be a minute, then we'll go down to the club for a swim and a beer . . . if that sounds OK.'

'Sounds fine.'

In a checked shirt with the sleeves rolled up to the elbows, pale moleskin trousers and studded brogues that clipped like a tap dancer's as he marched across the stone floor, John looked more like an English farmer just in from the fields on a hot harvest day than a long-term aid worker. He was well spoken and held himself in a formal manner but he seemed friendly and generous too. As we reached the end of the corridor and entered a conservatory that looked out on to a lavish garden, he told me he didn't expect payment from guests residing in the house and I was welcome to stay as long as I wished. He showed me to a spare bedroom. I washed my face and changed and returned to the conservatory.

If his musical and literary tastes were anything to go by, John was a man of extreme contrasts. Improbably stacked on a bookshelf next to such titles as *Encyclopaedia of Islam, Afghanistan: fragmentation of a nation*, Machiavelli's *The Prince* and, I was delighted to see, Rudyard Kipling's *The Man Who Would Be King*, was a stack of *Viz* magazines and in the cassette box next to Mozart and Schubert lay Billy Idol and the Macc Lads. He was also obviously something of a photographer. Hung on the walls were framed pictures of dramatic Afghan scenes. One poster-sized print of a game of buzkasi – a wild contest between forty-odd men on charging steeds for control of a dead goat (or Russian prisoner, depending) – was simply superb. Noticing a bottle of Laphroig single malt whisky on a side table I smiled; it was good to know we had things in common. I sat down in one of the wicker chairs and waited.

When John returned I complimented him on his comfortable home.

'Ha ... you haven't heard the mosque yet!' He stuffed a towel and goggles into a small bag. 'One of the microphones is practically in my bedroom. It wouldn't be so bad but I'm sure the muezzin's got TB. Coughs up half a pound of gunk every time he calls the faithful to prayer – not so pleasant at five in the morning. I've only been here a couple of months,' – he looked reflectively round the room – 'but I've been in Peshawar for nearly five years now.' You could tell it was something he was proud of. 'Came over to do some mountain climbing before going into the army, got offered a job with a Norwegian aid agency for three months and stayed three years.' He smiled wryly, 'Then I joined the Swedes and ... well, kind of gets into your blood.'

*

On Circular Road, opposite an area of wasteland where a fleet of smart jeeps and four-wheel drive vehicles sat idle, was the entrance to the America Club. Outside the guard house sat a sentry, his AK47 resting across his lap. Behind a thick set of steel gates was the closed and closeted world of the expat – no Pakistanis were allowed in.

Around the pool a few creamy-skinned women in swimsuits rested on sunbeds or on chairs under parasols, some with small children, others reading or talking. There was a pale bloke in some fetching, chocolate-brown trunks doing lengths and at the far end under a grand mulberry tree a couple of men lounged at a table, obviously much better off for the Fosters beer they were guzzling; one shouted a cheery hello to John.

There are over eighty NGOs working out of Peshawar on the Afghan cause, many of which employ a number of expatriate staff. They and their families all need feeding and watering and generally entertaining – that night a band of aid workers calling themselves FBI was doing a gig – and this was where they came. After a few weeks or months working in the destroyed cities or crumbling villages of the country that now lay but sixty kilometres away, I imagined they deserved it.

John came out of the changing rooms in a pair of skimpy blue Speedos and slipped on his goggles. It was a worrying sight. He wasn't especially tall, maybe 5'10", but he had the body of a well-worked bull. Constructed out of pure hard muscle, his thighs and calves were built like pistons, his chest like a barrel and his biceps were thicker than my neck. He dived in and started powering his way up and down the pool. Feeling rather puny, I splashed around in the shallow end for a few minutes, trying to keep out of the way before climbing out, changing and grabbing a beer and a fag. Plenty of time to get fit, I mused.

'So how is it in Afghanistan at the moment?' I asked, half an hour later, once John had rejoined me. 'What about the Taliban launching their jihad?'

'Yeah, like that makes a difference.' The sarcasm was obvious. 'Words, that's all. War in this part of the world is always a jihad.' He pushed a hand through his thick hair and leaned forward. 'They say the government has made some advances into Gor province in the west near Herat but apart from that things are pretty quiet. Mind you, that can change any moment. Afghanistan is like a pan of simmering water, the heat gets turned up – a new alliance or something – and it boils very fast. Gulbadeen Hekmatyar and his group Hezb-i-Islami have just done a deal with the government, so that could spark some fireworks, but apart from that it's hard to say. There's been talk of an offensive for a while now but what has become of it nobody knows.

'What, the government attacking the Taliban?' I asked. 'To try to knock them away from Kabul?'

'Possibly. If they could. But there's a rumour that the Taliban might strike first, up through Jalalabad, to hit Kabul from the relatively unprotected east.' He thought a moment and chewed on a clump of his beard. 'At the moment the war is a stalemate but that can't last for ever. Something will eventually have to give. We shall see.'

A waiter in a smart white shalwar kameez and burgundy waist coat came over with two more beers. The light had now almost gone, the mosquitoes were starting to bite. John asked for one of my cigarettes and I felt relieved.

'What are they like?

'The Taliban?' A resigned smile passed his lips and he sat back. 'Well, a friend of mine describes them as having the look of a hippie and the mentality of a skinhead.' He opened his can and took a large gulp. 'I try to stay as neutral as possible when it comes to Afghan politics, best way to stay out of trouble. And my main areas are in the north, in Badakshan, away from the Taliban, so I haven't had too many dealings with them. There was a funny article in the paper today from Herat saying that they're sacking everyone who can't tie a turban or grow a beard.' He shrugged and then grinned at the thought. 'One thing's for sure we don't want them taking over Kabul at the moment. It would make our trip to Nuristan pretty bloody tricky.'

'What do you think, about Nuristan?' I asked excitedly, leaning forward in my chair. 'Is it possible? Do you think we can do it? Can you come?'

'I don't see why not.' He studied the cigarette hard as though it held some hidden answer, then flicked the ash on the floor and looked up. 'I've decided that I'm going to quit the Swedish Committee. Can't be dealing with them any longer. I need to do something new.' He went on to explain that over the past few weeks he'd been thinking a great deal about his work, his future in the world of aid and a few other things besides, all of which had had a bearing on whether or not he would be able to join me. Having decided not to renew his contract with the Swedes, he thought he could go to Nuristan, think more about things there, and decide what to do with himself when he returned. For me it was fantastic news. 'Trouble is,' he went on, 'I'll be working quite hard until the time we go. It'll mean you'll have to do a fair bit of the organising: getting letters, some contacts and things.'

John rattled off a list of names, none of which rang any bells or lingered in my brain for more than a moment. We'd travel, he said, using letters of introduction. In this way the headman of one village could make us known to an ally in the next so we'd be passed along a chain of friends. It was, he explained, similar to how the mujahadeen operated during the war with the Russians. As he saw it we would need a translator, a security guide, a couple of porters and a whole host of other things which, perhaps naïvely, I had not envisioned at all. The way John talked the undertaking sounded more akin to Burton and Speke than Carnehan and Dravot. Answering my questioning eyes, he said, 'I'm afraid we can't just blunder into Nuristan like your two mates Peachey and Danny, Jonny. The way to stay alive in this country is to have things organised. After all, I don't suppose you want us to suffer the same fate as befell them, do you?'

Reluctantly, I accepted that he had a point.

'From what I've heard they're a tricky bunch the Nuristanis, not quite as homicidal as they used to be, but tricky just the same. Planning and contacts will be all important.'

Not really knowing what on earth he was expecting of me, I agreed. Letters from political leaders, commanders, mullahs? An expedition group complete with interpreter, porters and security men? Was he really expecting me to organise all that? I looked down at the floor and chewed pensively on a fingernail.

'Don't worry. It won't be so hard,' John said, lighting up another cigarette. 'I'll introduce you to some people. You'll soon get up to speed.' He then took a long drag and blew the smoke out slowly. 'But it isn't a holiday, Jonny. Afghanistan's hard: a big boy's country, for big boy's games. It sure ain't trekking in Nepal.'

I leaned back and put the can to my lips. The beer tasted cool, refreshing; the first I'd had for a while. Oh well, I thought, if this is the way it has to be done, so be it. It was tomorrow's problem, not today's. With John I surely had a far better chance of achieving my goal. I held up my beer can and thumped it into his. 'To Nuristan,' I toasted.

'To Nuristan,' said John. 'Piece of piss.'

Early the next morning I caught a bus down to the old town – I wanted to have a new shalwar kameez made up. Like many of the subcontinent's bustling bazaars, the streets around Qiss Khani, the storytellers' bazaar, are a swirling kaleidoscope of colour, cultures and creeds, only here it's all on a far larger scale than anything I'd seen before. The jewellers don't have stalls next to the cloth merchants, or the leather sellers close to the vegetable traders. In old Peshawar, squashed into the narrow streets and sunless alleyways, the merchants have their own bazaars. It's a noisy place buzzing with life but also possessing an edge of danger. It's a place where the sweet smell of hashish emanates from darkened doorways, where men with weathered skin and shimmering eyes don't only whisper, 'change money? hashish?' into your ear but quickly add, 'brown sugar, veeery good, old Buddha, buy guns'. It's a place where street sellers push bullet belts and holsters, and the police wear flak jackets; where baggy-shirted hawkers selling razor blades, knives and combs, discreetly offer automatic pistols. And it's a place where the sound of gunfire often punctuates the tumultuous din – a storybook town, echoing the world of Harun-al-Raschid.

Beyond the small-time dealers lurks the murky world of large scale international smuggling. Drugs, gems, ancient artefacts, weapons and even enriched uranium, all pass through the Peshawar bazaars. Standing at the mouth of the Khyber Pass, through which countless migrations and marching armies have strode, Peshawar will always be a frontier town.

I found some cloth, this time a shade of olive green, and was directed to an old Afghan tailor who took an hour and a half to turn it into a new shalwar kameez. From a stall next door I bought an eight-pocketed Afghan waistcoat, a woollen roll-up Chitrali cap and a mud-coloured patoo – a blanket-cum-cloak carried by all Pathans. As I turned to leave, four women draped in black burqas floated by. They reminded me of the horsemen of the apocalypse. I hoped it was not an omen.

Soon after midday I headed back to University Town, where I had arranged to meet John to discuss our plans.

In a cool office, air conditioner whirring in the background, John was standing opposite the biggest map I'd ever seen. In fact, as I looked closer, I realised that it wasn't one map but twelve smaller ones pinned three high and four deep to a colossal pinboard; a sheet of transparent plastic had been rolled down over it from the top. The 1:100,000-inch twisted mass of black contour lines depicting Nuristan looked more like a Jackson Pollock painting than a discernible map. But with coloured felt-tipped pens John slowly transformed it into a more comprehensible land of valleys, villages, peaks and passes.

'Have you got any plans as to the route you want to take?' John asked, putting the pens to one side. I had to admit that I did not. Until the previous day I hadn't been sure that the whole crazy venture was going to be possible at all. As long as I followed Peachey and Danny over the Khyber Pass and into Nuristan from the south, I didn't mind a jot. Though I sometimes forgot, Kipling's story was fiction and from there the footsteps of my friends became impossible to define.

'OK,' said John, choosing the green pen. 'So you want to start in Jalalabad . . .' He marked the town with a cross. 'And presumably finish with the Kalash.'

'Finish with the what?' I asked, bemused.

'The Kalash,' said John, turning towards me. 'In *The Man Who Would Be King*, they set out from Marwar Junction and travel to Kafiristan. So I imagined you'd want to end your journey there . . . with the Kalash, the last of the pagans living in the Hindu Kush?'

Scraping my jaw off the floor, I stared agog. 'You mean there still is a Kafiristan. There *are* pagans still living in the Hindu

Kush? I thought they'd all been wiped out years ago. In the jihad. The Amir ... Abdul Rahman.' The two books I'd read had made no mention of this tribe John referred to, at least none that I'd picked up on.

'On the Afghan side of the border they were. But on what was then the British side of the Durrant Line, one small tribe survived. The Amir couldn't get to them.' His eyes widened. 'I thought you'd have known about them. I just assumed that was where you would want to head for – Kafiristan as the Pakistanis still call it. Give the story a relevant ending.'

With great excitement I jumped up, rushed to the map and looked where John was pointing. With his green pen he marked an area in the top right hand corner just over a high pass on the Pakistan side of the border, some 200 kilometres north of Peshawar. I could make out three narrow valleys, a few small villages, forests and rivers. It was perfect. I could hardly contain myself.

'Well yes, yes!' I stammered. 'Of course, that's definitely where we must end then. In one of those valleys. Kafiristan. Fantastic.' So there were pagans still living in the Hindu Kush. Kafiristan had not been totally wiped out. The Kálash weren't exactly hidden, unknown and awaiting discovery as I had fantasised – in Pakistan, John explained, as a minority tribe with different and interesting ways they were actually quite celebrated – but they were there just the same.

'In the old days, you see,' John went on, 'Kafiristan was a much greater size than Nuristan is today.' He circled an area that reached Swat and Chitral in the east and the Panjsher Valley, above Kabul, in the west. 'But slowly Islam pushed in from all sides forcing the Kafirs higher into the mountains. Then the Durrant Line was established, the Amir invaded his side and only the Kalash were left. Amazingly they've survived ever since. There are a couple of works published here in Pakistan about them. You'll find them in one of the bookshops.'

It seemed incredible, miraculous even, and I stared at the map with my mouth wide open and my heart and mind racing. Until that moment I hadn't really known where I was heading other than Nuristan. Now the journey had a true goal, a purpose and an end. Kafiristan was real again, it existed, its people still dancing to a pagan song. 'Yes,' I said again, nailing the map with my index finger, 'we'll finish here.'

'Well *you* can.' Confusing me again, John now pointed further north. 'I have a great friend who lives up here, in Garam Chasma. If he's around at the time, I think that's where I'll go.' He looked at me once more and, seeing my concern, sought to reassure me. 'It's no problem. If I do decide to end up there it'll just mean splitting up for the last part of the journey. A couple of days. That's all.'

I agreed; whatever. My quest now had a physical goal and little was going to worry me. Or so I thought.

'OK,' said John, concentrating again. 'Well, I imagined we'd take a flying coach through Khyber, up to the border. Whether legally or illegally we'll just have to see at the time, but permission to travel though the Tribal Areas has been much easier to get recently.' West of Peshawar, sandwiched between Pakistan and the Afghan border, is an autonomous region known as the Tribal Areas, where, just as in the British times, government authority does not reach. With their own administration, laws and enforcement of justice based on tribal traditions, since the days of Alexander, and probably before, the tribesmen of this rugged strip of land have been ruled by no one. For successive Pakistani governments taking them on in their wild rugged land has always seemed too great a headache. To travel through the region today special permission and an armed escort are required. In the Tribal Areas kidnapping is rife. Alternatively, as Tim McGirk, the *Independant*'s man, had suggested, we could travel in disguise and keep our heads down. We would have to wait and see.

'Once across the border,' John went on, 'we'll take a minibus to Jalalabad, where we'll stay for a few days, getting everything in order. Now, in Nuristan itself' – John picked up a green pen and indicated the province some seventy kilometres north of Jalalabad – 'it seems there are three main valleys: the Ramgul, the Pech, that leads into the Parun, and the Bashgul.' He pointed them out. 'Now of course we can't write anything in stone, we don't know what will happen from one day to the next but if I'm going to do the trip, I'd like to do something pretty decent. I don't want just to nip in and nip out, I see no point in that. It would be nice to do something a bit special.' John's physique and the fact that he was an experienced walker and climber suddenly started to concern me. I lit a cigarette to calm my nerves, and, not wanting him to sense my tension, agreed enthusiastically. 'The two fixed points are setting out from Jalalabad and arriving some time later in Pakistan: Kafiristan or Garam Chasma, whichever, yes?'

I nodded.

'Good.' He put the red pen's tip on Jalalabad and started to scrawl.

As John began plotting the route, we talked. He listened to my suggestions, even asked for my advice and seemed to agree with most of what I said. I was trying to steer him away from the west of the province to keep the length of the journey as short as possible. I had absolutely no experience of trekking or altitude: the nearest I'd got to the mountains was on skiing holidays, and the last of those had been some six years earlier. I was also conscious of bad knees, a right ankle I had recently sprained and a none too lively set of lungs. He would stop for a while earnestly to discuss my concerns and seemed to take them on board. But when, after a couple of hours, we stood back to look at the proposed route I could see that I had not been as forceful as I'd thought. Zigzagging like a drunken bastard, the line he'd drawn was about as long as it could be, given the confines of the provincial borders; a sort of south-west–north-east traverse.

From Jalalabad it followed the Alingar River north beyond Metah Lam to a place called Nalyar where the track finished. From there the only option was to travel by foot. The red line led us up the Ramgul Valley, past Lake Mundol – apparently a stunning place where John was determined to go fishing – to Pushol. From here the trail turned due east over the Kantiwar Pass, down the Kantiwar River to the confluence with the Pech River and then south to the village of Wama. In Wama, John informed me, there was an aid clinic where we could rest. That was good news. If I'd made it that far I didn't doubt I'd need one. From there – about half way though the journey – we would double-back north again, retrace our steps for some fifteen kilometres along the Pech River to the entrance of the Kantiwar Valley where we'd turn north-east up through the Parun Valley and over the 4800-metre Paprok Pass to Gama. From there, if he so chose, John could travel north to

Garam Chasma to see his friend while I continued east to the Bashgul Valley and out to Pakistan and the valleys of the Kalash – or Kafiristan as it's still known. Traversing each of the main valleys of Nuristan this was a journey of some 400 kilometres through a totally lawless land. There were at least three passes of over 4500 metres – about the height of Mount Blanc, Europe's highest mountain – on our path. I was beginning seriously to wonder whether I had been so lucky meeting John. The guy was patently barking. 'Something a bit special?' It would probably be the longest journey ever undertaken in the province!

'You don't think we're biting off a tad more than we can chew?' I asked diplomatically. I felt threatened. John was used to Afghanistan, used to the dangers, used to trekking for days on tiny rations. I was not. I had no idea whether I'd be capable of such a huge undertaking; a journey of this length had never been my plan.

'No, piece of piss,' John replied nonchalantly. 'In Badakshan we walk thirty kilometres a day, no problem. Even allowing for the steeper terrain this journey will be fifteen days' walking, tops. Take a month, five weeks, whatever you like . . . plenty of time to potter about.'

Realising there was little to be gained by attempting to change his mind – he was obviously a man with fixed ideas – I gulped hard and forced a smile. Despite my reservations, I was very conscious of the fact that with John my chances of reaching Nuristan were far better than they would be alone. I had only a limited knowledge of the culture, a tiny smattering of the language, and a fairly rudimentary grasp of the politics and though I had a few other contacts in Peshawar, none was remotely comparable to John. In view of his revelation about Kafiristan, just for a moment I was tempted to blow out Nuristan all together and travel directly to see the Kalash. But no, I was determined to follow in the footsteps of my two heroes, Peachey and Danny. They'd gone the hard way, through the country from the south. So would I. And to achieve that and, more importantly, survive to tell the tale, I needed John's help. Whatever his crazy plans, I had little option but to smile and go along with them. I couldn't afford to scare him off.

The matter concluded, a contented John sat down. 'So what are you going to do with yourself now?' he asked. 'It'll be a while before we can leave.'

'I thought I'd go up north,' I said, leaning back, still gaping at the map. 'Head up to the Northern Areas or something. I guess I should spend some time in the mountains . . . acclimatise.'

'That's it. Go and do some Great Gaming, hey?' He motioned to my clothes, 'You've certainly got the gear for it. And you could do me a favour while you're at it as well. Put some flowers on old Uncle George's grave.' He stood up and grinned. 'You'll find him in Gilgit. Ask him for a bit of divine assistance, we don't want to end up the way he did.'

6 Playing the Great Game

'There are all sorts of Gods and Devils in these mountains.'

In a tiny graveyard, battered by the vicious wind that ceaselessly blows into the desolate mouth of the Gilgit Valley, lies a monument to the nineteenth century's secret war fought out between Imperial Britain and Tsarist Russia in the mountains and deserts of Central Asia; the Great Game as it has come to be known. Lying beneath a gnarled thorn tree, splattered by bird droppings, is a plinth of granite that bears the inscription: *Erected to the memory of G.W. Hayward, Gold Medallist of the Royal Geographical Society of London, who was cruelly murdered at Darkot, July 1870, on his way to explore the Pamir Steppe.* George Hayward was one of the Great Game's more illustrious players; coincidentally, he was John's ancestor.

I looked around for some flowers but could see none. There was very little colour at all. Over the barbed wire-topped wall that surrounded the graveyard the world appeared bleak and uninviting. The low grey rectangular concrete buildings were forlorn, the encircling peaks dark and moody. Even the sky was overcast, threatening rain which, judging by the aridity of the area, would probably never fall. There was the occasional splash of green in the form of a Himalayan oak or stately sycamore but without the sun even they appeared dull and listless. As I turned full circle, however, my eyes caught sight of bright pink petals poking above the wall behind: blossom from an apple tree. Standing on tiptoes I could just reach over and snap off a small twig which I forced into the hard ground above the headstone. The blossom looked sad surrounded by the dour memorials to Hayward and the handful of other Christians who had fallen hereabouts. Still, it was the best I could do. I tapped my ring three times on the grave, as I often do on Melanie's – hoping, I suppose, to attract attention – said the only prayer I could remember and asked George to keep a protective eye on his great nephew and myself on our forthcoming journey. Well, I figured it could do no harm.

Before leaving Peshawar, John had lent me a book, *The Gilgit Game* by John Keay, in which his uncle's extraordinary antics and lonely death are described. I'd read it on the twenty-four-hour bus journey to the north. First a soldier, then hunter, in the latter stages of the 1860s George Hayward had become an ambitious and successful explorer-cum-agent specialising in the Himalayas. Having completed a pioneering journey to Sinkiang in 1868 to 1869, he was awarded the RGS's gold medal. Sleeping rough, twenty degrees below, holding off starvation by eating raw his only yak and walking fifty kilometres a day over some of the world's most desperate terrain, he had proved himself a hard and courageous man with 'a pent-up deluge of determination and a disregard for consequence'.

Worrying that some of these characteristics might run in the family, I had grown all the more concerned about the journey I seemed to have agreed to undertake with the younger Hayward.

The following year, sponsored again by the RGS, and encouraged by the British government, George Hayward set out from Gilgit to reach the Pamirs. His mission, ostensibly, was to reach the 'high Pamir' and discover whether Lake Karakul was the source of the mysterious Oxus River. But, as was usually the case with such undertakings, there was a political angle, too. The government hoped to extend the British sphere of influence. In those days deceit and treachery among the local tribes was commonplace. The rulers of Chitral, Gilgit and Yasin, in an area then known as Dardistan, and the Maharaja of Kashmir, all had reasons for not welcoming the expedition. No doubt they simply wanted to keep the British out and be left alone to quarrel among themselves but Hayward himself was hardly the ideal guest. The book described him as both tactless and arrogant; he certainly hadn't won many friends. Time and again Hayward was warned that murder was afoot and time and again he chose to ignore it. Then one morning, just before dawn, in a clearing of trees near the village of Darkot, according to an eye-witness, the solitary man was rushed by ferocious tribesmen. Having been dragged out of his tent, a knife at his throat, he'd made one last plea. To be allowed to watch the sunrise. Standing on a grassy ridge, his face burnished by the new-born sun, he stared at the sky, the mountains and the tumbling glaciers, the willows and the pines one last time. Then, accepting death in the manner befitting a true Victorian hero, he returned to his captors and uttered the words, 'I am ready.'

A nutter, no question, but a great explorer too.

I had little doubt about the ability of John Hayward to stride out powerfully in the manner of his ancestor – in fact, to walk fifty kilometres a day, sleep rough in sub-zero temperatures and eat a dead yak would, I guessed, be rather appealing to my new partner – but I sincerely hoped that the arrogance and intransigence of his great uncle would not also form too large a part of John's character. What worried me more, however, was whether I had the strength, determination and physical ability of a real explorer. I knew I was capable of roughing it, I'd done enough of that in my time. What I wasn't so sure about was whether my body was up to the challenge of such a rigorous adventure: at least three 4500 metre passes on a journey of some 400 kilometres. Three years of almost continuous city living – an over-indulgence in the good life with precious little exercise – might well have taken its toll. In Africa I had a motor bike to cart me along, here all I'd have was my feet. There was only one way to find out: do a dummy run.

Having cleaned the slab of stone with a handkerchief and up-rooted the nearby weeds, I left.

Surrounded by a dark and barren girdle of mountains, Gilgit carried a sense of oppression, imprisonment, of a town cut off from the world. It was a relief to be off the stifling plains but the wind that tore through the valley cut like glass, forcing me to push along head down, squinting to keep the grit from my eyes.

All along the main street a row of single storey stalls sold a mass of cheap Chinese goods, 'fallen' from jeeps passing through on their way to the bazaars in the south. In the restaurants' glassless windows naked chickens hung in rows like some gruesome decoration.

Lying less than 300 kilometres from the murky, ill-defined borders of China, Afghanistan, Tibet, India and the former Soviet state of Tajikistan, now, as in George Hayward's day, Gilgit's strategic importance is immense. Since the opening of the Karakorum Highway and the Kunjarab Pass the old trade route between Kashgar in China and the subcontinent has flourished again with millions of dollars worth of goods travelling in both directions. But continue east or west around the giant arc of Himalayan mountains and in the mess of remote frontiers, you'll come across many hot spots and no-go zones, including the area where the long-running war between Pakistan and India for the Siachin Glacier is fought. At 6000 metres, it is the highest battlefield on earth. For the last few years Gilgit has also had trouble of a more local nature. On a regular basis two of the three main Islamic sects, the Sunnis and the Shias, clash, often with appalling loss of life: in 1988 more than one hundred civilians died in street battles. The trouble is always worst around the religious holidays when sectarian passions run high. The festival of Id ul Zuhara was two days away. Armed authority was omnipresent.

From Gilgit there seemed to me only one good route I could use to test my ability in the mountains whilst not unduly straining myself. I saw no point in pushing myself so hard that I broke down. Before my Africa journey I had started pumping weights to build up my strength but succeeded only in pulling two muscles, rendering me useless for a month. Not again. What I really wanted to discover now was whether I could cross a high pass – the passage leading through the mountains from one valley to another. I needed to know whether I was fit enough, but also whether my body could tolerate such high altitudes. If I started throwing up, shaking, or blubbering like a baby, I'd know Nuristan was not for me and could call the whole thing off. With the walking I was relatively confident – how hard could it be? – and resolved to let it take care of itself in Nuristan. But as for climbing a pass, I really hadn't a clue if I was up to that.

The route I had in mind led westward from Gilgit, up the Gilgit Valley, past the entrance to the Yasin Valley – at the top of which old Uncle George had met his unseemly end – over the 3800 metre Shandor Pass and into the old kingdom of Chitral. From Chitral Town – which at one time was known as the most remote corner of the British Raj – I could return to Peshawar by jeep. But as I sat in the garden of my shabby hotel discussing the plan with a helpful local called Jahingar, I discovered that I had a problem. The winter had been particularly harsh, with record amounts of snow falling: Shandor still lay buried beneath a knee-deep white blanket. Even so, Jahingar was sure that from the last village in the Gilgit Valley the journey to cross the Shandor Pass and down to the first village on the other side – a distance of some twenty-eight kilometres – could be achieved in about ten hours. Though no foreigners had done it yet this year, locals had been traversing the pass for a month. The main problem I had was my lack of decent equipment. Having spent most of my time on the plains where summer was well into its sweltering stride, I was not exactly burdened with thick coats and woolly socks. But 3800 metres, around 12,500 feet, is a long way up, a thousand metres higher than I had ever been before and my shalwar kameez and woollen patoo would obviously not be sufficient. And if it snowed again – judging by the current climatic conditions, a distinct possibility – well, things could get tricky. I had to hope for good weather and reasonable supplies in the town.

In front of the Park Hotel shop I found a handsome, thick-set man of late middle age deeply engrossed in *Princess in Love*, Anna Pasternak's kiss-and-tell tale of Diana, Princess of Wales' affair with James Hewitt.

'This man, he is a real bounder,' he said, holding the book up for me to see. A blue polkar-dot cravat was neatly tucked into his red check shirt which in turn was pushed into a pair of beige cords. His face was kind, a mass of lines, and was clearly part Tibetan. Turning the book to look at the cover, he took another glimpse of the dastardly man. 'Did the Princess really have sex with him?'

'So they say.'

'I don't know.' He shook his head, looking worried. 'OK, I understand these af-*faairs*, as you say, happen, but why tell the world about them?' He threw the book on to a cluttered desk and stood up, shaking the displeasure from his face. 'So what are you after?'

'Everything.'

It was a remarkable shop. Occupying a narrow room built on to the hotel's outer wall, it was crammed with everything you could imagine a trekker or climber might desire: snow shoes, crampons, teach-yourself-mountaineering books, Fray Bentos steak and kidney pies, a deer's head mounted as a hunting trophy and an ancient Afghan rifle. Most was second-hand stuff bought from mountaineers, trekkers and tourists who hadn't the space or inclination to drag the equipment home with them. As it was still early in the season most of the gear hadn't been touched for six months or more and carried a thick layer of dust.

Almost all of what I felt I needed Dad Ali Shah found amongst the mess: sun cream, mug, cooking pot, calor gas stove – there would be little in the way of spare food along this route so I would have to carry some emergency supplies – and a cheap Chinese sleeping bag. The bill for the lot was well under a thousand rupees, about £20. He also gave me a letter to his friend Mir Akber Khan, the wazir of Gupis – a kind of district commissioner – who lived in a village half way along my route. The only thing that he couldn't provide was a jacket but this I found at a second-hand store in the bazaar. Quite how a green, fake-fur-lined, canvas jacket, first used by the American military in Korea, then, judging from the inscription across the back and right breast, by the inmates at Penton Penitentiary, Louisiana, ended up on the streets of Gilgit, I have no idea. But I'm mighty pleased it did. Over the next few months I was to become quite attached to it. After a nominal haggle we settled on a price of 150 rupees. From another stall I bought some food – canned cheese, soup, pilchards. I was all decked out for under £25.

As I was wandering back along the pallid streets to my hotel I stopped at a mobile fruit stall to buy some oranges. As the hawker turned to weigh them on his clumsy scales an impish lad snuck up behind and, with eyes fixed to mine, almost daring me to call the alarm, picked up two. Slipping the fruit into his kameez pockets, he turned and scarpered away, laughing as he went.

———◆———

A huge man wearing only a pair of brief nylon running shorts charged towards us out of the shadows. 'You thieving baaaastards!' Eyes bulging and wearing a heart-attack expression on his face, his left hand was clenched into a giant fist and in his right was a thick cricket stump. We froze for an instant, then exploded into a full sprint, tearing up the street like men possessed. As I saw our car waiting on the corner, engine running, the letters SAPD flashed before my eyes. Suddenly the meaning was clear. I let out a whoop and quickened my pace.

With only ninety bucks between us and five hundred miles left to drive, desperate measures had been called for. An important birthday was coming up fast for me and one tank of gas less to buy would mean more valuable drinking funds. And besides, I'd had enough of being a waiter, picking grapes and selling paintings door to door. This was supposed to be the lucky country. It was time for some free rides.

At first our mission had gone all right. With a swift hand that had told me he'd done it many times before, Barry undid the petrol cap. Pushing the tube down into the tank, he squatted close to the ground and began to suck in short, powerful bursts. Heart thumping, I kept scanning the street, watching for danger. But it was the middle of the night on the outskirts of a small town: no one was around. I found myself grinning, adrenaline pumping hard, feeling the buzz. This was what I'd dreamed of as I'd sat in the suffocating confines of the classroom for all those years: to be wandering the globe, wild and free, taking life as it came, having adventures, living my own movie, Jonny Bealby plays James Dean . . . Quite where I was heading I hadn't a clue and neither did I particularly care.

Glancing in through the car window, I noticed a badge on the dashboard inscribed with the letters SAPD. The reflection of the street lights made it hard to see what was written underneath. Coughing and spluttering, Barry withdrew the hose from his mouth and stuck it into the can as the fuel started to flow. He hawked and retched spitting out petrol. 'Jesus,' I hissed. 'Keep it down. You trying to wake the whole fucking street?'

Arrested ten miles out of town, the end of my teens was marked, with few celebrations, in the company of the South Australian Police Department.

———— ◆ ————

In the courtyard around the bus a throng of festive holiday-makers gathered. Men with flowers in their hats hugged one another with even more vivacity than usual, held each others' hands, talked rapidly and laughed. It was Thursday noon, the day before Id ul Zuhara. Commemorating Abraham's attempts to sacrifice his son to Allah, the festival represents one of the main events in the Islamic calendar and everyone was buzzing. Along with a mountain of baggage tied on to the roof were goats and wicker baskets full of scrawny-looking chickens all destined for the celebratory pot. I threw my bag up to a lad who secured it with the rest. Inside, women sat patiently at the front with their children on their laps or fidgeting by their sides. Some wore only veils, others the full burqa. I found a seat by the window and sat down. This was the last bus up the valley for four days. Rather than wait in Gilgit for the holiday to pass I had decided to be on my way.

Through the lower valley the packed bus thundered, sending a great plume of dust, like a rocket trail, billowing out behind. Next to the gushing emerald waters of the Gilgit River the stone road wound its way between giant boulders and narrow cliffs, many marked by political graffiti. Ragged children played in the sun which had finally appeared, while their mothers washed clothes and laid them on the pebbles to dry. Ingenious irrigation channels, some carved into the rock, others made of hollowed out tree trunks, fed the crystal water into cramped fields of green wheat, maize and alfalfa. There were thin rope bridges hanging precariously across gorges and one steel-roped aerial runway, where a man sitting on a plank beneath the rope was pulled across the river by two others on the far side. How the first one had got there I couldn't guess.

At times the valley widened and the river calmed, giving rise to more small stone dwellings and expansive agriculture but it was never long before the canyon walls rose up around us again, sending the river into a raging torrent and the track back on to a narrow ridge.

At Gupis where the bus turned north to Yasin, despite three kind offers to be a guest for the holiday, I alighted, grabbed my bag from the roof and walked up the dusty street. The sun had already disappeared behind the Hindu Raj mountains to the south, casting our side of the valley into cool shadow. Adjacent, the taller snow-peppered peaks of the Hindu Kush still sparkled with brilliance.

'Where are you go?' said a young man sitting in front of his shop on a wooden veranda that stretched the length of the tiny bazaar. The other stalls were closed except for two at the far end where a group of turbaned men played cards. There was no one else around. 'Come here, sit.' He motioned towards a tatty charpoy pushed against the wall. 'Do not you be standing on ceremony.'

I laughed at the extraordinary comment and lowered my bag to the ground. 'Where did you learn an expression like that?' I asked. As I sat down the frayed rope creaked against the wood.

'At school. I am knowing many.' He grinned proudly, and clapped his hands like a magician announcing another trick. 'As the dogs bark so the wise man sings.' I failed to hide the confusion from my face; evidently some of his sayings had not survived the translation. I took out my cigarettes and offered him one which he accepted and we lit up.

'Is there a hotel in town?'

'Hotel is closed . . . Id.' He was in his early twenties, had a long wide nose and great black fringe that fell in front of his eyes. Over his grey shalwar kameez he wore a multi-coloured herringbone cardigan. His disposition was both happy and self-assured. Casually, pushing his tongue into his cheek so as to get greater purchase, he picked at a spot.

'Oh,' I said and took a drag. 'So there's no place here where I can stay for a day or two?'

'Of course, you can stay with me.' To my great relief, he left his complexion to fend for itself, jumped up from the floor and joined me on the rope bed. I thought it might collapse. 'It is holiday. You are most welcome with my family.'

'Thank you,' I said, and started to rummage through my pockets. 'That's very kind but I have a letter here for the wazir. A friend in Gilgit said I might be able to stay at his house.'

'Harr!' cried the lad throwing his head back, greatly amused, clapping his hands once again. 'That is what I say, you must stay with us. I am Inam Akbar Khan, son of Mir Akbar Khan . . . the wazir, he is my father.' He sat back. 'It is better who you know, than what you are knowing. Yes?'

'Indeed it is Inam,' I said. 'Indeed it is.'

Behind a high stone wall the wazir's house was the grandest of six dwellings in a garden of lush grass, vegetable patches and fruit trees that led down towards the river. Flat roofed and wooden framed, it was constructed in the shape of an 'H', the stone work plastered over with a mixture of mud and lime. As with all houses of importance in this part of the world there was a guest room filled with carpets and cushions. In this case some photographs of relatives and a poster of Amsterdam enlivened the pale walls, along with a set of horns from a markhor, a large goat-like creature that inhabits this area.

No sooner was I seated than the room began to fill with all the male descendants of the clan. All that is except for the seventy-six-year-old wazir who was resting. The majority of the men were Inam's uncles and cousins. His grandfather, Inam explained, had been an important voice in the area before Pakistan was created, when the region had had more autonomy. He had sired seventeen children – eleven sons and six daughters – of whom Inam's father was the eldest and Sher Akbar, a roughish faced English teacher who had seated himself next to me, the youngest. 'I am the full stop in my family,' Sher Akbar said with a smile that revealed tobacco-stained teeth. 'The last bat in the team.' I was relieved to hear they had been born of two wives.

They brought me tea and an evening meal of rice, dhal and eggs, which they were keen to share with me. Sher Akbar said that as I was a Christian – ahl-i-kitab, a person of the book – it was fine to do so but never would he do such a thing with a Hindu, whom he considered with utter disdain, or a Jew, a race he felt were cunning and deceptive. I let the hypocrisy ride and for a full half hour left him to lambast viciously Imran Khan for marrying someone he was convinced was a Jew. With the festival of Id uppermost in everyone's mind, the majority of the evening's conversation focused on religion, which I have never felt very comfortable discussing. To me one's faith is private, not something to be argued hard in cheap debate or preached self-righteously. Besides there's seldom much point discussing such things with those of a different persuasion. You'll rarely make much impact. I was relieved, therefore, when soon after nine, they decided to leave me to get some sleep.

'Mister Jonny,' said Inam, as he was departing, 'do you play cricket?'

When I answered that I did, the big smile that was never far from the surface broke across his face again. 'Good. Tomorrow my family play family from village across river – same every Id. We use you as secret weapon.' He slapped me on the shoulder, 'But remember, it *is* the winning that is important, to hell with the taking part.'

The following morning, as the women were preparing bread, I followed Inam and Abdul Aziz, his best friend and cousin, on their way up into the village to their mosque. From the side valleys, across the river and from the main road poured a multitude of men and boys, their ages spanning almost a hundred years. Some arrived on foot or horseback, others on scooters and bicycles, in jeeps or crammed on to trailers that were pulled by cabless tractors. Like Christians at Christmas they were dressed in their finest clothes. Many stopped to shake my hand, offer their salaams and with broad smiles bid me 'Happy Id'.

Just beyond the bridge the procession split into two, with Inam, his cousins and the smaller portion of the crowd continuing on to the Sunni mosque at the top of the village while the majority cut down to a green-roofed hall down by the river, the Ismaili place of worship. In the thirteenth century, Taj Mughal, king of Badakshan, from across the border in Afghanistan, seized both kingdoms of Chitral and Gilgit and tried to convert the inhabitants to Ismailism, a splinter of the Shia sect. As his reign lasted only thirty years, his success was only partial, but still today there are large communities of Ismailis in the area. There was no sense of animosity though between the two groups today. They greeted each other like the friends and neighbours they were. Leaving them to their worship, I sat outside Inam's shop. The sun shone through a cloudless sky, making the river and snow sparkle like jewels. Both muezzins sang the azam; calling the faithful to prayer.

Back at the wazir's house, following the traditions of Id ul Zuhara, a goat was slaughtered, strung up and skinned. Inam and Abdul Aziz took great delight in performing the butcher's duties and insisted on having their photographs taken in many varied poses with the cleavers and knives as they dismembered the beast ready for the pot. The kidneys were taken away only to be returned twenty minutes later lightly fried and served with chai and chapatis. Having been given the role of official photographer I was dragged around by Sher Akbar to meet and snap everyone, including the reluctant wives and daughters. Purdah, or the seclusion of the women from any external social engagement for the sake of family honour, is strongly adhered to in these parts and I was quite surprised to be asked into the kitchen room, never mind to take the women's photographs. Evidently they were too.

Inside the dark kitchen they pounded dough into the shape of dinner plates, and placed it on an iron disk that rested on bricks around the central fire. A shaft of sunlight fell like a beam of gold through the hexagonal hole in the roof, illuminating the smoke as it made its escape. The ceiling was black, stained by 200 years of use. They all stood up and, having been virtually forced to do so by Sher Akbar, posed modestly while I took their photo. It was one of the very few times I saw Muslim women in their homes.

In the orchard behind the main house, talking to an apple tree, was a grey-bearded man, dressed in a baggy shalwar kameez of deep green, a flat hat and leather jerkin. His shalwars were very short, reaching only halfway between his knees and his feet, revealing stripey, red and white socks and a pair of two-tone, brown leather platform shoes. How these seventies, glam rocker shoes had found their way into the lower reaches of the Hindu Kush I couldn't think – surely even Oxfam has some taste.

'You like apples?' said the wazir with a look that told me it was best to answer in the affirmative. 'Apples are the fruit of Paradise,' he said, checking a bud. 'They grow in the trees, they lie on the grass, they flow in the rivers. Red apples . . . English apples . . . big, red eaters.' We were standing under a number of the trees which still had some snowy white blossom. Many of the branches appeared to have been bandaged with surgical tape. The wazir looked particularly fondly at these, holding one gently, admiring the bloom.

'Grafting,' he said, after a few moments. 'Pakistan apples small and weak, only little on each tree. But English apples strong and many. This tree,' he beamed as if introducing me to his eldest son, 'this tree from England, given by man working for government. Now it is six years old I take pieces off it and graft them on to my Pakistani trees. This way we get many apples, eat all winter till April.' He then turned and made towards his vegetable patch.

Just after midday the feast was served. It looked delicious but sadly I have never really appreciated the virtues of goat meat. It's the only animal I know that tastes like it smells. When you eat beef, you can't actually taste the cow that was sometime previously wallowing in a shed. Similarly, a cooked hen tastes of something completely different to the smell of a farmyard chicken. But a goat tastes exactly the same as the smell of a manky, shit-covered mountain animal. It's also very tough and stringy with unchewable gristle laced throughout the meat. As a traveller, being faddy often means going hungry and therefore I'll eat anything, but goat is the one food I really struggle with. However, within seconds of the feast arriving a great mountain of the leathery flesh was piled on to a plate for me. Can you imagine a stray traveller being taken in on Christmas Eve back home and then refusing to eat the festive meal? Not very polite. So, trying not to breathe, I struggled through the meat, my teeth bouncing up and down as though on a piece of rubber, while those around me, oil dribbling from the corners of their mouths, ate their fill in concentrated silence.

By three the sun had disappeared, covered by billowing clouds. Soon after, it began to pour. 'Is raining cats and dogs,' said Inam, coming into the room, shaking himself down like a wet Labrador. 'Are you ready? Put on your coat, it's time to go.' Evidently there was no such thing as rain stopping play in the Northern Areas.

As we walked though the village, the young team magically emerged from behind walls and trees, out of low doorways, even from under a broken jeep. I didn't fancy our chances greatly – a more rag-tag team of miscreants would be hard to imagine. One of the group was no taller than four foot, with frail arms and a bad limp. Another was well over seven feet and built like an ox with arms like tree trunks and hands like hams. He had green eyes and a great mop of ginger hair but possessed a strangely tiny head as if it hadn't fully appreciated how much the body had intended to grow. He wore only a thin and dirty shalwar kameez and might as well have been naked for all the warmth it must have provided. Inam led us down through the rain, which had now calmed to a steady drizzle, over the new roped suspension bridge and on to the scene of battle: a flat expanse of grass next to the river.

Waiting for us was the Gaut XI, a team of equally unpromising ruffians from a small village downstream, who, I soon learned, were all related to Inam's family. In fact all of the players were in some way related. If Inam's enthusiasm was anything to go by, this gave the occasion added importance. 'Remember, we win,' he whispered to me before the start.

The Gaut XI won the toss and elected to bat first. The goats were cleared – that's to say stones, often the size of small boulders, were dispatched with extreme velocity and accuracy, in their direction – a wizened man bent double with age was made to stand next to the single stump at the bowler's end under the pretext of being an umpire, a home-made bat was given to the first batsman and the game began.

It didn't take long for me to appreciate the difference between the game I was used to and their innovative version. Soon the tennis ball was being regularly replaced by a rock which was thrown, not bowled, at the batsmen. By the attitude of the first lad to face the very much harder missile I can only assume that this was all part and parcel of cricket, frontier style. Deftly clipping the rock off his legs, much to Inam's annoyance, he made two quick runs, never complaining for a moment that the rules had been infringed.

The wind blew and the rain fell, yet no one seemed too bothered. Those not batting huddled under one long shawl behind the wicket while we fielders stood turning away from the elements, doing our best to stop or catch the ball or rock if it ever came our way. Occasionally one of the goats would wander back across the wicket only to be chased away. The game would be held up for ages while the ball was retrieved from a particularly tangled mess of thorns or rough grass, and arguments would ensue over the amount of runs scored or overs bowled. The umpire, quite obviously unused to so many shrieking youths, just capitulated to the loudest voice – inevitably Inam's. After a particularly vitriolic scream for LBW by Inam, duly given by the umpire, whom I doubt very much could even see the batsman let alone the exact point of impact of the speeding ball, it was agreed that they had scored ninety-five from the fifteen overs allotted to them.

As the mist fell and the drizzle turned again to rain, Inam and Abdul Aziz opened the batting, both using the plank of wood more in the manner of a Viking invader than a cricketer. Still, the result was impressive and when Abdul was out for twenty we were well on course for an easy victory. The Gaut XI, sensing defeat, started to employ some frontier tactics of their own. Just as the bowler was about to throw – I don't think I saw a straight arm all afternoon – the others in the team, especially the wicket keeper, would scream as loudly as they were able in the hope of forcing the batsman into playing an ill-timed stroke. It worked time and again and soon our advantage had all but vanished.

But then in came the giant Inzaman ul-Hak, the lad with the tiny head, to steer us to the brink of victory. Inzaman could not be ruffled by the jeering around him and, having tucked his sodden kameez between his legs, clobbered both ball and rock alike around the outfield. True, he lacked the style and panache of his more illustrious namesake who bats at number four for Pakistan, but the result of the powerful agricultural hoiks was that with five overs to go we only needed eight to win. Cowering under the shawl with the rest of my team-mates I had just about given up the idea of batting when Inzaman was brilliantly caught at the second attempt by a young lad in a Penn State sweatshirt fielding somewhere akin to deep square leg. It was an impromptu position, designed to prevent the ball entering the water channel and disappearing into some distant wheat field.

Suddenly, at number eleven, I was in, with the team's, not to say the Gupis branch of the family's, honour resting uncomfortably on my wet and shaking shoulders. The first delivery emerged through the murk too wide to hit, the second likewise but the third I managed to knock back over the bowler's head, narrowly avoiding being caught in the process, and scored two runs. We now needed six to win.

For a split second I really couldn't work out what had been hurled at me. Not one but three objects came spinning out of the gloomy twilight. Luckily, the two boulders shot past, one on either side – had there been a slip or leg-slip the chances are they would have lost their teeth – leaving the tennis ball winging its way through the centre towards me. With no thought whatsoever, eyes quite possibly closed, I took a wild swing to leg and by some miracle connected with the ball. As luck would have it, it flew between two bearded lads who had refused to stop holding hands all afternoon –

this had caused them quite a dilemma when it had been their turn to bat – past a goat, bounced back off a rock and dropped just behind square leg into the aforementioned water channel.

Great cries of anguish exploded from the fielders as they charged over to catch the bobbing ball before it disappeared for good. But by the time they had either changed direction, let go of their friend's hand or put down the large chillum that they'd just sparked up, it was too late and the ball was gone. Our team cried and clapped, hollering with mirth and mockery as I leisurely ran the six runs needed to claim victory.

Having taken the scores from the umpire, Inam made a few indecent but friendly gestures to his cousin, the captain of the Gaut XI, and led his team back over the river. As a veil of darkness descended over us we sang victory songs.

'Wazir XI zindabad (live for ever)!'

'Inam Khan zindabad!'

'Abdul Aziz zindabad!'

'Mr Jonny zindabad!'

As we reached the far side of the bridge, our faces and hair dripping wet, Abdul turned to me and said, 'Cricket, it is good game, yes?'

But before I had a chance to answer Inam turned and shouted, 'No, no. It is the Great Game.'

7 Struggle over Shandor

'If a King can't sing it ain't worth being King.'

Loaded down with fishing rods, shotguns, bags of sweets and bottles of drink, Inam, Abdul and myself climbed aboard a cousin's jeep, the driver and vehicle requisitioned without question, and set off up the valley. They had kindly agreed to take me as far as Phandar, from where I hoped to procure a guide-cum-porter to help me walk over the pass.

It was another bright day. The fierce wind that had pushed the rain clouds from the valley had blown itself out and now in the sun it was both hot and still. Bouncing up and down over the ever-changing route was slow work, at times running on pebbles and small rocks at the river's edge and at others riding a high ridge, no wider than the jeep, thirty metres higher. Often, we had to employ reverse gear to negotiate sharp corners safely and occasionally we had to jump out to remove boulders and rocks that had fallen from above. Despite the river it was principally a dry land, like a moonscape, bare of even the most rough and hardy vegetation. Struggling beneath the gigantic cliffs, it seemed incredible that the British had once worried that a Russian army might march across this land on its way to wresting the Raj from their grasp. Even today, it would be almost impossible. In George Hayward's time, positively laughable.

Just before noon we stopped on a flat area of shingle where the river became wide and shallow to let Inam and Abdul, who were keen to treat the journey as a fun day out, do some fishing. Unlike a local village boy, who stood in the middle, knee deep in the freezing water with a rod made from a willow branch, they positioned themselves on some flat rocks at the water's edge. They assembled their black plastic rods and, having placed some of the previous day's goat meat on hooks, cast into the water.

It didn't take long for them to start bellowing with excitement. Abdul pulled out the first catch, Inam the second and third and within half an hour we had six succulent river trout all approximately a pound in weight. When the British first came to the area towards the end of the nineteenth century they brought with them some of the trout they had introduced to Kashmir. Stating that anybody caught fishing the river in the first three years would go to jail for seven, they gave the fish the chance to become established. Now the river teems with them. I gutted, headed and tailed the catch and cooked up lunch on my newly purchased gas stove.

Phandar was a village constructed out of pale stone, on the edge of a wide glacial river plain where goats, highland cattle and shaggy ponies grazed. Shallow terraced fields worked by oxen encouraged by solitary men climbed steadily on either side. Small orchards of apple trees were ablaze with blossom and groves of spindly poplars and willows were turning green. Locals call Phandar 'Little Kashmir': it was easy to see why.

We alighted outside a dingy chai stall. In a woodshed next door three half-rotten charpoys and a kerosene lamp constituted the hotel where I put my bags. Having found Rehim Bek, yet another relative of Inam, who assured me he would either come with me over the pass or find someone else who would, the boys turned to go.

'You will miss us now,' said Inam, with an impish grin. I had to admit that I would. From the jeep, he took one of the two shotguns they had brought with them, loaded it and thrust it into my hands. 'Come, you must kill something.' He pointed at a group of sparrows sitting in a stunted leafless thorn tree by the river.

'I don't want to kill anything, Inam.'

'It is the way we say goodbye.' He started to walk towards the tree. 'It is for your pleasure.'

Not wanting to offend, I took the gun, crouched on a rock, pulled back the hammer and, deliberately aiming high, squeezed the trigger. Not having fired a 12-bore shotgun for a very long time I had completely forgotten about the immense kick or recoil the gun imparts and, much to the amusement of all present, as the deafening bang rang out across the valley I fell over backwards on to the soggy grass.

With tears of mirth still leaking from their eyes, Inam and Abdul hugged me a fond farewell. As the jeep turned Inam leaned out of the window. 'Remember, Mr Jonny,' he shouted above the roar of the engine, 'it is not goodbye but . . . '

'*Au revoir*,' I yelled back.

It was an easy walk along the gently rising, winding track. It became even easier when a man came past and offered me the services of his horse. Even with the heavy bank of mist that swirled ominously overhead, from the saddle the views were sublime, stretching for miles through snow-covered side valleys and up and down the main mountain gorge. In places the track ran close to a river which thundered mercilessly beneath tunnels of ice or crashed over waterfalls. Then the path would skirt away to the edge of a towering ridge, hundreds of feet below which other rivers wriggled like trails of silver smoke. Having the luxury of being able to view it all from the back of a horse only added to the pleasure. But as we passed the village of Gulakmuli, where the track climbed steeply through a narrow defile of orange splintered rock, it started to rain. The rain soon turned to sleet and then to snow and before long we were marching through a violent blizzard. Having first been thankful to the horse for saving me the arduous trek, now sitting on it left me exposed and cold. I had no gloves, so pulled the sleeves of my jacket down over my hands and sat on the reins. I pulled my hat over my ears and kept my head down, tilted away from the icy blast but it made little difference. The snow piled upon me, melted easily through the forty-year-old coat and left me numb. Normally I welcome snow with the excitement of a five-year-old, but not this time. Even the pleasant musty odour that rose in a steam from the rugged animal gave me no joy. Ayub, a twenty-five-year-old, English-speaking relative of Rehim Bek's who had agreed to act as my guide and porter on the journey over the pass, grimaced too. Each time I asked him how far it was to Barset, the last village in the valley, he just said, 'Soon,' and turned his head away from the gale.

All around, the world was white. We were now well over 3000 metres; what had fallen as rain lower in the valley up here had already left a thick blanket of snow. A thousand metres higher it could have been snowing for days. How on earth would we cross the pass now? In a few more hours we would be unable even to turn around. Eventually we pulled up outside a one-room house. Under the short veranda the door was locked, there was no one around.

'What is this place?' I asked Ayub, trying to shake the flakes from my clothes and stamping my feet.

'Is hotel.' He rubbed clean an area of the cracked window at the top of the door and peered through. Seeing nothing, he shrugged and turned to look as far out across the desolate landscape as the mist and snow would allow. Beyond the track I could just make out another flat-roofed dwelling where smoke was seeping from the short central chimney.

'We wait. If nobody come I have relative live here we can stay until snow finish.'

Unsurprisingly no one came. Even this hardy mountain race saw little reason to wander about in such weather and, after a damp, shivering hour, we collected our possessions and walked back up the track the way we had come, towards the distant house.

Though the wind had calmed slightly the snowflakes still drove at an angle into our backs. Climbing over snow-covered walls and freezing water channels, the ground creaking under our feet, we scrambled along the edge of the fields.

Outside the house Ayub asked me to wait while he stooped through the shallow door to find his aunt. After a minute there were loud cries from within and a moment later two grubby boys, aged about seven and ten, came rushing out. Seeing the stranger they stopped short and, with their heads cocked, studied me. Underneath the dirt and snot, that rose and fell in unison out of their little red nostrils, they were beautiful boys. Both were pale with Anglo-Saxon features, the elder even had sharp blue eyes that darted quickly between his brother and me. Over their grimy shalwar kameez, they wore torn ski jackets that had probably started life on the backs of two smart kids on the slopes of Val d'Isère or Tignes, and on their bare feet were torn plastic football boots.

Evidently satisfied, they took me by the hand and led me round the corner into a pleasant whitewashed room, about ten foot square. Rough goat-hair carpets covered the earth floor above which there was a willow-branch-and-mud ceiling. A glossy poster of fifteen oiled body builders flexing their muscles was stuck with tape to one of the walls and on a shelf where three tatty books lay on their backs was a vase of plastic flowers. Two thick quilts were folded in the corner, otherwise the room was empty. Having removed my boots, I pulled one of the covers over my shoulders and sat down. The boys, their glance not leaving me for a single moment, did likewise.

Within a few minutes Ayub returned with his aunt – well, brother's wife's mother's sister, if I understood correctly – who was carrying a pot of steaming tea which she placed on the floor. She was a strong looking woman with deep lines extending from her mouth and eyes and across her forehead. Her hair fell in two thick plaits under a red pillbox hat which she wore tilted backwards. Her old shawl was thin and holey and her clothes threadbare. She had soot marks on her cheeks and her fingernails were black with grit; she looked closer to fifty than the thirty-two years old Ayub told me she was. But despite all that it was easy to see where the children had inherited their beauty. Her mouth was wide and sensual, her cheek bones proud and her bright eyes shone with life and vivacity; though I couldn't understand what it was she was saying, the expressions on Ayub's face told me she had a good sense of humour too. Her husband had died of pneumonia at the beginning of the winter, so now she and her eldest son had to farm the land and raise the children. She also had a nine-month-old daughter. She poured the tea into a chipped china cup and, with a gracious smile, handed it to me.

'This salt tea,' said Ayub. 'Sugar expensive, salt better.'

I don't know if it was my surroundings and the way I was feeling but it tasted fine, sweet in a strange kind of way, not really very different from sugared chai.

As there was no window or electricity the door had to be left ajar to let in light. Through it I could see a gnarled apple tree on a ridge beyond a low wall. Over the next four days, as I lay in the same spot, practically inert, I watched that tree sink further and further until its entire two-metre trunk was buried in a drift. At first I worried about the pass, about the amount of food I had and about the burden I was being to Ayub and his relatives. But before long, sitting numbed by the cold, staring vacantly out through the door at the wintry world, my thoughts faded into an empty void. Time's relevance became less and less until it meant almost nothing at all. Occasionally I was brought tea and the boys popped in to see me. I ate cheese from a can and boiled my soup. I stared at the floor, at the walls, at the ceiling, which had started to leak. I stared outside. But none of it meant a thing. Five hours, five days, five weeks, it would have made little difference. I was awake–asleep, suspended in time. It's how I imagine incarceration must be.

Through the emptiness my mind began to slip back. Warm beneath the quilt, I withdrew into my head, capturing images from long ago. I saw myself as a child, going to school, fighting with my brothers, playing on my parents' farm. I pictured times as a young man loafing around Europe and Australia. Living in Sydney, I'd learned to play the guitar and dreamed of becoming a rock star. Back in London, I'd formed a band. In my mind's eye I saw the gigs and remembered the buzz and excitement that had come with creating, performing, living the fantasy. I sang the songs to myself, tried to recall the lyrics.

Alone in this silent world, I flicked through the album of pictures photographed on my mind. I saw my old car, my flat, my friends, jobs I'd done: working on pop videos, in recording studios, decorating, dispatch riding. And I thought about Melanie. As I was drawn deep inside myself, my mind became clear and focused. I saw her face, could feel her warm skin, smell her smell. I heard her voice, her laughter. I talked to her, reliving our holidays, our travels, our life together. *'So,' she said, leaning back against the hotel bed, a mischievous smile curling her lips, 'when are we going to get married then? In Goa at Christmas or back home in the spring?'* It was as though I'd fallen backwards through a crystal ball into a fantasy land. I sometimes wasn't sure whether I was awake or asleep: dreams and illusions spun like thread.

And through the visions came appreciation. I had been a wanderer until I'd met Melanie, happy and content, enjoying my life, but deep down always searching for something more, some elusive force that would fill a void within me, a hidden entity that would make me whole. In Melanie I'd found it. There'd been no more need to wander; through her I had come home.

———◆———

'Why you not have sex last night?' The Kashmiri commissioner's grey hair was thick, blow-dried into a bouffant quiff; his eyes dark, suspicious. 'You have argument?' He studied me closely. Aware of other policemen standing stiffly behind my chair, I turned, desperate to find a friendly face; no one would hold my glance.

'What is your occupation?' the commissioner asked.

I didn't know. I didn't know what I was, who I was, where, why anything. I didn't answer.

He pointed towards my earrings. 'These, these things.' Leaning back in his chair, he placed his hands together as though in prayer. 'Are you homosexual?'

I laughed, almost hysterically, and rubbed the palms of my hands down my thighs.

'Did you kill her?'

I stared dumbfounded.

He shrugged. 'Hold him until the results are known.'

The police cell was gloomy and quiet. With only one small barred window positioned high in the paint-chipped wall, the air was stale and as dusty as the floor. I sat rigid on the hard wooden bench rocking gently back and forth; despite the warmth I shivered uncontrollably. Words hammered in my head. Dead body. Embalming. Autopsy. Dead body. Embalming. Autopsy. I closed my eyes and saw Melanie's lifeless body.

I gradually became aware of a metallic buzzing, reverberating in short bursts, transmitting from the corner of the room, by the door. In the confined space the noise grew, frenetic and desperate. Straining my eyes I saw a large cockroach, beached on its back. I watched it for a moment as it spun round and round, like a child's toy. I then stood up and walked slowly towards it. Sensing danger, the struggling creature went into another frenzied reel, kicking its legs, driving with its wings. To no avail. It stopped exhausted and lay still in the dust. I crouched down and watched it. It's long antennae were all that moved. I picked it up and turned it over. It scurried silently through a crack beneath the door.

———◆———

The village 'hotel' reopened and I moved in. Having eaten most of my rations I had little choice but to leave the kind family who had no food to spare. It would be some time before the short summer months provided a harvest and stocks from the last were now all but gone. Feeding themselves was difficult enough. This was the hardest time.

Each day I sat on the hotel veranda, huddled under a quilt and shawl, looking longingly towards the sky, hoping to see some encouraging sign. Occasionally I would glimpse a patch of blue, the weak wind would cease completely and the snow lessen to desultory flurries. At these times I would venture out on walks down to the river or visit Ayub's young nephews and build snowmen with them or help their elder brother and mother clear snow from the roof with wooden paddles. But the calm never seemed to last and before long a white pall of swirling mist would tumble from the mountains again, shrouding the valley and depositing yet more snow, leaving me huddled once more in the warmth of the hotel. What the pass would be like, I didn't dare to think.

Then, finally, I woke to find a clear sky. Ayub came bounding up from the village with an excited expression plastered across his face. He was as eager to be getting on as I was. He had a wife and young child just across the pass living in Chitral.

'Weather is best, moon is good. If no snow more we leave tonight.'

'Moon? Tonight?' I asked, baffled. 'Don't you mean morning?'

'No, we leave at one, night, early. That way the snow frozen, we no sink in but walk on top. In day now impossible.' He nodded, eyes wide, waiting for my approval. 'I come here at one. You be ready.'

I promised that I would.

Dressed in every article of clothing I possessed, including a spare pair of shalwar trousers wrapped round my head like a scarf, socks over my hands and plastic bags in my boots, I stepped outside into the wintry paradise. The night was still, not a breath of wind or trace of movement. Rising over the Hindu Raj, on the southern side of the valley, the moon illuminated the scene like a celestial floodlight. Throwing back the mellow rays, the snow-covered cliffs and peaks that lined our way were as bright as day, as if they were glowing from within. I could see only a few stars, parts of the major constellations, though the sky above appeared inky black. Icicles that hung from the roof sparkled, and all around, the snow blinked like diamonds. It was the night as day, reflected through a silver mirror.

I heard Ayub long before I saw him. His movement disturbed a sleeping dog which let out an echoing howl. As he approached up the track I noticed plastic bags wrapped around his lower legs, and rubber galoshes covering his shoes. Over his baseball cap he had tied a scarf and had a large piece of cloth tucked in about his neck. He picked up my half empty rucksack – part of our deal – and, with only a smile for a greeting, started out down the track.

It was easy going. The ground was frozen hard and though we had to take care not to slip, we walked at a decent rate. The track took us north over a small river and levelled out on to a great white plain that stretched for fifteen kilometres to the foot of the pass. From here there was no path to follow. No one had crossed over Shandor since the recent snows and what tracks there were had now disappeared. I stepped in behind Ayub, walking at the end of his long moonshadow, and relaxed into an easy gait. The only sounds were the ruffling of our clothing and the cracking of the ice crust that covered the billowing snow.

Then, booming out of the silence like the Cry of the Valkyrie, came a shrill and piercing scream, followed by the sound of galloping hooves. Startled, we both stopped and turned and saw a lone horseman charging across the plain. From a distance he looked like one of Ghengis Khan's moguls, or some crazed Cossack with murderous intent. He reined in as he approached, coming to a shuddering halt a few feet away. Great clouds of steam billowed from the animal's flaring nostril, its flanks were covered in sweat. The horseman made an impressive picture, dressed as he was in a Russian fur hat and worn military coat. He had a great black beard and shinning eyes, moistened by his cold ride, and over his shoulder he carried a gun. Just for a moment I expected him to draw an unseen scimitar and cut us to ribbons but thankfully there was nothing to fear. Apparently he had heard that a foreigner – or feringhee, as we are known in these parts – was crossing the pass and thought he might want to rent a horse to make the task a little less arduous. Remembering that this was supposed to be a test of my endurance, I declined the offer. Without concern, the horseman wished us luck and trotted away.

Marching on across the sparkling land, I felt a rush of excitement surge within me. The plain was as flat as a polo field and having spent nearly eight days at a similar height, becoming accustomed to the altitude, my breathing was steady and clear. Far from what I had imagined, the walk was no strain at all. It was easy and for the first time in a long while I was filled with that rare but familiar travelling buzz; a feeling of joy and wonder so acute that looking around I actually laughed out loud. On either side the glowing mountains majestically framed our route and before us hung the moon. Beneath our feet the glistening snow billowed like clouds and above us shone the stars. Besides us there were no humans up here. Calm and pure, it was a land above and beyond the troubles of mankind. It seemed as though we were walking in heaven. I knew the trek would become tough at the end, as we climbed to the top of the pass. But for the moment striding out across the surreal, extraordinary landscape I felt that life could reach no higher peak. Remembering Danny's song as he'd walked in the mountains on his way to Kafiristan, I started to sing:

> The Son of Man goes forth to war,
> A golden crown to gain;
> His blood-red banner streams afar,
> Who follows in his train?

Suddenly Ayub stopped, squatted close to the ground and gestured me to silence. 'Look,' he whispered and indicated some tracks in the snow. 'This wolf, maybe mountain fox, fresh.' He stood up and peered around but neither of us could see or hear anything unusual. The earth was as tranquil as an ocean bed. Five minutes later, he pulled up short again and this time pointed into the distance, slightly to the right, beneath an overhanging cliff. Straining my eyes I could just make out the movement of an animal. It was too far away to tell what type it was but judging by the size of both the creature and its tracks it was too large to be a fox.

After three hours we had covered the fifteen kilometres and were at the end of the plain where the ground rose steeply towards the pass. Behind our backs, the eastern sky was starting to brighten, before us the moon still paved the way. Remembering some advice I had been given about drinking water to avoid altitude sickness, a condition that kills more than a few trekkers each year, I opened my bottle only to find the contents frozen solid. After a five minute break – Ayub would allow no more, it was essential we were off the snow shelf before the sun melted the surface – we began to climb.

Within seconds my feet felt like lumps of lead, my breath rasped in and out at a frightening rate and the smile of joy that had covered my face on the walk across the plain was replaced by a pitiful grimace. Everything I carried seemed to double, triple, in weight – my camera, water bottle, bum bag – all dragging me closer to the ground. Despite the rising sun, my hands went numb, my beard froze and my teeth began to rattle. Feeling more like a clown than a heroic explorer, I plodded onwards at a tragic pace, watching Ayub disappear beyond some far off ridge. For a second or two I actually wondered if I could make it.

Without warning, my stomach and bowels suddenly contracted in pain. Realising what was coming I stabbed pathetically at my shalwar trousers with my frozen fingers. The knot was tight. My fingers, as useful as wooden tent pegs, couldn't release the tie. Feverishly I pushed and pulled and at last my trousers fell. As I exposed my rump to the freezing air I cried out with relief.

Half way up the ridge Ayub was waiting. Already carrying my rucksack and his own small bag he insisted on taking my camera and water bottle. Embarrassed though I was, I also let him lend me his gloves. Plonking one foot just in front of the other and stopping every ten paces to catch my breath I staggered on. In agony and anguish I continued past the great white boulders and citadels of rock that bordered the path and finally reached the top. Doubling over, hands on my knees, I looked up to Ayub and smiled again.

The soldiers at the Shandor Pass security barracks were surprised to see us but made us welcome, finding us a place by their fire and making us a warming cup of tea. Seldom has a drink tasted so fine.

Bored by the mundanity of their work they asked a lot of friendly questions; it was a hard posting, six months on the pass with just a handful of mates and snow for company. When they made me sign the book, I saw that I was the first Westerner over the pass that year. I smiled as I thought of those to come, thundering across in jeeps, up to see the polo on the highest polo ground in the world – the pitch was still recognisable even under all the snow – or to fish the lake that was now indiscernible from the plain that surrounded it.

By ten we had descended 1500 metres and could see dwellings, terraced fields and blossom on the trees. A few minutes later we heard the cries of children's voices and the engine of a jeep. My feet were half crippled and my legs felt like jelly, my head ached and my back was sore. I was exhausted but I didn't care. Though I had certainly struggled I had not thrown up, I wasn't shaking, or blubbering like a baby, and I had crossed the pass. I had climbed to almost 4000 metres and walked more than thirty kilometres, completing the journey in under nine hours. I had proved to myself I could do it. Still, creeping though my euphoria a grim thought persisted: the journey through Nuristan was 400 kilometres long with at least three passes, two of which were closer to 5000 metres than 4000. The prospect made my head spin.

PART THREE

Across the Land of Light

8 To the Back of Beyond

'We're going through the Khyber with a regular caravan. Who'd touch a poor mad priest?'

The flimsy metal pole dividing federal Pakistan from the locally administered Tribal Areas swung easily to the vertical, allowing the column of trucks to continue west towards the Khyber Pass. Immediately the stalls by the roadside changed. Gone were the fruit and vegetables, the sweetmeats, the cuts of bloody meat, the baskets of nuts and sultanas. Now great blocks of black hashish, looking oily in their transparent seals, hung in the glassless shack windows, along with opium, refined heroin and guns of many styles. Armed men in turbans with bearded faces and dark eyes sat propped against walls, against trees, or rested on flimsy charpoys. Some talked in conspiratorial groups, while others pulled smoke through dented silver hookahs. There were no police, there was little law. It was still Peshawar yet it was another world.

Once past the check-point, our van pulled out from the rear of the Red Cross convoy, which was laden with wheat for Kabul, and moved up towards the front. There were sixty kilometres to the Afghan frontier, another twenty to Jalalabad. John sat with the driver while, behind, Ismael Azizi, our translator, and I bounced up and down with an old timer from the Khyber Rifles. As part of our armed escort, the aged soldier had been supplied by the authorities to protect us from local thieves and kidnappers; I hoped his four colleagues riding in the jeep up front were better suited for the task. Looking as old and haggard as the land through which we passed, he might well have been doing the same job in British times. He was soon asleep, leaving his gun to loll worryingly across his lap, varying its aim between Ismael's gut and my groin.

A few miles out of town we passed under a large stone arch,

Khyber Gate, and out into a rugged land. Plains of pale rock, boulders and dried earth stretched away to the distant hills. Sparse, dust-coated thorn trees, wild grass and fern-like tamarisk lined the road. Scattered villages with mud brick, flat-roofed dwellings occasionally sprouted out of the dirt but there were no humans about. Only the mangy goats, pi-dogs and a wobbling horizon gave movement to this pointed landscape.

The first time I'd met Ismael I'd thought nothing would persuade me to take this Nuristani refugee on a long journey through his dangerous homeland. He had the face of a hit man. A long hooked nose, broken in two places, protrudéd from beneath a narrow forehead and his eyes were as mean as bullets. His angled jaw was as sharp as a chisel with a thin black beard accentuating the hard lines. At first he had been quiet, even churlish, taking the proposal of our journey with all the enthusiasm of a Pathan offered pork, but over the course of half a dozen meetings he had opened up. It was just as well. Translators with English, Pashtu, Dari and a Nuristani language don't exactly grow on trees.

Already the sun was high, pounding everything with its sledgehammer rays, forcing the temperature up to fifty degrees centigrade. The draft of air caused by the van's slow momentum gave little relief, but still I was happy. I was on my way to the Khyber Pass and the border with Afghanistan. Perhaps more importantly, I was finally heading to Nuristan, the land of light.

Since scrambling over the Shandor Pass I had been busy: procuring provisions, organising letters to ease our passage, putting a group together as per John's instructions and growing out my beard – from a goatee to full-faced – which was no small feat in the heat of mid-summer, I can tell you. It did seem a mite ridiculous that I, with such limited Afghan experience, should be the one to organise things but with John busy elsewhere there was no real choice. Rushing around in Peshawar – and a few other places besides – it took me over a month but by the time John was ready to roll I was reasonably pleased with the progress.

Though John had now officially quit the Swedish Committee they had asked him, on a consultancy basis, to prepare a report on the current situation in Nuristan. This was good news. First, by travelling at the behest of an official aid agency we had been able to gain permission to travel through the Tribal Areas legitimately, but also it was the best insurance we could gain against being kidnapped. 'There are only three real dangers in Afghanistan,' John had told me sometime earlier. 'One, you're unlucky and get hit by a rocket, stray bullet or step on a landmine. Two, you piss someone off, make them lose face, in which case you're in real trouble. And three, someone decides he wants to kidnap you. With the weight of an international agency behind you, he might think twice. Without, you're either a blank cheque or a political pawn.' As ancient warriors the Afghans are a proud people with a well defined code of behaviour. Slaughter and carnage, as prevalent today as they were a thousand years ago, are still usually fuelled by political or ethnological reasons or because someone has broken the code. Unlike some other parts of the world where senseless murder is commonplace, in Afghanistan killing for its own sake is rare. We both suspected kidnapping was our greatest danger.

Soon the road began to climb, round and round in sweeping coils, taking the convoy between the craggy rocks and narrow defiles. No vegetation grew up here. With starched white cliffs and jagged ridges, it was a cruel country littered with relics of its barbarous past. As the fastest route to enter the subcontinent from the west, the Khyber Pass has for millennia been a place of violence and wars. Carved into rocks or painted across them are countless plaques depicting the heroics of those who have fought and fallen attempting to take or hold the pass. Atop the serrated bluffs and steep rising hills are ruined forts and picket posts. Alexander's armies, and those of the Mongols, Moghuls and the Afghans, have all passed through here on their way to loot the fabled riches of Hindustan, more often than not fighting as they went. Peachey and Danny had come this way too; not only disguised as a mad priest and his servant bound for Kafiristan but also a few years earlier with General Roberts' army to seek retribution for the destruction and slaughter of the British mission at Kabul.

'Aye, and a good deal more troublesome it was then too.' Danny's voice was with me again. 'In those damned red coats we was an easy target for them murderous sharp-shooters hidden up amongst the hills.'

I turned sideways to get a better view. Looking up towards the cliff tops, shimmering bright under the sun's fierce rays, it was easy to imagine the nightmare of running the gauntlet of the Afridi tribesmen in more brutal times. They've controlled the pass for thousands of years, and will probably control it for thousands more.

Today the route is the main artery in what many describe as the world's most porous border. It is through this pass and countless other mountain trails that snake across this unguarded frontier that a river of smuggled goods flows. Ancient artefacts, opium, enriched uranium and a multitude of household appliances all pass this way. A constant stream of bicycles free-wheeled past us down the road heading towards Peshawar. Brought into Pakistan on transit papers from China, so avoiding tax and duties, they are taken by truck to the Tribal Areas from where they are re-imported for nothing save a little back-hander. The lads riding them the sixty kilometres to town received one hundred rupees a bike. Some rode one and carried another on the rear rack. At each of the seven check posts great mountains of brown cardboard boxes containing TVs, washing machines, hi-fis and videos were stacked waiting for the right bribe to be paid before they could continue on their way to the more affluent homes of Islamabad, Karachi and Lahore.

The border was in chaos. Crowds of men, women and children, whole families, jostled one another as they forced their way through a steel mesh gate that divided the two countries. Three Pakistani soldiers stood among the rabble looking flustered, wielding their bamboo canes with impressive vigour, but all they seemed to care about was stopping the army of raggedy children who scurried to and fro taking petrol and diesel to the war-ravaged country in plastic containers that were strapped to their backs. No one crossing in either direction showed any identification. As aid worker and journalist – the ruse I'd used to gain an Afghan visa – we had permission to cross, but had we not, I doubt it would have presented too much of a problem. Wearing our local garb – John, too, preferred to dress like an Afghan – we'd have simply pushed our way through like everyone else. Many of the crowd were refugees returning home after years in exile, others were leaving, forced out by some new round of fighting. One fat lady, draped in a dirty green burqa was being pushed across on a wheelbarrow. Sitting regally surrounded by a bright confusion of pots and pans, she appeared like an old peasant queen riding on a palanquin.

There was much noise too, the blabbering of people, revving of truck engines and bleating of sheep. And through the mayhem hot dust rose. We had our passports stamped and walked through the mêlée.

On the Afghan side of the gate we were immediately set upon by an officious government soldier who started shouting loudly, demanding to see our documentation. He was young, no more than sixteen, with a wispy beard hanging under his chin. It took John nearly an hour to calm him down, during which time the soldier made a half-hearted attempt to arrest us. We explained patiently who we were and what permission we had. Eventually we boarded a battered minibus and headed down the dusty road to Jalalabad with no harm done. Still, it was a gentle reminder; we were now in a war zone and anything could happen

———— ◆ ————

Ordered to lie in the dirt with our hands behind our heads, I sensed the soldiers' guns pointing at our backs. I could taste the dirt in my mouth and feel the grit pressing hard against my cheek. Could one of my fellow passengers be an agent carrying weapons to the rebels? Had the soldiers been tipped off? Jesus! Was I about to die here, now, after all that had happened; shot like a dog?

A week earlier I'd struck a deal with the gods: a negotiated settlement to end the unbearable depression I had lived with since Melanie's death when the world had flipped upside down. I couldn't commit suicide. After only a moment's contemplation I realised I would never have the guts to carry out such an act, nor was I sure I even wanted to. So instead I travelled to warring El Salvador where the odds of encountering some form of danger and violence were high. If I was to die then so be it, my troubles would be over, the pain gone. If I survived, I could take it as a sign that life would one day be worth living again.

It had been incredibly exciting travelling beyond the gringo trail, seeing a country close to the edge. I'd felt tremendously charged, as though simply being in this dangerous land made me important, special somehow. A car bomb had exploded a block from my hotel and I'd narrowly avoided being involved in a shooting. Neck draped in cameras, pockets stuffed with film, notebooks, pens, even a fake press card, I'd lived the illusion of being a war correspondent: P.J. O'Rourke, holidaying in hell; Jimmy Woods in Salvador. Up close and in my face, life here had forced me to open my eyes and see the world again. It had also answered my question: I didn't want to die. At another shout from the commander we scrambled back to our feet. I brushed myself down and boarded the bus. I felt alive, fiercely alive, as though I was starting a brand new life. I knew it was time to go home, to try to start living again.

———— ◆ ————

We arrived in Jalalabad early in the afternoon and made straight for the Emergency Relief Unit (ERU) guest house. Andrew Graham, a great bloke who I'd met in Peshawar, who had helped me organise things while John was away, ran the small but efficient NGO and had kindly given us permission to use the guest house while he was in England.

Greeting us on the veranda, a beaming smile exploding across his face, was Haji Pordhal, a thirty-three-year-old, ex-Mujahadeen Tajik commander. He wore the ubiquitous Chitrali flat cap, a mottled brown shalwar kameez and a many-pocketed 'journalist's' waistcoat. Only one of the pouches contained any pens or paper, however. The rest were brimming with armaments: hand grenades, spare magazines, bullets, a knife and God knows what else. There was an AK47 draped over his shoulder. He extended his arms and hugged me warmly.

'Jon Bibly Sahib,' he said, continuing with the full plethora of Afghan greetings: 'Chitouri' (Are you fine?), 'Jon Jorast' (Is your body good?), 'Mondana Bashi' (May you never be tired), 'Khair Khairyat' (Is all well?), and 'Al Hamdulillah' (Praise be to God). The formalities over, he motioned to my dress. 'Like Nuristani,' he said.

I beamed. At last I'd got it right.

Andrew Graham had introduced us in Peshawar saying he would give us good security on the journey. I had agreed at once. If Haji Pordhal was anywhere near Nuristan, I wanted him on my side. He was a war-toughened warrior, but behind his sparkling blue eyes, I could see there was a man of honour.

'I see you've found your Billy Fish,' said John, referring to the Kafir chief who'd stood loyally beside Peachey and Danny on their journey. I agreed that I had.

Beside Haji stood Masood, one of Andrew's chowkidahs, or

watchmen, who was also coming with us and Ahmed Gul, who sadly was not. As ERU's main man while Andrew was away he had to remain in Jalalabad. I had met him a few times with Andrew in Peshawar and we embraced affectionately.

Haji Pordhal then introduced us to three men he'd brought down with him from his home in Darr-i-Noor – a village in Kunar Province, on the southern fringe of Nuristan – who would act as porters and I noticed John's brow crease in consternation. I have to say he had a point: a more sinister looking rabble would have been hard to imagine. Majid Khan had the face of a murderer, pure and simple. He had fat black lips and stained black teeth and the hair from his beard climbed up his cheeks almost to his eyes which were cold and shifty and overshadowed by thick eyebrows. His nose was like a boxer's, splayed across his wide, asymmetrical face. When I went to shake his hand and offer the Afghan greetings, he leered disgustingly, as though he'd just thought of an unspeakable sexual act involving himself and a donkey. Then he turned away, laughing. Mohammed Alam, Haji's younger brother, was patently as mad as a balloon with pale, vacant eyes and a distant expression but Sayeed Qayum looked the most worrying of the lot. He had a cruel mouth that, even when he smiled, curved down at the edges in a look of utter contempt and his eyes were devious and cunning. It was the face of a bully and as the only one appearing to be playing with a full deck of cards, he seemed the most dangerous to know.

Still, being an eternal optimist, and wanting John to be impressed that I had at least managed to organise a crew – even if that crew looked more like a gang of thieving cut-throats than the solid and experienced expedition hands that John was both used to and expecting – I acted as if all was fine, reminding myself of the expression about books and covers. Besides, when I went to my room, I found that I was sharing it with three large scorpions and that's a fairly good remedy for taking your mind off most things. After the initial shock I pulled myself together and squashed them. It really has to be said scorpions are the most stupid of creatures. They just sit there and wait for your boot.

Over the next couple of days we got everything in order or, to use one of John's favourite expressions, squared away. John took on the role of boss, organising everything as meticulously as he does when running a convoy of medical supplies over an active frontline for his aid agency. If he wasn't out trying to gather letters to or from every commander within a 500-kilometre radius – 'Keys to fit locks, Jonny,' he said, 'the right key opens the door, the wrong one lands you in a whole heap of trouble. Best to have all the right keys, hey?' – he was making notes, drawing up contracts for the group, counting, re-counting and dividing money, covering everything he possessed in transparent, sticky-backed plastic and studying the maps. He was a professional and having embarked on the mission there was little room in his mind for friendship and frivolity. Like a captain of a commando unit on the eve of a covert attack, John's manner had hardened; in the country he loved he wore his serious hat. Most of my time was spent on provision runs with Ahmed Gul.

Jalalabad was a pleasant town. Its wide streets were lined with giant peepul and neem trees, the buildings, often two- or three-storey affairs, were largely free from war damage and the climate, though hot, was dry and manageable. There were orchards of orange trees and olive groves and great swaths of green wheat fields and rice paddies irrigated by the Kabul River; it was easy to see why it had been used as the winter capital by the old Afghan royal families.

Even though rumours persisted that the Taliban were preparing to swing round from their southern frontline and take the town before striking at Kabul, the atmosphere in the bazaar was largely placid and subdued. To everyone's surprise the all-out offensive, reported for months, had still not materialised. The government army had made one half-hearted attempt to push the Taliban out of their positions on the southern outskirts of the capital, but the attack had failed and the war had sunk back into a stalemate. Most seemed convinced, however, that the deadlock could not last for ever. Sooner or later something would have to give. In the meantime, life in Jalalabad remained peaceful. Thanks to the efforts of the hugely corrupt local shura, or governing council – an independent group allied to neither the government nor the Taliban – there had been almost no fighting in the town for over a year. The reason for this was simple: business, whether legitimate or illegal, works a whole lot better when people aren't killing each other.

In the bazaar we bought provisions. Though it is manifestly a part of Afghan culture to see to travellers' needs it was important that we took some rations of our own. By using the chain of letters we would generally be guests of local commmanders and village bigwigs who could afford to offer us hospitality but occasionally we would be forced to burden less affluent people with our presence. Though wherever possible we would pay for our food, it was also important that in these situations we did not deplete their minimal stores. At the very least, when crossing the passes from one valley to the next we would have to camp in the aylaks, or high summer pastures, where we would be forced to fend for ourselves. There are only two or three shops in the whole province of Nuristan, no hotels or bazaars; what additional food we needed we'd have to carry. We bought seven kilos of flour, two of tea, four of sugar, a jar of Marmite – really! – and sixteen packets of BP5s. This high protein biscuit made by the Norwegians, originally in case of nuclear war and now given out by aid agencies, was an easy and efficient way of carrying food. When I suggested to John that a large jar of peanut butter might be in order, he looked at me as though I'd just farted. 'I don't think so . . . ' he retorted, 'we'll travel on bread and tea and whatever else we're given.' I bought one anyway and feeling like a naughty schoolboy, hid it in my bag.

Before the contracts could be drawn up the wages had to be agreed upon. It was important, John felt, that a hierarchy was organised within the group where, by having a set job, defined on a piece of paper, everyone knew their place. Thanks largely to me, it was here that we had our first real problem. When I'd met Haji Pordhal in Peshawar, I'd told him that we could probably pay whatever Andrew Graham paid his staff, which was $4 a day for himself for taking care of our security and $3 each for the porters. Though John thought Haji's fee fair, for the porters, he reckoned, $3 was far too much.

'In Badakshan where I have worked for many years,' he told Haji, in English, with Ismael translating, 'to honour one man's work for one day we must pay one seer [seven kilos] of wheat. Is this not so?'

'Sahih ast,' agreed Haji, who sat cross-legged on the living room floor, as usual his bottom lip bulging with ground tobacco and wood ash, a mixture called nazwar. His open face studded by his dazzling blue eyes made it almost impossible for him to look truly grim, but he seemed to be trying.

'One seer of wheat in the bazaar costs 20,000 Afs [about $2],' – again John paused to let Haji agree – 'therefore how can I pay so much?'

'This price you quote is for menial work,' countered Haji impassively. 'Road repairing, building, work with your aid projects. It is not for carrying heavy loads over the mountains into a dangerous country.' He pointed to all the equipment stacked against the wall. There was quite a pile. 'I have told them the price . . . how can I now say it is changed? If you do not want us we can leave.'

I could see that this riled John but being experienced in the ways of local negotiations he tried not to let it show and continued to haggle calmly. In the end it came down to good Afghan diplomacy.

'Haji Sahib,' said John after twenty minutes' hard bargaining, 'you are big man, well respected. You have done big jihad against the Russians and know many people.' Haji smiled and nodded. 'I am a man who has been in Afghanistan for five years, I too know many people and have respect.' Again Haji nodded. 'We do not know each other but we know many people the same, people who respect us both. I want you to be happy – if Haji Sahib not happy then I am sad – but I wish to be happy also and I think $3 is too much.' He stuffed a great mound of beard into his mouth and chewed in contemplation. Above us a ceiling fan spun slowly. Outside a bird sang. After a moment he continued. 'We will buy your men boots and socks, two cartons of cigarettes, water bottles and torches and pay them one hundred rupees [$2.50] a day. It is a compromise. We can both be happy.'

Haji Pordhal thought for an instant and then laughed, slapping his hand on his knee. He turned and spat the remnants of his nazwar out through the door. 'You work in Badakshan,' he said in English, 'you talk like Badakshi . . . Al Hamdulillah.' Invoking

Allah, he stroked his beard in the Afghan gesture of 'deal done', then stood up and left the room.

John looked at me and smiled. 'Face, Jonny,' he said enigmatically. 'In Afghanistan it's all about face. I saved mine and let Haji save his.'

That evening, after the contracts had been signed, while John was out in the bazaar having his head shaved in true Afghan style, my friend Ahmed Gul came into the house. Having hugged me warmly, he slipped a thin silver ring from his finger telling me it had been a gift from a very great religious man. He handed it to me as a talisman. Then, from the pocket of his dusty kameez, he withdrew a small black pistol and a box of ammunition.

'I don't need this AG,' I laughed nervously, really quite surprised. 'We'll be fine.'

'Mohammed, praise be upon him,' he said, a narrow grin flickering across his face, 'he say, "Trust in Allah . . . but tether your camels at night." ' He winked and added, 'If you get into trouble and mullah's ring no good, the gun might help . . . take it.' He forced the cold metal object into my hand, along with a box of bullets. A Colt .25, it was both light and unobtrusive. Having watched as I slid the weapon into an inside pocket of my waistcoat, he wished me the protection of the merciful and was away into the night.

The jeep thundered out of Jalalabad along the road to Kabul. The sun creeping slowly above the eastern hills stretched the shadows of the trees into jagged shapes across the flat valley floor. The dawn mist had cleared, leaving the light sharp and golden. Sitting behind the driver, I lit a cigarette and wound down the window. With the true journey finally underway, I was filled with curiously mixed emotions: both tremendous excitement and a sense of foreboding. I pulled hard on the reassuring smoke. At Sobikhel, twenty-five kilometres out of town, we turned north at a military check-point, towards Mehtar Lam, crossed the Kabul River and continued along the right bank of the Alishang. Far off, beyond the quiet plains, the mountains of Nuristan rose up black before us like a mysterious fortress, a lost world. We sat in silence, each man absorbed by his own thoughts.

The first stage of our route had changed. The journey north up the Alingar to Lake Mundol and Pushol, in the Ramgul Valley, had still seemed the most obvious trail but at the last minute John had had an inspired idea. The Swedish Committee had two clinics in Laghman Province on the Alishang River just below Nuristan's south-western border at Dawlat Shah, where the road ended, and Farish Garh. John agreed that, in return for transport, which had proved somewhat problematic, he would inspect the two medical centres. Entering Nuristan by way of the Alishang, the more western of the two rivers, over the Karik Pass, and then travelling down to Mundol, made the trip longer but I had long since given up worrying about distance or passes. The whole idea still seemed so ridiculous that to stick another sixty-five kilometres and 4500-metre climb to what we were already attempting didn't appear to make much difference. And, as John pointed out, it was an unusual way in. The number of Westerners to penetrate Nuristan in the past twenty years can practically be counted on the fingers of one hand, and John was sure none would have come this way. From Mundol the journey would continue as originally planned. Though John now knew that his friend was around in Garam Chasma, he was still unsure which way he'd finish his journey. For me there were no doubts: if I made it 400 kilometres across Nuristan, I would end with the Kalash in Kafiristan.

At Mehtar Lam we stopped for breakfast. Sitting on platforms covered in rough blankets two feet above the ground, we ate goats' cheese, naan bread and drank sweet green tea. For eight of us the bill was a little over a dollar. But there was another reason we had to stop in Mehtar Lam. We had to pay respect and seek permission from two important men: Abdullah Jan Wahidi, the political governor, and Commander Osman, the military leader of Laghman Province. Without their approval we would be lucky even to reach Nuristan. The paperchase that would, with luck, lead us safely across the country was about to begin.

Laghman Province was run by Gulbadeen Hekmatyar's Hezb-i-Islami. At their offices we found the governor, Abdullah Jan Wahidi, sitting in a tatty room surrounded by surly mujahadeen. Three clerks tapped slowly at the keys of their ancient typewriters and swarms of mosquitoes whined overhead. Abdullah Jan was a fat man dressed in white with a shiny face, pale grey eyes and hennaed beard. On hearing we were travelling under the auspices of an aid agency he dictated a letter slowly for one of the scribes, who, I noticed, had painted fingernails. Having given us the permission to travel further north and an introduction to the commander at Dawlat Shah he took us outside and invited us for lunch. It was only nine thirty and John was firm: 'Could you please thank Jan Wahidi Sahib for his time, his assistance and his generous offer,' he said, for Ismael to translate, 'but with his kind permission, we still have a long way to go and wish to move on.' This was a sentence with which I was going to become very familiar.

We shook the governor's podgy hand, praised Allah and left.

'Right,' said John, turning in his seat, having issued instructions to the driver, 'now we enter the power game. If we don't go and see Commander Osman he will find out we've been here and be angry, perhaps make problems for us. But if we do go we're saying to Jan Wahidi that we don't think his letter is enough, which might insult him. Still,' he took off his cap to wipe his shining head with his dishmal, a cotton cloth carried by all Afghan men, 'keys for the locks, that's the most important thing . . . Out of form, we'll drop by.'

As it turned out, Commander Osman was in Pakistan, where many of the rich commanders seem to spend their time. His assistant gave us two letters for the commanders of Dawlat Shah and Farish Garh, and succulent segments of a giant water melon. Having bought a few last-minute items at the bazaar, namely nazwar for Haji, we left town heading north.

Soon the land began to rise; on each side the valley walls rose steeply above us. By the foaming river large areas were cultivated with wheat, maize and alfalfa and higher up, irrigated once again by ingenious water channels carved into the rock face, smaller terraced fields climbed like steps on a giant's staircase. At the lower end of the valley the wheat was ripe. In some places it was being cut with scythes and de-husked by men beating bundles over upturned oil drums. But the higher up the vale we pushed the greener the crops became and as we arrived in Dawlat Shah, late in the afternoon, they were weeks away from harvest.

Commander Abdul Malik, a jovial forty-year-old, had learned of our imminent arrival and greeted us warmly. Quite how he knew we were coming we never found out – mountain semaphore, John called it. In front of his house, which was two storeys high and stood away from the rest of the village, was a brand new Toyota land cruiser and, draped in a ripped tarpaulin, a B21 rocket launcher truck. The long, thin boxes made of green painted wood that had held the rockets were now being used as pillars to support a flat roof on to which dry wood was stacked and beneath which cows lay chewing idly. A rag-tail group of the commander's militia sat under a mulberry tree sucking on nazwar. Much to my surprise, two light bulbs hung from one of the branches. Having bought his own dynamos, the commander's was the only house in the village to have electricity. Laughing heartily, hugging each of us in turn, Abdul Malik ushered us inside with all the bravado of someone entertaining visiting dignitaries and sat us down to a feast of roast duck, buttermilk, thick warm bread, curd and tea. Sitting cross-legged on the floor in the manner of the area, we all scooped the food from communal bowls. Two of the commander's sons stood subserviently above us passing a tin cup of water to whoever was needy. Trying hard to keep my left hand away from the action, I ate voraciously. It was as well I did. It was the last decent meal I was to eat for weeks.

When everyone had finished, Haji raised his hands to the heavens, stroked his beard and praised Allah. I watched as everyone followed suit; I could see I had much to learn about Afghan etiquette. By not complying I had told our host his hospitality sucked. They were important lessons to know; stick your feet out in the wrong direction, put your bread down the wrong way up, touch the food with your 'soiled' left hand and it was tantamount to asking your host if you could just nip upstairs and shag his missus. John had taught me a few rules and, leaning back against the wall, doing my best not to attract attention, I went over them in my mind. Luckily, if the commander's actions were anything to go by, my *faux pas* had passed unnoticed.

'Londanaz,' he cried, towards John and I. Realising that my partner was uninterested, studying a map, I leaned forward again and smiled politely. 'Dar Londanaz, you have red buses, I think.' Laughing heartily, he slapped Haji on the back. It was obvious he found the concept hilarious. It seemed that strangers only rarely came through Dawlat Shah, especially in the form of two feringhees, and now that they had, he intended to make the most of it. 'And the Princess Diana . . . she beautiful lady. I see her in magazine while making a visit to Pakistan.' He had never heard of Prince Charles.

'I have ten children,' he told us proudly. 'Five boys and five girls. The Russians kill many of our people, I am doing my best to put them back!' He rambled on, laughing, slapping his leg, pressing us all to accept more tea and boiled sweets – taken in place of sugar – reminiscing with Haji about the jihad, talking politics and asking me many questions about London and home. John sat in the corner with the charts, jotting things down in a note book, leaving me to answer.

'BBC Wooild Seeervice,' said the commander, imitating the radio announcer's voice, 'az Londanas.' He repeated it over and over as though cracking a tremendous joke. It was hard not to be seduced by Abdul Malik's cheery bonhomie. Nevertheless, I began to feel rather weary. It was hard work having to field and reply to all his questions, laugh at his jokes – which often seemed to lose their edge under Ismael's translation. This was my first night with a powerful local warlord and I didn't want to say the wrong thing. Causing offence, making people lose face, John had told me, was an easy thing to do. Each answer and question of my own had to be measured. The only thing to silence the commander was the World Service Dari news. When it came on air, it was almost a religious affair. Everyone stopped and listened intently to the day's events. It was the only reliable source of information they had.

At eleven o'clock, with the prospect of an early start facing us, John looked up from his maps and asked Ismael to thank our host for his generous hospitality but explain that with his kind permission we should like to sleep.

After the commander had reluctantly gone – taking Haji with him whom he kept up all night – John turned to me and said, 'I just hate talkative fucking commanders. They get on my tits.' He lay down by the wall and pulled his patoo over his head. When I looked out of the window I noticed a new moon setting. I went to sleep with a smile on my face.

9 Running Scared

'... and together we starts forward into those bitter cold mountainous parts, and never a path wider than the back of your hand.'

I couldn't believe it when I heard Haji singing the azam. I thought it was all part of some strange dream. Forcing my eyes open I lay there in the darkness watching the faraway stars, listening to the beautiful but haunting voice drift serenely up the valley. It seemed to act as a catalyst to the birds who added their song to the sacred lament, then to the cockerel and a dog who started to howl. Around me bodies began to stir. Reluctantly, I hauled myself up, wandered silently outside, where I scooped up some cold water from the irrigation channel and splashed my face.

Through the milky light of dawn dark figures tramped, down the stony track beneath mighty sycamores or straight into the maize fields to go about their ablutions. Over the river lay a wispy mist out of which the mountains climbed. Up the valley to the north the higher peaks were transformed in moments from deep violet to shimmering pink. In what seemed like an instant, daylight broke and my heart surged.

We didn't leave at five as planned. The jeep that was supposed to take us the three kilometres to the clinic had developed a flat tyre and it took the best part of an hour to change it. In addition, the porters were having problems dividing their loads. It would have taken either John or myself about thirty seconds to remedy the situation but John was insistent that it was their job, their responsibility and as such they should do it themselves. It was easy to see where the problem lay. Crafty Sayeed Qayum was trying to carry as little as he could get away with and seemed to be instructing his close friend, simple Mohammed Alam, to follow his lead. This left the slightly ostracised Majid Khan carrying much the heaviest load in by far the worst pack – a military duffel bag. Sayeed Qayum told him the loads were equal. Eventually, Majid Khan believed him.

With the jeep fixed, away we went, up the steep, zigzagging road to the top of a crescent-shaped ridge where two steep-sided valleys converged forming a mighty 'Y' in the earth's crust. At the juncture sat the clinic. It seemed like an odd place to have built it, not really in any community but stuck out on a limb between the upper and lower parts of Dawlat Shah. Even at this time in the morning there was quite a crowd waiting to see the doctor, but it didn't fool John. They had simply been told to get their arses there pronto by our friendly commander to make the place appear necessary and used. If John's report was negative, stating that the place was a shambles and was not being utilised in the way that it should, the Swedish Committee might decide to close it down. Bad news for the commander. It is on such premises that power often resides. Not to mention the fact that as commander he can pilfer the drugs and sell them at a good profit. John spent an hour wandering from room to room, inspecting medical supplies, ledgers and equipment and asking questions before drawing his conclusions. You didn't need to be an expert to arrive at some fairly hard truths. Every surface was covered in dust, cobwebs clung to walls and tables and many of the metal appliances were starting to rust. Then we hauled the bags out of the jeep and set off up the track to Farish Garh, below the Karik Pass, some twenty-five kilometres away.

The group had now swollen to the size and appearance of a small army. Commander Abdul Malik, still the epitome of joy and good humour, had decided to accompany us some of the way and had brought with him five fully armed mujahadeen as an escort – one of whom was his fourteen-year-old son. We marched in single file. 'It like jihad,' said Haji, with a contented smile.

Shaded by giant walnut and mulberry trees, the track led down towards the river through hamlets of a dozen or so dwellings. Two or three storeys high, each house was made of a wooden frame and layered stone and covered in a pale mud. On the flat roofs pink and white mulberries dried next to neatly stacked bundles of firewood. Old women wove goat hair carpets on large wooden looms and grubby-faced, bare-bottomed children hung from trees or teetered precariously on the edge of the numerous water channels out of which sparkling water trickled. Then the path climbed out of the tiny habitations, leaving the river below a quiet and distant murmur.

High up on the side of the mountain we walked on the slate-covered lip of the water channels that skirted the contours of the land, often the full length of the gorge. The paths were narrow, in places no wider than a couple of feet, gripping the edge of the ridge and falling away sheer to the gurgling waters a hundred metres below. Once, not watching my feet but looking around, I stumbled and fell and for a worrying moment dangled over the abyss with only a few holly oaks and pines between me and oblivion. Haji, walking behind, as sure-footed as a mountain goat, grabbed at my shirt and hauled me back. 'This bad, bad thing, Jon Bibly Sahib,' he remarked, grinning broadly. 'You learn flying 'nother day.' I took a lot more care after that.

With many of the men away in the aylaks, the terraced fields were worked by women. Wearing pink shawls, voluminous green pantaloons and rough goatskin boots tied up with leather thongs, they toiled hard controlling the irrigation and weeded the crops with miniature hoes. Some wore silver necklaces and bangles that jangled merrily as they worked. As we marched by they stopped, looked up at us and smiled. Most were young, fair and petite with creamy skin and angled eyes. They were Passais: a tribe of Persian extraction. Through the years their blood has been mixed with the Hazaras – descendants of Tumur Leng and Ghengis Khan who passed through the region many centuries ago – and hence the slight Mongolian look. One girl in particular caught my attention. Not noticing us at first, she sat on the soil singing happily as she uprooted unwanted plants. Like Haji, she had a clear voice that, drifting on the breeze, merged with the song of the birds and the river. When she saw us she stopped, her eyes creased and she started to giggle. She had the sweetest face.

'Eyes front!' came Peachey's voice. 'Remember what happened to poor Danny. In parts like these women means trouble, same today as they did do then.'

Having already experienced a failed marriage from an earlier journey into foreign lands, Peachey's warning was not really necessary. I wasn't keen to repeat the experience. But on this trip, where contact of any sort with females had been very limited, it was uplifting to see such friendly women, especially this one who laughed and sang and just for a moment I let my eyes and thoughts linger. Remembering, however, that such behaviour was not befitting a good Muslim girl, she pulled up her veil and returned to her task. I sighed a little and walked on by.

After a break for bread and cheese Commander Abdul Malik turned and headed home, leaving only his son to accompany us. We continued on up the valley towards Farish Garh. John took the lead and pushed on at a frightening pace, grim-faced, thrusting at the ground with a great staff he carried, and soon we were well spread out. On the first stage of the walk the porters had been larking about, running, pushing each other, demanding their photograph be taken, stealing fruit from the trees, shouting and laughing like lads on a summer holiday. John had become angry and reprimanded them. This was further retribution and now they grimaced with pain and puffed like old men, taking breaks regularly. With Haji, Ismael and Masood close behind, I passed them slumped against some rocks. I forced a determined grin on to my face so as to avoid the complaints I could see were welling up in their minds. My legs had long since stopped belonging to me, they felt like pieces of rubber.

The land became dryer the higher up the valley we climbed, the hamlets dropped away and the fields stopped. The mountainsides were bare and pale, the colour of dried oats, rising up steeper as the valley narrowed. With the sun at its zenith, pressing down from a clear sky, it was hot work and I was wet through. At each of the natural springs or clear streams we stopped and drank hungrily. Given the terrain, I found it hard to believe that we would soon be coming to another hamlet, but then we turned blindly round an abutment in the cliff, high above the valley floor and there, sitting on an escarpment of rolling plains, was a village surrounded by a fresh green land. It was a beautiful sight. I stopped again and took a photograph.

———◆———

A scrum of writhing bodies, cameras, lens, flashlights, mobile phones. Two snappers swearing at each other, pulling at jackets, grabbing bags. Others taking advantage, squeezing through to steal their places. A door opened, the back entrance to the night-club. The mob surged forward. In an instant the dark wall burst brilliant white. From nowhere an elbow struck my stomach. Gulping for air, I slumped against the wall. I looked up and watched, amazed, as even more photographers pushed past me, forcing me back. The cameras in their hands were like guns. Giant lenses levelled, aimed and fired. Zap, zap zap. Harsh white light tore from the flashes like laser beams. Elbows working hard to keep others behind. 'Over 'ere love, come on give us a smile.' Now all I could see was a wall of thirty men. For a moment I contemplated trying to climb a lamp post, to get some shots from higher up. Instead I lit a cigarette, moved away and watched the circus from the rear.

Back in town after my trip to Central America I'd had a few photographs, even articles, published. A friend working in an arts and entertainments press agency convinced me that joining the paparazzi would be a good way to make some money and keep my eye in at the same time. 'We'll let you know where and when the stars are going to show. You've got the cameras and a bike and we know the photo desk editors. We'll split the proceeds fifty–fifty.'

What a mess. Shaking my head I turned my back on the feeding frenzy and trudged up the narrow street to where my bike was parked. The band – split up, re-formed – had just finished for good and so the dream of fame and fortune had gone; yet still I was working dead-end jobs. Where my life was heading I hadn't a clue. The elation I'd experienced in the war zones of El Salvador was now long gone. I didn't feel important, special, any more. I felt small and threatened, worthless, going nowhere again. Having packed my gear into the top box, I put on my helmet and drove away.

——— ◆ ———

While John did his inspection the rest of us sat in the clinic examination room, exhausted – we had covered the twenty-four kilometres in a little over six hours.

'Body pain,' mumbled Majid Khan to me. 'Peel, peel.' It was the only English he knew. He held out his hand, his sinister face saddened with doleful eyes. I wasn't surprised he was hurting. There were scales in the room which I'd surreptitiously used to see what each of the porters was carrying. His pack weighed nearly twenty-seven kilos, a good five kilos more than the others. I handed out a couple of Ibuprofen tablets to each of them. John came in and called me aside.

'Give them once and they'll expect them every time,' he said, warningly. 'I pushed on hard today to see how they'd cope, see if they're up to it. If they can't hack it we might as well know now. Besides, they don't need the pills, they think any medicine is good for them.'

I explained about the weight discrepancies.

'That's their responsibility, Jonny, their problem. Don't interfere. Let them sort it out.' As he returned to his inspection I realised we were starting to develop a 'good cop, bad cop' relationship with the group. I could see resentment already forming in the minds of the porters. It was harder work than they had expected and from John they had not received the praise and adulation they thought they deserved. It was obvious we would have to tread carefully. If we pushed them too hard they were liable to jack in their jobs and force Haji to take them home. The serious mood that had consumed John since entering Afghanistan now seemed to be developing a darker edge. And I felt he was starting to cut me out.

Though perhaps not cast from exactly the same mould, during the few days we'd spent in each other's company back in Peshawar, John and I had got along fine. We'd chatted generally, discussed the journey at length, even had a laugh or two. He'd told me something of his home, his family, about some of his hair-raising escapades while working for aid agencies, and though it could never be said he'd worn his heart on his sleeve, I thought I had formed a fairly good idea of what he was like, what made him tick. Now I wasn't so sure; he was beginning to feel like a stranger again.

What, I wondered, were his reasons for the trip? What did he hope to gain? Being so wrapped up in my own quest, I hadn't given John's motivation much thought. I'd just assumed that to him it was little more than a holiday to a previously unexplored domain where, as he'd said, he could think more clearly about his future. But now I sensed that he too had a more profound inspiration propelling his journey. Remembering him earlier, stone-faced and wild-eyed, marching hard with that determined gait, it seemed almost as though he was out to prove something to himself; as though there was some inner voice pushing him, testing him, driving him harder. That perhaps by forcing himself physically he could find the answer to some emotional riddle. What that riddle was, I hadn't a clue and as he kept to himself, consumed, it seemed, by inner thoughts, I doubted I ever would.

We waited, leaning against the walls of Commander Mohammed Malik's guest room. Hard foam cushions, covered in patterned cloth, added to the comfort as did the deep red carpets but with the only window jammed shut the small room was both dim and airless. Two holster belts, heavy with automatic pistols, hung from a rack on the wall next to Islamic posters. Resting on a shelf next to the door was a tacky plastic model of the mosque at Mecca with a clock fixed into the side. With purdah strictly adhered to in Afghanistan, any house larger than a couple of rooms will have a special place for the men of the family to entertain their male guests. Often it's the best room in the house, as had been the case in Dawlat Shah. I guessed the same would apply here.

We had walked for two hours already that morning, up from the clinic to the house of Commander Mohammed Malik from whom we had decided to procure an extra porter for the pass and a guide to show us the way down to Bandul, the first village in Nuristan. We'd been told it was important to take two people. Whoever came with us would have to return and if he travelled alone his chances of being robbed and murdered were much greater. High up in the mountains, especially between mantikas, or districts, there is no law, no authority. Crossing from Laghman to Nuristan was like moving from one hostile kingdom to another. It seemed the code of the Afghans didn't reach this far.

Commander Mohammed Malik sat impassively at the far end of the room with three ugly henchmen around him. Well into his fifties, our new host had a long grey beard cut square in a fringe. His shalwar kameez was dirty, with a large dark stain where the material stretched to accommodate his expansive girth, and his waistcoat was torn. At first he had appeared friendly enough in an avuncular sort of a way but as the time ticked slowly by his appearance became more sinister. His eyes, which had seemed harmless, even warm, turned mean and cold and the lines that burst from them in deep grooves hung heavier.

Nothing much was said. Mostly we sat in silence: the porters sleeping, Haji stitching up a grenade pocket on his waistcoat, Ismael and Masood, now bosom friends, whispering and giggling like a couple of schoolgirls and John studying maps. I wriggled restlessly and swatted flies. Occasionally Mohammed Malik would make a comment to Haji about the war, asking for the current news and about his jihad – everyone gave Haji great respect. He'd served in Saudi Arabia with the Muslim coalition force during the Gulf War and though he had never been called upon to fight, while he was there he'd made the pilgrimage of Haj to Mecca. It was a story he liked to tell and one others loved to hear. Once Mohammed Malik apologised to us for the poor hospitality. 'There is no bazaar up here,' he said, 'we have little.' Politely John explained that we were sorry to be putting him to so much trouble. But most of the time if he talked it was in a murmur to one of his men who came and left with worrying regularity. Seeing no reason for the prolonged audience I began to wonder if we were actually being held. At one thirty, as I suspected it might, the Mecca clock screeched a metallic, 'Allahhh ou'Akbarrr . . .' And everyone left to pray.

'What the hell's going on?' I asked John, my last shred of patience long since disappeared. We'd been sitting there for almost four hours.

'It's just their way,' he replied, unconcerned. 'They'll give us lunch and then we'll do the deal. Don't worry, it's not far to the aylaks.'

When everyone was back the food arrived; it was goat. I forced some down for form's sake, wondering rather despondently how many times I was going to be obliged to eat this repulsive meat, and again leaned back against the wall. The discussions, when finally started, did not begin well.

'Three days ago,' said Mohammed Malik, running a dirty yellow comb through his beard, 'one of our men went to Bandul to kill another man. There had been problem with land in the aylaks. This is not good time to be crossing Karik. Men in Bandul will be looking to take revenge.' A low-pitched murmur resonated round the room; even Haji looked concerned. To be honest I couldn't have cared less. I'd have been quite happy to cross a pass into hell if it took me away from that ominous place. John obviously felt the same.

'We have no choice,' he said, firmly. 'From here we must go over the Karik Pass, it is the only way. We come in peace as aid workers to help the Afghan people. Their dispute will not be with us.' He looked at his hands and then up again. 'Your generous hospitality has overwhelmed us, but now we must ask for more. We need you to provide us with a porter and a guide to show us the way.'

Mohammed Malik looked out of the window and thought for a moment. His three lackeys sat cross-legged at his side grinning stupidly. I couldn't help thinking that the village might benefit from a bit of outside blood. One of the sidekicks had a nervous twitch which sent his jaw into spasms, making him look as if he was trying to remove some invisible item from his chest with his chin. They all had black hair to their shoulders cut like a Norman helmet – Mick Jagger in the early seventies or Joey Ramone whenever.

'It is possible,' said Mohammed Malik noncommittally, returning his gaze to the room. He had a small mouth that barely moved when he spoke. 'How much will you pay.'

Before John had a chance to answer a fourth lackey came in and whispered something to Mohammed Malik. As I was beginning to realise, many of the male folk of these parts were nasty-looking characters but I'd have had few qualms introducing any I'd seen to my younger sister, if it would have kept this one away. He had pale skin and short auburn hair but each line of his weathered face was steeped in treachery. Dark, soulless eyes gazed dispassionately from under narrow brows. As far as I could tell he had no teeth except for one yellow fang at the front that had a hard time staying inside his empty mouth. Most frightening of all was a deep purple scar slanting from left to right across his pointed nose. I almost gasped aloud.

'Honoured host,' said John graciously, once the new addition had sat down next to his boss, 'it is not for me to say, it is for you to tell us what you consider a reasonable rate for your men to accompany us.' I hoped to hell John didn't mean these men.

'This I cannot say. It is up to you.' And so the formal sparing continued until eventually John, having again expounded his Badakshi theory about a seer of wheat, said that he considered

30,000 afghanis a suitable rate for such work. It would take them two days to deliver us to Bandul and return which would make 60,000 per man. At this the commander looked grave and asked the newly arrived cut-throat what he thought.

Spitting nazwar in the vague direction of the window, then wiping the spittle on the back of his sleeve, Cut-throat held John's glance with his sinister eyes. 'Never . . . ' he said. It was a look that loosened your bowels. 'You must pay 200,000 afghanis . . . each man.'

Whether John was fed up, as frustrated as I was at having been made to sit and wait for over five hours, or whether he just felt affronted by what he considered an absurd price, I cannot say. But from his hard-set jaw it was obvious that he was not best pleased. Suddenly he turned towards me and with a face like thunder boomed, 'Well Jonny, it looks like we're the afternoon's entertainment, hey? Ismael, if you could thank our host once again but say that if that is how they feel there is obviously no point in discussing this any longer. With his kind permission, we would like to be on our way.' He jumped to his feet, picked up his bag and made for the door. 'Face', it seemed, had been lost; John had felt insulted. What concerned me more was how Mohammed Malik might feel. To risk upsetting the brittle emotions of trigger-happy commanders sitting on the edge of nowhere seemed like a rash move. Was the tactlessness of old Uncle George re-emerging in his ancestor?

We walked in silence, beyond the last house, where the maize and the pine trees fell away to leave a dry landscape, harsh and hostile. I could sense John fuming. The path ran beside a swirling brook between great white boulders that were strewn about like giants' snowballs. A chill wind blew down from the pass that was veiled beneath a thick dark cloud. Occasionally, a boom of thunder echoed down the valley.

Coming the other way was a man in his forties. He wore laceless plastic shoes, thick trousers, bound at the bottom with hide, and a rough jacket. For a change, it didn't look as if murder was uppermost in his mind. His face, though tough and lined, appeared bright and cordial. As luck would have it, he had a friend who lived over the pass, just before Bandul, and if we gave him 100,000 afghanis for the two-day return journey, he would be happy to show us the way.

By the time we reached the aylaks, the sun had fallen behind the western ridge. The wind blew down hard from the pass, across the snow and haggard earth: I couldn't imagine a more lonely place. I took my patoo from my bag and pulled it tightly round me as we all sat down. John stood away, the expression on his face not encouraging conversation.

Looking down the valley from the stock pen where we rested I caught sight of five armed militia heading our way. My heart nearly stopped. I stared harder, hoping I was wrong. But even at a distance of a few hundred metres there was no doubting who the men were. At first they didn't come to the stone pen on whose roof we sat and just for a moment I thought they might have other business at the aylak and our presence was merely a coincidence. But they were just asking where we were. Kalashnikovs hanging menacingly over their shoulders, with our old enemy Cut-throat leading the way, Mohammed Malik's men came over and sat with us.

They seemed friendly enough at first. They posed for photos, talked to the rest of the group and asked me a couple of questions about home, but when Haji called John and myself over to a rock away from the rest I could see that he was worried.

'I do not like this situation,' he said, pushing his prayer beads through his hand two at a time. 'Why have they come up here now, just to talk? It is not good. We must be away from here and over the pass early tomorrow.' He frowned.

John sat on a rock, his face unmoved. 'You may be right Haji Sahib, but they will not try anything here, in their own mantika. Kill one and they must kill us all and this would bring many problems for them. No, they wouldn't be so stupid.'

Haji shrugged, his mouth closed tightly. Beneath his beard his jaw muscles flexed.

'No,' John continued calmly, 'if they wish trouble on us they will wait until we are on the pass so they can blame it on the Nuristanis.'

'They seem quite friendly,' I said, trying to inject a note of optimism into the conversation, but immediately wishing I hadn't.

'No one is more dangerous than a stranger who's a friend,' spat Haji, in a hard voice, staring at the ground. He then looked at John and held his gaze. 'We must be more polite.'

The sky was clear and black, filled with a million stars, shimmering bright like splinters of ice. The wind had dropped, the animals were still, the only sounds the whisper of the distant river, the crackle of the fire and the ceaseless muttering of the five mujahadeen as they squatted in a circle, their evil faces turned orange by the flames. I lay in the shadows between Ismael and Masood, unable to sleep. What were they saying? Could they really be plotting our murder, wondering whether to haul us out onto the open ground, here, tonight and execute us with a single bullet in the back of the head, or just shoot us while we slept? Or had they decided to wait till morning when we were on the pass? Without the language I couldn't tell. To slaughter us in cold blood simply for the brusqueness John had showed their boss did seem a little excessive but in that wild spot anything felt possible. They were savage people, no question about that, and if the commander considered he had lost face . . . Well, whatever John reckoned, they could kill us with ease.

My face hidden by the shadows, I watched as Cut-throat stole glances in our direction. That motherless face was capable of anything, of that I felt sure. Praising Ahmed Gul, I wriggled deep inside my sleeping bag and felt for the cold reassurance of my hidden gun.

We were up with the dawn. Relieved to find myself still pulling in air, it wasn't a struggle; I was eager that we should be packed up and on our way as fast as possible. The sooner we were over that pass and into Nuristan the better. Which seemed kind of ironic, considering the murderous reputation of its inhabitants.

I crawled out of my sleeping bag and stepped gingerly over the inert forms of the mujahadeen who lay where they'd sat, wrapped in their thin patoos around the dead fire. Their guns hung by straps from wooden pegs or were propped against the wall. I had half a mind to empty the magazines.

Outside the stone hovel it was icy cold, with a strong wind

ripping down from the pass a thousand metres above us. The bottom half of the approach was covered in a dirty snow sheet that even from this distance looked treacherous. At least the dark clouds that had boomed like artillery the previous evening had moved away; beyond the wall of peaks where the sun lay hidden the sky was already a piercing white.

Around the other stone dwellings hardy women were busy stoking fires while their men sat, sheltered by low stone walls, milking cows and goats. The animals seemed as restless as the rest of us; the sound of their baying and kicking hooves merged with the wind into a haunting rhythm.

We were all nervous, even John, who in addition was sullen and taciturn. Having told the porters to remove some gear from each of their packs to give to the guide who'd agreed to carry a small amount, he roared at Sayeed Qayum when the hapless porter appeared to do just that. Apparently he had gone into a part of the bag John had designated off limits. Sayeed Qayum seethed with anger at the perceived injustice, his dark eyes darting all around like a choleric devil, and as he stomped past me he spat something in Dari I didn't comprehend but understood well enough, 'If I had a knife I'd cut out the heart of your friend and feed it to the wolves.' Great, I thought, not only do the mujahadeen probably want us dead, but now the porters agree. I was beginning to wonder how great an expert on 'face' John was. I slapped Sayeed Qayum on the back, smiled understandingly and promised to shoot a whole roll of photos of him. But within seconds I had forgotten all about the porter's hurt feelings; the row had woken the mujahadeen who were now sitting up, carrying cadaverous complexions, hacking copious amounts of phlegm into their mouths and firing it at the fire. And I'd thought they appeared bad in the firelight? In the stark light of dawn they barely looked human.

The thin path led along the right-hand ridge between the rough grass that climbed on one side towards a jutting cliff and fell away gradually on the other towards the river. Here the going was almost flat. Even at this altitude the walking was easy but it wasn't long before the path swung round over the river and started to climb. I took a last look towards the flat valley, breathed a sigh of relief that

Cut-throat and his boys weren't following us, and turned towards the ascent.

Only now did I appreciate just how steep the mountain was. Leaning forward at an angle close to forty-five degrees my back and calf muscles began to take a strain they had rarely experienced before. Within moments my lungs were heaving like bellows, the cold air rasping through me as though I were running the last stage of a marathon. My feet were heavy and plodded before me like two giant pendulums. It could barely have been harder had I been shackled with a ball and chain. Despite the wind I was soon sweating like a horse. I wasn't carrying much – my camera, canvas shoulder bag and water bottle, from which every few paces I drank greedily – but as on Shandor everything seemed to be weighing me down, forcing my knees to buckle and legs to shake.

When we hit the snow-face the climb became worse. Sheltered almost continuously from the melting effects of the summer sun by giant cliffs that rose up vertically on either side, the whole route, from one side to the other, was covered in a thick sheet of ice. The only way to scale it without slipping and sliding down was to traverse across and back again – like a sailing ship pushing at a headwind – trying to secure a firm footing before starting each stride. I had a wooden pole which I used to gain extra purchase but it was pathetically slow work and soon the rest of the group was a long way above me. I realised there was nothing to do but keep plodding forward but somehow I just couldn't seem to find the right gear. I'd known it would be hard, I'd struggled on Shandor, but I was making heavier weather of it than I felt I should. Every few paces I stopped, sank over my pole and gulped at the ever thinning air.

'Take smaller steps and try not to stop,' shouted John from up above, his voice almost lost on the howling gale. The rest of the group had come to a halt under a jagged ridge to let me catch up. 'Slower, slower but keep going . . .' he yelled, 'and stop drinking that water, makes it twice as hard.' I cursed him feebly for all his strength and mountain experience. He was as fit as a goat, not even out of breath, just like the rest. I realised how pathetic I must look all red in the face, soaking with sweat and swearing like a pirate, but I didn't care. All I could think about was the pain in my legs and chest, cursing the fact that I was born and brought up on land reclaimed from the sea. After a moment that thought gave me heart. I must have been the first person from Lincolnshire to fight their way over the Karik Pass.

'Once we get off the snow-face and up on to that grassy ridge we'll stop for some tea and bread.' Sheltering beneath the ridge, John pointed to the right. It was only now that I realised there were actually two routes, one going straight on, which, so the guide informed us, cut west towards the Panjsher Valley and not to Nuristan as I had supposed, and a second that did a dog-leg to the east. It was both higher and further. I whined like a cuffed dog.

'Jon Bibly Sahib,' said Haji, smiling at me, 'look like Nuristani, walk like Punjabi, yes?' I forced myself to grin. We set off again.

Much to my relief I found John's advice good. By walking behind him, following exactly in the tread of his boot, I didn't become so out of breath and was able to keep going for much longer distances. 'The secret to walking in the mountains,' explained John, a few yards ahead, 'is to get your heart, lungs and feet all working in rhythm. If any one of them is out of sync, it's a bloody nightmare. Stick behind me, you'll be fine.' Once I got the stride of my feet working in unison with my breathing, my heartbeat seemed to follow. I could feel the rhythm, all three vital parts working like a metronome. I still wasn't as fast as John and soon he was a fair way ahead again but now I was OK. I didn't need to follow his exact steps, I could do it on my own.

Beyond the snow, where the ridge branched to the right, the land opened out. The towering walls that had stood threateningly above us now fell away, giving the sun room to shine. Feeling its warm, healing rays on my face was exhilarating and as Masood lit a fire and prepared tea, I felt good. Even John now appeared calmer, more at ease. Looking up I could now see the pass beyond another smaller snow field not so far above. And peering down it seemed as if we'd walked for . . .

'Shit,' said John slowly and took a large gulp of tea. It was Haji who'd spotted them first and was holding out his arm, pointing. Walking in a line, as tiny as ants, were five dark figures, standing out vividly at the start of the snow-face; they were heading our way.

'Mujahadeen,' said Haji quietly. And we all sat and stared. My calmed heartbeat doubled again.

'Is it definitely them?' asked John, squinting for better vision.

'Who else would it be?' answered Haji. 'See, they all carry guns.' Even from this distance it was easy to spot the weapons slung over their shoulders. I had been thinking on the morning's walk that perhaps we had all been a little paranoid the night before. John's action with the commander, though certainly hasty, was surely not enough to have us all killed. I'd reasoned that John was probably right: even if the commander could make it look like Nuristanis pulled the trigger, it would still bring problems to the area, and to him. But now here were his men marching up the mountain towards us, getting larger, more real and menacing with every stride they took. Why should they be following us? I could think of no positive reason. I stuffed a Marmite-covered chapati into my mouth, washed it down with the last of the tea and stood up. Within moments we were off again.

The going was better now and we could move a little faster. The sun, scraping the surface of the rocks as it rose higher above the pass, attracted us like a powerful beacon. Ismael and Haji were walking behind me, quiet and pensive. Every few minutes one of us would turn to check on our pursuers. At one stage they disappeared, taking a different route. For a moment we thought we'd made a mistake, they weren't after us but were headed for Panjsher. But then we spotted them again high on a ridge above the snow-face, taking a harder but shorter route. As I turned to get on, heart pumping, lungs creaking, I realised with a desperate sinking feeling that what I had taken to be the crest of the path was in fact a false summit. The real one was now visible another 200 metres higher, beyond another bowl of snow. Used to the terrain, with lungs like sails, the mujahadeen were eating up the ground at twice the rate that we were. There was no question of us reaching the pass before they caught us. After a while John stopped.

'There's no point in trying to out run them, we'll wait here and see what they want. They're unlikely to try anything. We're safer on this side of the pass anyway.' Even so Haji forced a bullet into the breech of his Kalashnikov. I put my hand into my side pocket and, wondering if I'd really have the guts to use it, felt for my gun and released the safety catch. We sat in silence like condemned men. I took out a cigarette and lit it.

Suddenly John laughed a short hard cackle of mirth and handed me his camera. He had removed the wide-angle lens and replaced it with a powerful telephoto. The men were now only 250 metres beneath us, and, having come round the top of the snow-face, were in the full glare of the sun. 'Those guns, Haji Sahib,' he said, as I aimed the camera, 'I don't think they'll be blowing anybody's head off today.' I pulled them into focus and laughed too. He was right. I suddenly felt quite weak. The larcenous rabble who were going to butcher us in cold blood were in fact no more dangerous than a bunch of school children. The weapons weren't guns but picks and shovels. Haji smiled, whispered 'Al Hamdulillah,' and withdrew the bullet from the breech.

When the group reached us, they stopped and chatted for a few minutes. They were Passai woodmen on their way to find work as builders in Bandul. They wore moulded plastic plimsolls, dirty shalwar kameez, waistcoats and flat caps the colour of the earth. Their possessions wrapped in patoos were strung across their backs. While we talked, one of them – a man in his mid-forties with a dark face as creased as a walnut and great tufts of hair sprouting from his ears – knocked the axe head off the shaft he was carrying, and, by dropping a stone into the tapered hole and filling it with tobacco, he turned it into a chillum.

An hour later we reached the top of the pass. Ismael handed me a bottle of goat's milk, smiled and slapped me on the back. I had forgotten how thirsty I was and wolfed down the refreshing liquid. Having drunk my fill I passed the bottle back, wiped my lips and stared towards the east. There, tumbling endlessly away in a great sweeping valley, cutting a swath through an embrace of rocky peaks, was the country I had held in my mind's eye since first reading of Peachey and Danny's travels. Nuristan, once Kafiristan. The name may have changed but the image in my head had not. For more than ten years I'd harboured a dream to be standing here. What would I find? What would it be like? Bubbling with expectation, a broad grin creased my tired face. One of the last true wildernesses on earth, Nuristan has always been a secret and mysterious land, a place of myths and legend, of danger and reward. Untouched as it is by Western hands, almost unseen by Western eyes, I wondered if it was here that I'd find an adventurer's utopia, a wanderer's Shangri-La.

Nuristan. Land of Light.

10 A Land like Narnia

'That's how we came to our first village . . .
just as though we'd tumbled from the skies.'

We hadn't been going long before it started to snow. Flurries at first that became heavier the further we descended. There was no path as such; we simply had to find our own way, more often than not, hopping from one giant boulder to another. From above, the mighty rocks had appeared black, like great nuggets of coal, but now that we were on them I could see that the undersides were red, the colour of terracotta. It was as if someone had come along and splashed them all with creosote. They were sharp and jagged, making every step a potential disaster. With the steep downward momentum it was hard not to go too fast and risk losing your balance. I had to keep forcing myself to slow down and take care; a broken leg here and we would all be in trouble.

After a while, the snow turned to rain, a cold drizzle, driven by the wind, that stung our faces. Wild flowers of violet and yellow grew amongst the coarse grass but the conditions were too unpleasant to see much beauty in them. High above the tree-line it was a bleak world, wild and barren. The shrill cry of the marmot – a beaver-like animal – was the only proof we were not alone.

Early in the afternoon, we struck upon a herd of goats and a few cattle and then, wedged under a cliff, a low-roofed dwelling. Made of stone and turf, it was little more than a cave, with smoke seeping through a hole in the roof. Outside, secured with chains, were two fierce dogs, striped like tigers and a similar size. Barking fiercely they announced to the valley that strangers were coming.

A man and his teenaged son, who were up here in the aylaks for two months making cheese and butter to see their family through another harsh winter, crawled from the entrance and invited us in.

Their features were rather European. As fair-skinned as John or I, both had green eyes and mousy hair, aquiline faces with sharp noses and square foreheads, proud jaws and wide mouths. Like everyone in the region they wore the shalwar kameez but over the trousers they donned oversized shorts, of a similar cut to those worn by ice-hockey players, but made out of a thick dark felt. They were kind and boiled water for our tea but seemed only moderately interested, or surprised, by our arrival. As we sat, squashed like pilchards in the tiny smoke-filled hovel waiting for the rain to stop, it appeared for all the world that feringhees regularly came this way. The father chatted garrulously about his goats and cattle.

When the rain relented a bright sun pushed through the clouds and soon the sky was clear; in a few hours we had gone from deep winter to the middle of summer. Before too long we were well below the tree-line. Giant green pines scattered across both sides of the valley climbed high above the path which was littered with their dead, rust-coloured needles. The trail led down to the widening river that coiled its way through crops of young green maize and mountain wheat. We walked along low water channels lined with flowers: dandelions, buttercups, daisies, tiny pink roses, reeds and wild grasses, and the pungent fragrance of honeysuckle filled the air. With the sun falling towards the western sky, the guide pointed. There, on the hillside, a thin trail of smoke climbing vertically from an invisible flue, was our first real Nuristani home.

The owner was an old man who, alerted by another chained dog, shuffled across the bare courtyard to greet us. Leaning on a twisted pole, he had a great beak-like nose, hooked and bowed, watery eyes sunk deep in his head and a long and pointed hennaed beard. He wore a bottle-green turban tilted backwards, forcing his angled ears out horizontally. As the late afternoon sunlight struck him across the shoulders, the ears were burnished into the shape and appearance of transparent leaves. I shook his hand, touched my heart and offered the plethora of greetings. I'd never met a goblin before.

'This is Sher Gul,' said the guide. 'My friend is away at the moment, up in the aylaks. This is his father.'

'I am a poor man,' said Sher Gul in a frail voice, tilting his head up to look at us, 'and I have little to offer but I would be honoured if you would be my guests. Otherwise I can take you into Bandul.' He pointed to a track that led down towards the river and a wicker bridge. 'It is only an hour away . . .'

John glanced at me questioningly and I nodded. The thought of this man walking ten minutes, never mind an hour, seemed preposterous. And we were exhausted. It had been eight hours since we'd crossed the pass, twelve since we'd left the aylaks above Farish Garh. 'If you could thank Sher Gul for his kind offer,' John said to Ismael, 'and tell him that we would be honoured to be his guests.'

The house was made of horizontal timber and flat stones. The lower tier was for winter stabling, when the herds return from the high pastures. Surrounded by a low stone wall, now it was packed with yellow straw, dry wood, a goat and some chickens. He led us up the ladder – a slim tree trunk with grooves cut in it – and on to a small open-sided veranda where his wrinkled wife sat on a low stool rocking a baby swaddled in a cradle. The woman wore dark baggy leggings and had a scarlet shawl draped loosely over a pillar-box hat. Despite her advanced years, as we trudged past she pulled the shawl over her nose and mouth. In the corner, beside a small smouldering fire hung a doubled string pebble bow, an engraved axe and a three-pronged wooden fork. Behind the woman, leaning against a wicker screen, were two inflated yellowish goat skins which looked like recently deceased corpses. I'd seen photographs of these before: half filled with milk then gently rocked, they're used for making butter.

We set down our bags in a dim corridor beyond the main entrance and took off our boots before falling into the guest room. It was a large room with a carved central pillar, the cracked walls plastered with mud and straw and the floor covered in thick and rough goat's wool rugs. Through the unglazed window a warm breeze blew.

'Hindustan or Inglistan?' asked our host, seated cross-legged on the floor, leaning against the pillar. Besides Afghan, in his mind these were the only options. 'Oh,' he said on hearing our reply. 'No roads and no cars, you have done well. Long ago some feringhees came over Karik, but not for many years.' When pushed to say how many, he shrugged and suggested twenty-five. He was a kind man, about seventy years old, and through Ismael's translation, he told us something of his life. He'd been to Jalalabad once in the fifties but he hadn't liked it much – too many people, too much noise – and had been here, surviving off the land, ever since. Isolated as he was, the war had largely passed him by. Occasionally, during the occupation, Russian helicopters had flown by looking for mujahadeen supply routes, but that was all. His grandfather, he told us, was a Kafir and had been converted to Islam as a young man. Interested in the roots of the Nuristanis, I asked where he thought his ancestors came from. Might he, I wondered, be able to provide confirmation of the legend of Alexander the Great's passage through the area?

'The mullahs they tell us we are the people of Quorresh,' he said, gazing vacantly out of the window at the sublime view. 'From Arabistan, the tribe of the prophet, praise be upon him.' He had a sharp, high-pitched voice, not unpleasant, that seemed to give what he said great passion. I'd not heard the story before. I lit a cigarette and listened intently as Sher Gul warmed to his theme. 'Many years ago, when Islam was young, our ancestors fled their land. They were Kafirs, believed in other gods, Gish, Imbra and others, so they couldn't stay. Led by three brothers they sailed on a sea and the big river for many days before landing in the south.' He leaned forward and gestured vaguely towards the hills. The Arabian Sea and the Indus? I wondered. 'Then they walk and walk across the deserts and through the hills. First they stop at Kabul, then Jalalabad. But as Islam spread so they pushed higher into the mountains until they reached this country. One brother was called Ram, he stayed in the Ramgul Valley, another, his name was Kam, he live in Kamdesh, in the Bashgul Valley. And the third was called . . .' he stopped talking and adjusted the angle of his turban. Unable to remember the third brother's name he cut the story short. 'Then Islam came and brought us here.' He smiled simply.

'What about Alexander,' I asked, exhaling smoke slowly. 'Sikander? Sikander Julkhan? Have you heard of him?' But as Ismael translated my question Sher Gul just shook his head vaguely, leaned back against the pillar and resumed his vigil through the window. Disappointed that the myth seemed unknown, I joined his gaze towards the hills and stubbed out my cigarette.

The light had faded and the room was dark and quiet. Sher Gul lit an oil lamp and brought us warm milk and maize bread, apologising again for having so little to offer. After tea we lay down on coarse rugs, wrapped ourselves in our patoos and, thoroughly shattered, headed for sleep.

'Shit . . .' I exclaimed and sat up straight. 'What the hell's . . . ? Jesus!' I turned on my torch and found to my horror that I was crawling with grim brown bugs. Some were so tiny as to be barely visible while others were a good centimetre long. They resembled miniature crabs, and seemed to nip almost as hard. On my chest, my back, in my hair, my beard and over my arms, they were everywhere. 'Christ, I'm covered in bloody bed bugs,' I said in dismay.

'Welcome to Nuristan,' said John with a grunt and rolled over to sleep.

It was a bright morning, the birds were singing and the widening river gurgled slowly by. Willows and birch lined the path that cut through fields of lush green crops. On either side the hills climbed to far away peaks scattered with towering cedar pines and holly oak. The nearer we got to Bandul the more people passed, heading to the summer pastures or to tend their crops higher up the valley. The men were tall and generally dark and handsome, appearing like Romanian gypsies. They still carried guns but weren't too intimidating. Often stopping to find out who we were and where we were going they seemed more intrigued by us than distrustful or threatening. Even so, we never divulged our route further than the next village; to do so would have invited robbery. The women had large silver discs hanging from chains around their waists and, like Sher Gul's wife, wore scarlet shawls. We never saw their faces though. The moment they noticed us they pulled down their veils, turned away and waited until we'd passed. I bounded along behind the curved form of Sher Gul. With a strange animal-like gait, amazing us all, he led the way.

Again the morning had been spiked with tension. This time the porters had refused to go on, realising my worst fears by telling us they'd had enough and wanted to return home. John, once again as tactful and flexible as a falling girder, had become embroiled in an argument with Majid Khan about carrying something extra. With

Sayeed Qayum still smarting from his public dressing down on the other side of the pass, the outcome was inevitable. For two desperate hours it looked as if we might lose the entire team, leaving John and me to travel alone – a prospect I did not greet warmly. But having been informed by Sher Gul that a band of notorious robbers lived on the Alingar, which offered the only way out besides returning past Commander Mohammed Malik and his fearsome militia, they soon changed their tune. I had failed to realise that having lived on the border of Nuristan all their lives, brought up on tales of the murderous tribes who resided there, the porters were more scared of the province than we were. Whether Sher Gul deliberately neglected to tell us that the most famous band of Ramgul bandits lived in Pushol, at the head of the valley, directly on our path, I guess I'll never know. Still, the whole episode hardly improved John's see-saw spirits. Much to my concern, he seemed to plummet to new-found depths, leaving him distant and fractious.

The village of Bandul was magnificent, much larger than I had expected. Clinging to a spectacular spur of rock that entered the main valley along the line of a fast-flowing tributary, it was formed by a great wall of mud-brown houses. In some places as many as eight dwellings were stacked precariously in receding layers on top of one another, the roof of the lower forming the veranda for the one above. Glorious walnut, mulberry and apricot trees climbed between the homes, their leafy branches often resting on the roofs and walls. Taking advantage of every inch of fertile land, beneath the village, just above the river, tiny patches of maize and millet sprouted. The morning sun burned the mud walls to a deep gold, smoke spiralled through the clear air and the shrieks of the children echoed up to meet us.

Having lost so much time, we didn't stay long. A young man with a manic look in his eye led us to a circular clearing beside the river surrounded by willows and hand-placed rocks; the village wezstal, or meeting place. Here he made us wait while Sher Gul and a boy went to inform the village elders we were coming through. With a square forehead, flat nose and mousy hair, our self-appointed host looked rather Slavic. With great animation he told us we had arrived the day after a double killing. Apparently a man had returned from working in the gulf and, rich from his well paid employment, had taken a girl for his wife without concern for the fact that she was already betrothed to another. There had been a fight and if the lad was to be believed – or Ismael's translation was accurate – the two men had shot and killed each other. From a cross belt stuffed with bullets, he proudly brandished a 1930s German Mauser and re-enacted the scene. I asked him where he had come by such a weapon, but he just laughed and waved it hazardously around, declaring proudly, 'It is mine.'

Twenty minutes later we were off again, heading towards the promise of a well-earned respite: a swim and wash in Lake Mundol.

After two hours the path started to climb in a pitted, snake-like coil. The Bandul Valley had narrowed now to little more than a sharp ravine. The vegetation had all but died away, the houses and hamlets left way behind. The dun-coloured ground was dry and rocky and hard as flint. Only the holly oaks now remained. Passing one, Ismael swiped at the twisted trunk with the small hand axe he was carrying. The blade bounced back with a 'kan*ggg*', as though he'd struck metal.

Suddenly, quite without warning – our sight being all but obscured by the terrain rising before us – we found ourselves on the apex of a mighty spur of rock that sat facing the junction of another colossal valley, the Ramgul. The rock face glowed yellow, almost orange, in the bright mid-morning sun and fell away in sheer walls to a wild turquoise river. In places it was calm, resting quietly in deep beckoning pools, but in others it turned white, hurtling like a demon in a desperate struggle through a confined gorge. I was transfixed.

'Amazing, hey John?' I said, hoping the sight might raise a smile in my partner.

'Sure,' he replied without emotion, glancing only for a moment over the stunning abyss before walking on alone.

I stood and looked worriedly after him, unsure what to do. Whether he was angry with me for gathering such an inexperienced and, to his mind, hopelessly inadequate team, was simply incensed by the morning's events or troubled by some inner torment, I wasn't sure but there was now virtually no communication between us. I hadn't realised to quite what extent the tides of my fortunes would be affected by the mercurial moods of my travelling companion. The power balance of our relationship had, it seemed, turned out to be as tricky and unpredictable as Afghan politics. It felt as though another, completely unexpected, set of rules and laws to understand and abide by had been introduced into our journey, as if the wrong move on my part could flip us from camaraderie into sullen neutrality, or worse. This was, I clearly saw, a pretty disastrous dynamic in a relationship between travelling companions. Even worse, the situation was making the entire group despondent. John was the leader: when he smiled we all smiled with him, when he was surly, the dark vibes affected us all. The trouble was he wasn't smiling. I knew I should talk to him to try and dissolve whatever the problems were. As his partner it was my responsibility, but I was nervous. He'd become cold and intimidating – as approachable as a ticking bomb. Besides, he was the experienced Afghan hand, he was the one who spoke the language, knew the customs, was used to travelling under such conditions: who was I to question his ways?

I waited on the ridge, and, when requested, gave each of the porters a couple of pills for their 'body pain', took their photo and then waited for Ismael to arrive. As he saw the Ramgul Valley he stopped, clapped me on the shoulder and burst out laughing. 'Oh, my God!' he exclaimed. It was much more the response I'd hoped for.

An hour later we stopped by a stream for prayers. John sat by himself in the shade of a holly oak, pensively picking his nails with a knife. Plucking up the courage, I walked over and squatted beside him.

'Is everything all right?' I asked, watching him anxiously. 'You seem a little . . .' Unsure which word to use, I let the sentence hang.

John turned and stared at me. Not a muscle on his face moved; his piercing eyes burned like lasers. 'What do you think?' he cursed, contemptuously. 'The whole group was prepared to leave us this morning, jack us in. If we haven't got their trust what have we got? Majid Khan was totally out of order. In any other circumstances I'd have sent him home.'

'I don't think it had anything to do with Majid Khan,' I said as calmly as I was able. Confronting John in such circumstances was a scary business. I swallowed hard. 'It was all to do with Sayeed

Qayum, yesterday. He's the leader, the other porters do what he says.'

'Sayeed Qayum?' He looked aghast. 'What do you mean? He went into the wrong part of the bag. I'd specifically told him not to and he did. You have to keep discipline, if you don't . . .'

'But can you see how it looked to him? He didn't understand that he'd done anything wrong, only that you shouted at him in front of everyone. I know you're the expert, John, you understand this country far better than I do, but . . .' I looked down at my hands not daring to say more. After a moment I looked back at him. 'And you and I, we must talk. We can't go on like this.'

John's face returned to rock and with a glare that made me shiver, he stood up and silently walked away.

At a small hamlet Sher Gul introduced us to a friend who he told us would guide us on to Mundol. Hunch-backed, still clutching to his gnarled stick Sher Gul, a hillman through and through, had outpaced us all and didn't even look tired. Having introduced us to his friend, he turned to leave.

'Coco jan,' said Haji using the term for uncle, 'you have been good to us. We would like to thank you for all you have done.' He was old and poor but the respect that everyone had for him was plain to see. John handed Ismael some money, who passed it on to Sher Gul but the old man refused. With moist eyes he declared it not to be his culture. 'You are my guests,' he said with a quivering voice. 'It is my duty.'

'Coco jan,' replied Ismael, 'it is not for the hospitality that we give you this money. We give it as a sign of our friendship and our respect for you.' Reluctantly Sher Gul accepted it and left.

Sher Gul's friend was tall and dark. Wearing large leather boots, black trousers and a low-collared, gold-embroidered black cotton shirt, he looked like a Turkish circus performer. Full of good cheer, he told us terrible tales about a band of robbers who lived in Pushol and whom we would be lucky to avoid. Hearing about feringhees, they'd be bound to want to rob us, he mused aloud. The robbers were seven brothers and were notorious throughout the valley, and far beyond, for their murderous raids. But that was not all. There was, if our cheerful informant was to be believed, another dangerous mob living near the village of Kwist which we were just entering. Here the path crossed the river and continued along the western bank. We had just traversed the rickety bridge when we heard the cry.

'Estada shodan! Tawaqof! Tawaqof!'

The man who leapt down the bank to stop us was short, had charcoal smeared around his eyes and spoke as if he'd just sucked on a helium balloon. He had a squashed nose, crooked teeth and an irate boil weeping pus from an inverted chin. The ubiquitous Kalashnikov was thrown across his shoulder. Flapping his arms as though trying to fly, he gestured angrily towards us. 'Stop,' he squeaked again, 'you cannot pass.' If Sher Gul had been a goblin, here was a troll.

'But we have a letter,' pleaded Ismael, holding up one of our many documents. It was addressed to the Jamiat (government) commander who we had been informed was in control of the village. He was in charge, however, only on this side of the river. As Ismael read the letter aloud to the illiterate man, we quickly discovered that he wasn't a common thief or, sadly, the Jamiat representative but instead worked for the Hezb-i-Islami commander who was in charge on the far bank from where we'd just come. By pure ill chance we'd stumbled in to the quagmire of Afghan politics. We'd read the wrong letter to the wrong man, used the wrong key, as John might have said.

Though Jamiat and Hezb-i-Islami weren't fighting each other anymore – their leader Gulbadeen Hekmatyar was now part of Rabbani's government, working in coalition against the Taliban – in out-lying areas relations between the two factions were still strained. For the sake of his party's credibility the lackey knew it was important that we showed equal respect to both sides. He told us therefore that before we could continue we would have to return across the river and pay our respects to his boss. But we all knew what that would mean. Being forced to sit for an age while Hekmatyar's henchman decided how best to push and pull us to his own advantage. Handled wrongly, it could take hours, even days – or worse. It was a delicate situation and though no guns were being pointed at this stage we were but a short step away from finding ourselves being held. The soothing waters of Lake Mundol seemed as distant a destination as the Arabian Sea.

Soon a crowd of men had gathered. The Jamiat commander was away, they said, otherwise he would have given us men to proceed unhindered. Reassuringly, they all joined the argument on the side of Haji and Ismael, shouting and screaming at the little Hezb minnow. One of them even grabbed two of our bags and marched off down the track, determined that we should pass through quickly.

'What does this man know?' he yelled to no one in particular. 'He is short, he is stupid. It is Rabbani here, not the cursed Hekmatyar.'

Though it made Ismael laugh, it didn't have the desired effect and only managed to spur the irate little man into action. With a dark face and raging eyes, he went stomping off up the hill to radio his commander and find out what should be done with us. There was no point in trying to pass quickly through the village once he'd gone. The Hezb commander would have allies up the valley. With one radio call, he could have a group of mujahadeen waiting for us anywhere he pleased.

'Go with him, Ismael,' said John, more bored than angry, 'and tell the commander, whoever he is, that we are harmless aid workers on our way to Mundol and wish to pass.' He then lay down under a large mulberry tree and closed his eyes. We hadn't spoken since our little chat. I wondered apprehensively what he was thinking.

Ismael did as he was bid but came back twenty minutes later saying ominously that the commander would not give us permission to advance until we had been to see him. He was angry, Ismael said, that we had tried to sneak through his domain unnoticed. By doing this we had insulted his party, his leader. Charcoal-face looked as pleased as punch. He stuck out his chest and having wiped pus from his boil on the back of his sleeve repositioned his cap at an altogether more important angle.

'Right,' said John, getting to his feet. 'I've about had enough of this. I'm buggered if I'm going to sit here all day. Come on, Jonny, we'll go and sort this out. Show me where the radio is, Ismael, I'll have a word with this commander.'

We walked off up the village, the lackey almost jogging to keep up. With John in his current frame of mind, I was more than a little anxious. If he came across as irate and managed to offend this commander in some way, we could easily find ourselves in all kinds of trouble. Still, I was pleased to have been asked along. At least we were talking again.

At the top of a hill we came to a small mud-brick room above which an aerial climbed. Inside, a green two-way receiver sat on a table with a microphone resting before it. John pulled back the chair and sat down while the lackey fiddled with the dials. After a moment the static broke to reveal the commander's voice.

'Salaam alaikum.'

'Salaam alaikum,' John replied. 'We would like to offer our greetings and best wishes and thank you for your kind offer . . .' Talking in halting Dari, he was concentrating hard. Sweat particles sitting on his forehead began to run; he wiped them away. After he'd finished his introduction, he flipped the switch and the commander's voice came back, wishing the goodness of Allah upon us.

'We are aid workers on our way to Pushol via Mundol,' John continued, once the commander had finished, 'and though we would very much have liked to take up your kind offer of hospitality, on this occasion we regret that we do not have the time. Therefore, with your kind permission . . .'

'Respected guests,' his voice came back thin, fighting through the static, 'it is my responsibility that you should come to no harm while you are in my mantika. There are many thieves hereabouts. It is better that you stay the night with me.' That's rich, I thought, as Ismael did his best to translate the conversation quietly into my ear. For now, I had no doubt, it was the commander who was the greatest threat to our wellbeing. We were pawns in a power game between commanders of different political ideologies. By staying on this side of the river and refusing to visit the other we were in effect saying that Jamiat was more important than Hezb-i-Islami and that the Hezb commander was less influential and powerful than his Jamiat counterpart. 'Face' was once more in jeopardy. With trepidation I listened to John's reply.

'Honoured friend,' he started, unable to keep some of the

exasperation out of his voice, 'as I have already said we are aid workers doing good work for your country. I have been working here for five years. General Hamimullah is a very good friend of mine and Gulbadeen Hekmatyar has himself given full permission to our journey.' Quite who General Hamimullah was I hadn't a clue but I liked the lie about Hekmatyar and smiled at John; reassuringly he gave me a wink. 'If I am to report to them that we were having problems in the Ramgul Valley, this may cause problems for you. This is something that I would not want. We may have to decide that no aid can come to this area.' Then the *coup de grâce*, a way for the commander to give in without feeling insulted. 'Having seen Pushol we shall be returning through Kwist in four days' time,' John lied again. 'We would be honoured to meet and discuss your views on the area then.'

There was a long pause. The words that broke the silence were heaven sent. 'Of course, you may proceed, I have never wished to delay your journey. It is only for your safety that I am concerned. I shall look forward to the meeting on your return. Give the information to my man. I shall see that you are brought here safely.'

John thanked the commander and having praised Allah, switched the machine off. 'That's how you deal with annoying commanders, Jonny,' he said, standing up and smiling at last. 'Take no shit but let them think they've won. Not only can we now proceed but we've also laid a false trail. By sundown tonight every thief and bandit in the valley will think we're coming back this way in four days' time while really we'll be heading safely over the Kantiwar Pass to Wama.' - He slapped me on the shoulder, obviously delighted with his powers of diplomacy. 'Brilliant, hey?' It was, without a doubt. As he turned away I let out a long and silent sigh.

Lake Mundol was even more stunning than I had imagined. From a ridge by the path we looked over the steep sides of the barren valley to where the water rested as calm and motionless as a mighty slab of polished lapis lazuli. Deep turquoise, the colour was so dense against the arid cliffs and pale sky the bottom of the valley looked as if it had been immersed in some beautiful oil or a rich enamel paint. Curving slightly, the lake stretched away towards the north, leaving the far end where the village was situated hidden behind a spur of rock. I stood agog, I had never seen anything like it in my life.

'Incredible, isn't it?' said John, changing the lens on his camera. 'It's the way the sunlight reflects through the water that gives it that intense colour, that and the minerals from the snow melt. Lake Topkhana in Badakshan is the same.' Greatly surprised by his friendly enthusiasm, I agreed earnestly.

Suddenly a deafening explosion filled the air, echoing from one side of the valley to the other. And then another followed. Confined by the steep cliff walls they sounded like atom bombs. I jumped a mile. 'What the hell was that?' I asked.

'Grenade,' exclaimed Haji with a happy grin.

'They're probably blowing the rock, making a water channel or something,' explained John, lowering his camera. 'Anyway, let's get on. That water looks too damn good just to look at. I need a swim.' So did I. Aside from splashing myself in irrigation channels or the rivers I hadn't had a proper wash for a week. But it wasn't the prospect of a refreshing soak that gave me the most cause for pleasure. Before hurrying on John turned to me and smiled. 'OK?' he asked.

Quite mysteriously the face of thunder that John had borne, almost permanently, for the past few days had mellowed to a more pleasant image. Suddenly it was as though nothing whatever was wrong with the world. Again we were partners it seemed and now that I sensed his dark mood ripple its wings and fly away, I felt emotionally and physically uplifted. Why it had gone and when it might return I hadn't a clue. I was just thankful for its parting.

As we walked along the path there was another explosion and, rounding a corner, we found out why. And the answer wasn't rock blasting. A group of boys, some naked, others in their shalwar trousers, stood dripping wet on a ledge some twenty feet above the freezing water. Shivering slightly in the afternoon sun, they held their hands close to their chests in an attempt to preserve some body warmth. Standing before them was a young man with a majestic blue shawl, embroidered with flowers and edged with lime green tassels, thrown over his shoulder. Checking to see that all was clear below, the man pulled the pin on a hand-grenade and lobbed it over the edge. A moment later a giant boom shook the water, sending a fountain of crystal froth ten feet into the air. Immediately the kids charged down a steep and rocky track to the lake's edge, or jumped off the ledge. Shouting and splashing, they proceeded to collect the catch – for this was fishing, Afghan style. Not able to control himself, Haji fired a burst from his gun into the lake well away from the children and let out a whoop of delight.

'This fishing I like, Jon Bibly Sahib.'

Beside the lake was a flat field of lush grass on which cattle and a small white stallion grazed. John told Haji and the porters to rest for half an hour and then go up to the village with the letter for the local commander, organise the accommodation and buy a couple of chickens for dinner. Whether a peace offering or not, it was a gesture that went down well with all. He then took his telescopic fishing rod from his bag and with visible excitement assembled it. This was the moment he'd been waiting for. He intended to enjoy it.

Just as he was ready to start, another explosion reverberated around us. 'Bloody heathens,' said John wryly. 'Come on, Ismael, you want to learn fishing the real way?' As John headed towards the far side of the lake, I heard him whistle.

The water was searingly cold, scooping the breath from my body as I plunged from the bank. Snowmelt filled the rivers that flowed into the lake and it didn't feel much above freezing to me. But once the shock had died away and my breathing was restored, it was sublime, and unbelievably refreshing after the long day's march. I swam out towards the centre of the lake and looked around me. The towering cliffs peppered with holly oak rose vertically to a clear sky where birds of prey soared high above. They say there used to be cormorants here, fishing on the lake; with the frequent explosions it wasn't hard to work out why there weren't any now. On the eastern side, still bathed in the golden sun, the children splashed happily in the water as they collected another catch, but over to the west the valley face was set deep in the evening shade. A couple of fishermen, with poles not explosives, stood in the shallows at the northern end where the lake shrank once more to a river, and cast their lines. Behind them the strange houses clung to the hillside above the water meadows that stretched like a carpet away into the distance.

The local commander was a neat spiv of a man, resembling a Colombian cocaine dealer, no doubt as hard and sharp as a hatchet. He was called Ali Jan. In his house, high up on the hillside, we ate our chicken and the fish John and Ismael had caught. The fish, shera mahi, or milk fish as everyone called it, was delicious, if a little bony, but there was only one each. The chicken on the other hand would have been considered inedible in any other circumstances. As ancient as the valley, what little flesh the crippled roosters provided was so tough I couldn't break through it, my teeth simply bounced on the meat as they had done on the goat. It was like trying to devour an elastic band – my boot would have provided more sustenance. Still, I reasoned, this journey had never been planned as a gastronomic tour. It was eat it or starve, so I ate, painfully chewing each lump of grizzled flesh, my imagination on full overdrive trying to imagine it was sirloin steak.

Once dinner was finished and Allah had been invoked, everyone wandered outside on to the flat roof for the day's final azam. I followed with my sleeping bag. John and I had decided that wherever possible we would sleep on the roof. Still scratching our bedbug bites we had little confidence that any of the guest rooms would be cleaner than Sher Gul's. Besides, so long as the rain held off, it was beautiful and warm under the stars.

'Haji no get bitten by bug,' said my warrior friend with his infectious grin as we made our way outside.

'How come?' I asked.

'Haji have Kalashnikov.'

Without a breath of wind, the valley was quiet and still. The sky was not yet black but a deep, rich blue, sparkling with stars. A half moon climbed from behind the opposite ridge, seemed to rest for a moment, then drifted off towards the heavens, silhouetting Haji – our travelling muezzin – as he prepared to lead the faithful in prayer. Facing the western skies, he began to sing. His voice was strong and rich, spiralling effortlessly down the valley. It floated over the trees, the river and reflected off the rocks in a rising and falling cadence as he called gloriously to Allah. He sounded like an angel. Behind Haji the others formed a line, bowed their heads and then fell to the floor in muted prayer. I fired a cigarette, leaned back against the wooden wall and stared up towards the shimmering heavens. I breathed in deeply, holding on to the magic of this incredible place and in a quiet whisper thanked my own god.

——— ◆ ———

The road in front of me disappeared, replaced by a wall of black. Everything slowed to half speed. I recognised the shape of a taxi cab, saw a young woman staring out from the back. I heard the beat of my heart and the rasp of my breath. Instinct hit the brakes and the bike began to slide.

I opened my eyes gazing up into the murky sky, rain splattering against my face. I could feel nothing. Slowly, noise returned: a slamming of car doors, a horn, footsteps and then faces above me, peering down. A man with a great red face was shouting. Feeling no pain, I sat up. The bike was lying in a heap, crunched against the side of the taxi. I knew it was my fault. Getting slowly to my feet, I shuffled towards the crippled machine, aware of the small crowd watching me. With help, I dragged it to the side of the road. People began to move away. 'Drop down to Battersea, Oscar Five,' the controller's voice had cracked across the air-waves only moments before. 'Pick up 29 Simpson Street. That's Simpson, as in American divorcee who caused the abdication of our monarch in the thirties. Roger.' The half-smile that had forced its way across my miserable face was now long gone.

Dispatch riding was a soul-destroying job, hardly better than pursuing stars with a camera. It paid well – £400 a week if I worked hard – but, my God, I earned it. Breakdowns, punctures, being sworn at by other drivers, ignored by receptionists and hassled endlessly by officious police, I worked in all conditions, narrowly avoiding death or paralysis three or four times a day. On the bottom rung of the workers' ladder I felt as though I belonged to a sub-class of modern untouchables, operating on the periphery of life. In warm offices people chatted, drank coffee, listened to the radio, did deals, serviced customers, produced things. They made a difference. Trapped inside a leather suit and full-face helmet I lived inside my head and the isolation got to me. Often I drove like a lunatic, fast and recklessly, without much care. I felt removed from the world around me, swamped by insecurities. In my tormented mind I'd become an outcast, Mad Max, a fucked-up warrior of the road, unable to see life as others saw it, unable to blend in, get on.

Back on the pavement, I slumped against the wall and fell to the floor, a broken puppet. I knew I was lucky not to have sustained any major injuries but still I started to cry. What began as sobs soon became an uncontrollable howl and within seconds I was bawling like a five-year-old. Tears streamed down my cheeks, tasting salty in my mouth; I didn't bother to wipe them away. I felt like a child, lost and confused. I realised then that I had truly had enough. For eighteen months I had been free-falling through a chasm of despair and now I'd hit the bottom. This was as low as I was prepared to go.

'Oscar Five, Oscar Five,' the voice came back through the radio once again. I wiped my eyes and took a deep breath.

'Got another pick up for you,' said the controller. '43 Lupus Street . . . that's Lupus as in Latin for wolf.'

———◆———

The next day we continued north towards Pushol and the Kantiwar Pass. It was an easy walk along the river bank beneath a clear sky. At Mangor we passed Mullah Halal: a large flat rock said to be stained with the blood of fifty mullahs who were ceremoniously butchered at the hands of the Kafirs a year before the forced conversion. By contrast, a few kilometres further on was the famous script written on a low cliff-face by one of Amir Abdul Rahman's soldiers to celebrate their victory over the forces of the infidel. At least that's what we had been led to believe it was and the words were indeed to that effect but the date, once we'd stood for ten minutes trying to work out the difference between the Muslim and Christian calendars, was 1931 which was thirty-five years after the Amir's jihad.

With the beautiful day and the prospect of soon being clear of the supposedly treacherous Ramgul Valley, everyone was more at ease; including John, whose desolate mood really appeared to be a thing of the past. Whatever it was that had been getting him down he now seemed reconciled to: the group was what it was, however amateur, the split with the porters had been put behind us and whatever other worries he had, at least for the moment, he'd pushed from his mind. Sorting out the Hezb-i-Islami commander in Kwist had seemed to be the turning point, fishing and swimming in Lake Mundol had done the rest. He still walked on his own and was sparing with his words but there was definitely a happier spring to his step. It was a profound relief to us all. With no confrontations for forty-eight hours, the group had finally reached some kind of harmony.

Worried about the infamous band of brother robbers, we passed Pushol on the far bank and pushed on towards the pass. Two herdsmen coming the other way, returning from the aylaks, their horse laden with butter and cheese, told us the bandits had been on a large raiding party over a neighbouring pass ten days earlier and had netted more than a hundred goats and fifty cattle. Perhaps they were engaged on a similar venture in another valley or were too busy celebrating the last to bother with us. Or perhaps, as John pointed out, they were waiting to ambush us north of Mundol on the fictitious return leg of our journey. Whichever was the case, no one we passed gave us any trouble.

Following the track along the foaming river, through the hay meadows, we climbed to high above the tree-line. It was hard work and I was still sweating profusely. I was forced to stop and take on litres of water from the river and springs. But much to my relief I realised that I was finding the walking easier. Unlike when crossing the Karik Pass, I could now feel my legs, hard, firm, solid beneath me; my bad knees were giving no trouble and neither was my twisted ankle. Even my breathing was more regular – my lungs somehow felt expanded. No longer did I linger at the back of the party. Now my pace was not much slower than the rest and we arrived at the aylaks in a merry group.

John looked pleased, striding around just below the pass with a contented grin half hidden behind his bushy beard. There was no cover here, the only stone pen was already over-crowded with four brothers from the village of Nilaw, their goats and a million fleas. At well over 4000 metres it was going to be a cold night, especially for the porters whose only defence against the biting weather would be their thin patoos. But John wasn't concerned. As I pointed this out he turned to look at them as they played by the river seeing who could throw a rock furthest.

'A sad inevitability,' he said, with a rueful smile. For all their whinging he knew they were tough. Huddled together, they'd handle it.

John took a couple of packets of BP5s out of a rucksack, passed me one and opened up the other. The nuclear holocaust biscuits, though filling and supremely useful on a trip like ours, weren't very appetising. They had the texture of sawdust and were probably not quite as tasty. From my own bag I withdrew the hidden peanut butter and handed it warily to John with a spoon. With an amused snort, he unscrewed the lid and scraped out a large dollop which he then placed on the biscuit. 'Not a bad idea,' he said a moment later, chewing heartily. 'Packed with energy. Umm . . . I'll remember that next time.' Feeling foolishly pleased, I took the jar and devoured a large mouthful myself.

John breathed in deeply, got to his feet and looked around. Down the valley to the west over another distant range the dying afterglow of the setting sun had fired the sky to a burning red. Mist lingered beneath us, changing shapes in the gentle breeze, but there was none above. Over the pass a huge moon rose.

'You know,' said John, taking it all in, 'the further I get from civilisation, from people and things, the higher into these mountains, the happier I am. I just love it up here.' He wandered off by himself and stood on a rock against the deep red skyline. Draped in his thick wool patoo, his head covered in his Chitrali cap and carrying his staff, he was a timeless figure.

11 The Garden of Indra

' "Now what is the trouble between your two villages?"
And the people points to a woman.'

For four long days we walked towards Wama – down steep ravines and up towering rocks, along vast valley floors and through narrow defiles, in forests of pine and across dead tundra – the thought of a rest at the clinic keeping us going. Many times we had to cross swirling torrents when sheer cliff-faces blocked our path. Compelled to remove our boots, we staggered out into the chilling water that often reached up to our waists, struggling to keep our balance against the river's powerful force as it crashed from the snow-line on its long journey to the distant plains. At one place John tried to follow Haji over a fast flowing rapid by jumping from one boulder to another. As he landed his foot slipped on a wet rock and he fell backwards. Lunging desperately, he threw out a hand to Haji who was standing ready to catch him. Haji took the weight but John's momentum pulled them back. For one wretched second it looked as though they were both going to fall into the freezing swirl. But Haji was strong. Belying his slight and sinewy frame, he was tough and his muscles were as hard as iron. He adjusted his footing in an instant and swung John to safety.

With a greater rainfall than the Ramgul Valley, between the splintered cliffs the land was green. The upland water meadows gave our aching feet and joints a rest. Willows marched in columns along the river's bank, their silver branches splayed like fountains. Wild lilies and lilac bloomed and fruit trees creaked under succulent crops. While pulling on my boots, having just crossed another stream, I looked about me at the idyllic land.

'Like Paradise, hey Haji Sahib?' I said to my friend.

'No. No,' he replied, poker-faced beside me. 'Paradise would have more bridges!'

Despite the Nuristanis' vicious reputation, to date only one feringhee has met with a violent end in the province; his name was Andy Skrzypkowiak (pronounced: Shipsoviak). An English journalist of Polish decent, Skrzypkowiak was murdered near the village of Kantiwar in October 1987, while travelling to film Amir Shah Masood and his guerrilla army. It was well accepted that Haji Gafor, a Hezb-i-Islami warlord and fierce opponent of the Jamiat military leader, who ruled the Kantiwar mantika like some feudal baron from a dramatic, hill-top fort, had had Skrzypkowiak killed. Quite why no one seemed sure. As always, there were plenty of rumours, ranging from the allegation that Skrzypkowiak had struck one of Haji Gafor's men to the assertion that he was a CIA spy working for Masood. Whatever the truth, Haji Gafor sounded like a dangerous character and one best avoided. Unfortunately that was impossible. He was, after all, one of the most powerful men in Nuristan and his lair lay on the only feasible route between the Ramgul Valley and Wama. For form's sake we had to drop by.

The man who entered the gloomy room had a bad limp. He wore the baggy, felt shorts over thin cotton trousers and a tatty, double-breasted pinstriped jacket. Taking off his cap he revealed a thick mop of black hair, greying at the edges. His face was pale, his expression blank. We stood up and he greeted us one by one, without enthusiasm, simply going through the motions.

'Haji Gafor is away,' started the man, once we were seated. There was no hint of a smile on his face, he was cold and impassive, no life in his dark eyes. 'He is in Kabul with Hekmatyar and the government. I am Commander Abdul Rashid, Haji Gafor's brother. What is your business here?'

John was as direct as our host – not rude but brief with an equally hardened face. 'We are harmless aid workers,' he said, quietly, with Ismael translating. As he spoke he handed over letters to authenticate his statement. 'We have been on a journey up the Ramgul Valley and are on our way to Wama. We seek no favours and ask only that you allow us to pass freely through your mantika.' John was desperate to be away. To him the idea of staying for a moment in the house of a man who'd killed a fellow Briton was abhorrent. We had already been forced to wait for more than three hours for the audience – during which time no tea had been served, a sure sign of impending doom – and once again I was beginning to wonder if we were in fact being held. Here the armed militia sat like guards by the entrance, looking fierce and hostile. They made no attempt at conversation, even with Haji, just whispered quietly to each other, eyeing us surreptitiously from beneath their furrowed brows.

Abdul Rashid sat motionless. What was going through his mind was impossible to tell. If he considered we were lying, that our letters were covers and we were in fact there investigating Skrzypkowiak's murder, he would be duty bound to hold us until his brother returned. Now forming part of the government, Haji Gafor couldn't afford to have old murder allegations dragged up. Even in Afghanistan, such things could cause problems.

Apprehensively, I glanced past the chicken wire that covered the window, across the flat maidan and up to the old square fort, sitting menacingly above us on a great rocky spur. Made of mud, rock, and timber, it had been constructed by one of the Amir's generals who'd torn through the valley a hundred years earlier, converting – or butchering – the pagans of the village where they stood. By the fort's mottled walls, I could make out more mujahadeen sheltering from the worsening weather.

The sky was thick and slate grey. Rain that had been threatening now fell in driving rods and a harsh wind blew, bending the corn and knocking fruit from the trees. It would take us at least four hours to reach Kusht, our next destination down the valley, and it was already past noon. Whatever Abdul Rashid chose to do with us, I could see we were stuck for the night.

After a while Abdul Rashid climbed awkwardly to his feet and limped out into the corridor, beckoning one of his militia. Turning their backs to us just beyond the door, again they began to whisper.

What were they saying? What did they have in mind? Why were they being so secretive if they believed that our mission had nothing whatever to do with them, or past crimes they may have committed? Unable to hear the conversation we had no way of knowing. Given the murderous fame they'd earned themselves it was all too easy to assume the worst. They'd killed one Briton, they could do so again. I sensed danger shrouding us like a cloak.

After a few minutes Abdul Rashid summoned Ismael, our only Nuristani, to the door. He asked him again who we were and what the real purpose of our journey was. Ismael was reiterating what John had already told him when Abdul Rashid stopped him and regarded him curiously. Suddenly he asked where Ismael came from and who his father was. Now what was he thinking? I wondered anxiously. But when Ismael told him, the commander's attitude changed completely. With his hand on Ismael's shoulder, he came back to the centre of the room, his countenance brightened considerably and at last he called for tea. Ismael's father, so it turned out, had been one of Abdul Rashid's greatest friends. An audible sigh seeped through the room.

'For many years,' Abdul Rashid told us, a sparkle returned to his dark eyes, 'back into the Kafir times, there has been a problem between upper Kantiwar and lower Kantiwar.' We were in the upper half of the village, the lower being a mile further down the valley. 'It has to do with land in the aylaks, both communities claim the land to be theirs. At times this problem explodes into war and people get killed, sometimes as many as twenty or thirty, sometimes, like last week, just three. It got so bad that a large jurga – a meeting of elders – was organised, this maybe . . . ' He pushed his cap to the back of his head and stared at the ceiling, 'maybe twenty years ago?' He looked at Ismael. Having received confirmation, he continued, 'Important men from all over Nuristan come to work out the problem, find an answer that both communities could live with. Mohammed Azizi, Ismael's father, came from Waigul. He stayed here with me. He was my friend.' He looked at Ismael and again rested a hand on his shoulder.

Ismael had told me that his father had been an important man. As chief political representative for his mantika of Waigul he had been greatly respected. When barely thirty years old he had been chosen to speak for his community at the Kantiwar jurga. But such a position also brought enemies. On returning to Waigul, leaving the jurga, when Ismael was only four years old, Mohammed Azizi had been assassinated by a lone gunman. The jurga had failed, the problem remained. Twenty years on, however, he had brought a détente to our strained party. It was a fantastic piece of luck.

The following morning we continued on towards Wama, through Lower Kantiwar which appeared deserted – the people all fighting for their aylaks no doubt – and headed into the forest. Almost at once the sides of the valley narrowed into a steep ravine. The river that had meandered sedately down through the flat water meadows was suddenly forced into a swirling torrent, changing its colour from deep emerald to a clear turquoise flecked with brilliant foam. The path, amid the giant pines, was hard and thin, never wider than a few inches across. At times the track ran beside the water, whose deafening roar made conversation impossible, but then it would climb and peace would fall, the thick fern and tangled creepers muffling our footsteps. Occasionally we'd hear the cry of a bird or rustle of an animal, a rabbit or deer perhaps, hidden by the foliage.

We stopped for lunch at the village of Kusht. To protect themselves from hostile invaders, since the earliest times it has been the custom of the region to build the villages high on the hillsides to make an attack easier to repel. We could see Kusht from far away, the pale smoke drifting through the trees at the top of a cliff and disappearing into the murky sky. When we reached the cliff we were all tempted to rest by the little stone shack used by travellers next to the rickety bridge at the confluence of the Pech and Kantiwar rivers. But the thought of an alternative to yet more BP5s for lunch, gave us the energy for the climb.

The old man who greeted us had a bald head and a great white beard that stuck out perpendicular to his weathered face. A white robe fell from his shoulders to the floor and around his waist was a thick leather belt bearing a dagger. He looked like George C Scott playing King Lear. His face was grave and depressing.

'I have blood in my stool,' he said in a booming voice that would have reached the gods at the Albert Hall. Looking at John, he grimaced and pointed at his stomach. John went for his medical bag.

From the old man's roof where we sat the views were breathtaking. We had climbed on to a promontory at a point above where two valleys met. To the north-east was Kantiwar from where we had come, to the south was Wama where we were going and to the north-west, partially obscured by the crest of the ridge, the Parun Valley and our route out. Here the houses looked more traditional. Built with flat rocks sandwiched by planks, or rough-cut branches of wood, they were left bare, not plastered with mud. A-frame hay lofts packed with golden fodder were perched in the holly oaks and beneath was stacked dry firewood. The mosque, elevated through the trees on a ridge beyond the village, had a loud speaker, powered by a car battery which was brought up from the south each month.

Apologising for having no meat, Lear placed before us three stone bowls of steaming cheese, covered in bright yellow, clarified butter which he called krut. It was delicious. As was the bread. Instead of the thick and stodgy maize chapatis we had grown used to we were given thin bread like a pancake or crêpe. When we had finished, the old man emptied his robe on to the plastic sheet: it was full of perfect apricots.

Before leaving I was suddenly caught short and so decided to go to the 'loo', which I assumed was, as always, down in a maize field. But as I descended the notched pole, one of Lear's sons stopped me and indicated that I should enter a small wood-panelled room. In the most ingenious design, a water channel had been diverted from the steep hill into this 'bathroom'. When the sluice gate was opened, a bath could be run, albeit with near freezing water, and the toilet flushed. I was very impressed.

In the afternoon the track was fine, for the most part flat and wide, running by the river. In fact it was an unsurfaced road, but no cars or jeeps had ever used it for it had never been finished. Each time the local construction team had come to a sheer cliff-face or ravine they'd simply left their work and started where they could on the other side, waiting for the day when the people with the real equipment could come in and finish the job. They'd been waiting a long time: this stage of the road had been completed before the Russians had invaded. Wherever we went, people clamoured for roads, hassling John mercilessly in his guise as an aid worker, realising that it was the lack of such an infrastructure that kept much of the land of light in the dark ages. They'll be waiting a long time more.

It was good to saunter along in the dappled shade for a while, enjoying the scenery without constantly having to check my footing. But soon the sun's pale face wasted away and the dour sky gave way to rain, drizzling at first, but becoming heavier as we travelled down the valley. Pulling my damp Chitrali cap down a little lower over my eyes, I trudged on, getting soggier by the minute, feeling increasingly uncomfortable. At lunch I'd taken off my boots to discover that my feet now bore the rare distinction of blisters on top of blisters. Added to that my right foot was sprouting splinters from a cactus I'd stepped on during one of our many river crossings; every time I thought all the sharp needles were removed, new ones would appear and two or three had started to go septic. I found it hard to ignore the growing pain.

At last we emerged from a narrow canyon on the river's left bank. Before us, rising in a great arc over the foaming waters, was a spectacular bridge, its cantilever structure supported by two huge grey boulders. On the far side sat the village. Stacked eight high, making as much use of the land as possible, the earth-coloured houses claimed the lower cliff and stretched along the river's far bank. Narrow dirt lanes divided the rows of houses, also joined by wooden aerial runways. In front of the buildings, beside a huge green mulberry tree by the river was a flattened meeting place. Despite the rain, people milled about.

'Wama,' I said excitedly to Ismael who was standing beside me.

He put a hand on my shoulder and grinned. 'That's not Wama, Jonny Sahib,' he said, smiling. 'This is Pul-i-Wama – "Wama by the bridge".' He removed his hand and pointed to the heavens. 'That is Wama.'

I followed the trajectory of his out-stretched finger, high up the almost sheer mountainside and nearly shrieked aloud. There, 300 metres above us, clinging to the face of the rock, in a place fit only for eagles and the gods, was the real Wama. There seemed no way up. Could these people fly? Through the gossamer veil of mist, I could make out rows of dwellings supported by leaning poles, looking for all the world as if they were about to collapse and tumble to oblivion. Above, dark clouds billowed menacingly. Just at that moment a thunder clap boomed through the valley and a mighty fork of lightning flashed across the sky – a Hollywood director could not have achieved a more thrilling effect. My face dripping, I stood enthralled. 'Jesus . . .' I whispered reverently.

Though impressed with Wama's beauty, I was relieved to discover that the clinic was not up in the high village but only a little way beyond the bridge. Thoroughly exhausted as I was, the thought of having to climb another mountain, even to a place as spectacular as this, would have been enough to reduce me to a blubbering wreck. We were all spent, and had been running on reserve for most of the afternoon. Tired and soaked but semi-euphoric at having finally reached our goal, we stumbled into the clinic and collapsed on to foam mattresses – foam mattresses! – and sat in silence, too drained to think, never mind speak. A kind Afghan doctor, who ran the place for a Japanese NGO, gave us tea and cigarettes, and, much to Majid Khan's visible delight, handfuls of painkillers; his body pain, he told us all, was very bad indeed.

The next day we did as little as possible. Having washed ourselves and our clothes in the river, bandaged our sores – John expertly removed all the cactus splinters from my foot – examined our bites, for we were all now crawling with fleas, we lay on charpoys in the courtyard of the clinic under the warm summer sun. A little-used jeep track made it as far as Wama which meant that it was possible to stock the small village shop. It was the only shop we came across in the province. It didn't sell a lot besides plastic plimsolls, razor blades, rice and a few manky metres of cloth but it did have some good biscuits which I bought and we all devoured hungrily – the peanut butter was now long gone. As each day passed I was doing my trousers up a little tighter. With all this exercise and so little food I was losing weight fast.

The owner of the shop, a friendly man called Nia Matullah, was also the local commander. He had a wide and smiling face with clear eyes and a kind expression and was no doubt as crooked as a cork-screw. With John in town he was worried. As in Dawlat Shah, Nia Matullah perceived John's presence as potential trouble, a threat to his cosy existence, and was keen therefore to give us what we wanted and be rid of us as fast as possible. He was delighted when John told him that he had to travel south to Gusulak on the border with Kunar Province where there was another Swedish Committee clinic he'd agreed to examine. For the two day trip, John was going to take Haji and Masood while I kept Ismael. The porters could look after themselves. Without any hesitation Nia Matullah agreed to organise a jeep for John – by radioing a relation with a vehicle further down the valley – and a guide to escort me and Ismael up to his friend, Mohammed Nebi, who lived on the cliff in the high village. It seemed such an extraordinary place, I was desperate to visit.

Even after a day's rest I found the path exhausting. First one way then the other it zigzagged up the cliff, as steep as a staircase in a castle tower. Our guide was a fierce-looking man called Abdullah Khan. He had a crooked face with a deep scar running across his right cheek and upper lip and over which his moustache fearfully failed to grow. Under a leather jerkin he wore a Sam Browne belt packed with bullets for the automatic pistol he carried 'cop-style' in a holster under his arm. He didn't wear the modern shalwar kameez but the traditional baggy trousers bound below the knee by thick cord, giving them the appearance of plus fours. His harsh appearance was deceptive, however, for on seeing me panting hard and struggling, he offered to carry my camera and water bottle.

Just below the village was a wooden platform with carved rails and supports. Constructed in Kafir times, it was a resting place for those, like me, with tired legs and heaving lungs. It teetered on spindly supports, which bent this way and that. I was amazed it had lasted so long. Wama, at least the upper half, was one of the few places in Nuristan not to capitulate quickly to the Amir's forces one hundred years ago and it was easy to see why. Climbing such a steep cliff the attackers had been totally at the mercy of those higher up. Only after a prolonged siege and incessant harrying by teams of mullahs and converted Kafirs had the village succumbed.

As Ismael and I sat by our guide, regaining our breath, the mullah wandered by. He was short and fat in white robes and was holding a black umbrella above his head for at this altitude the sun's rays are strong. 'May God be with you,' he cried in the most affable manner, coming on to the platform to embrace us affectionately. 'Please do not feel afraid in our village,' he chortled merrily. 'We are here to serve you. Anything we can do for you we will.' It was wonderful to be so warmly welcomed by this jolly Islamic Friar Tuck.

The platform looked south towards the dark mountain Kund, Garden Mountain, and beneath it was a carpet of bright trees. This was Indra Kund, the Garden of Indra. According to legend Indra was a great Kafir king, a mighty warrior and revolutionary leader. He was also a giant, responsible for many feats of extraordinary power: he positioned the two house-size boulders that support the bridge, flattened part of the mountainside to give land for growing crops and defeated many an army single-handedly. But his greatest feat was the making of his giant orchard. Maybe two hundred acres in size, irrigated by the most extraordinary water channels, the locals believed that Indra created it as a testament to the son he slew. (No one I asked could explain why he'd killed his son – Abdullah Khan believed it had something to do with an argument over milk!) Ismael had another idea: Indra made the orchard to grow vines for his beloved wine. As I listened to these tales of a Kafir hero, told proudly with bright eyes and passion, I realised that this was the first time I'd heard any such tales from the pagan past. In this remote yet devoutly Islamic village, Kafir legend still stirred the blood and the imagination of Indra's descendants.

After a simple but delicious lunch of walnuts, cheese and apricots on the roof outside the house of our host, Mohammed Nebi, we went to see the orchard which has survived for centuries. Accompanied by six armed men – which I thought a little excessive – we wandered along the water channels that hugged the mountainside just above the forest of fruit trees. The channels weren't rough ducts blown with dynamite and sealed with slated stone – themselves, often, remarkable feats of engineering – but carved conduits worn smooth with time.

Above the far end of the orchard there was another platform, where we sat and rested. Mohammed Nebi told me other legends attributed to Indra, which surprisingly included the killing of many a good Mohammedan. I asked him if he was proud of his Kafir ancestors and he told me he was.

'Indra give us this,' he said, pointing to the trees, and then to the terraces to the right and left. 'This is our life, of course I am proud.'

I asked him about Sikander and the legend of the great Macedonian warrior, but like Sher Gul he shrugged in ignorance and told the story of the Quorresh. No one I asked had heard of Alexander.

As we returned, Mohammed Nebi suddenly cut from the path and headed deep into the forest. At first it was a struggle through a mass of brambles and creepers, but it soon cleared and we could walk easily through the trees in the marbled light. There were fruit trees of many types: apple, apricot, pomegranate and of course mulberry and walnut. But hanging from the branches like giant snakes, were the once-sacred vines. With wizened creepers, the colour of rust, and wide, vibrant leaves they crawled through the branches of the trees like some giant spider's web. Large bunches of green and red grapes hung from them, getting fatter with each warm day.

In a clearing we came upon an old woodcutter sitting on top of a huge obelisk, using his axe head as a chillum. He was elflike, well under five foot, with a tapered beard and twisted nose. It was not the man, however, but what he was sitting on that Mohammed Nebi wanted Ismael and me to see. Holding on to a vine, he pulled himself up the huge boulder and gestured that we should follow. With difficulty I scaled the three metres and found an extraordinary thing. In the centre of the rock was a perfect square trough. Like the water channel it was carved with precision and smoothed with time. Capable of holding some fifty gallons of liquid, it was now full of leaves and brackish rain water. Suddenly Mohammed Nebi and the woodcutter started jumping up and down by the side of the hole, holding each other's arms. Laughing and singing, they began to jig, squashing imaginary grapes. Round and round the trough they whirled, only inches from the edge of the rock. Turning faces high and faces low, frantically spinning, almost losing control of themselves they whirled around the trough in dance. In the wild spot under the chequered sun and gambolling shadows it was easy to imagine Indra and the Kafir men making their festive wine.

Further along there was another rock with an even more ingenious design. This boulder was long and low, the shape of an old sports car. Cut into the back at one end was a large trough, at the bottom of which was a hole leading to a second trough. The grapes were crushed in the upper tier and the pithless juice would flow clear and seedless into the trough below.

'Are they ever used?' I asked.

'No . . . never.' Catching his breath, Mohammed Nebi gave a firm reply.

'But is wine still made?'

'Sometimes by the young men, but if the mullah finds out he gets very angry – he beats the youths.' It was hard to imagine the mullah I'd seen, old Friar Tuck, beating anyone. 'Me, I make grape juice, no alcohol.' But as he said it he couldn't help giving me a smile.

As dusk began to fall, we sat on low stools on Mohammed Nebi's roof drinking sweet green tea. On a flat roof below us, transformed by drying fruit into a patchwork of rich colours, an old woman stood staring out across the valley. She was wearing a beige coat made from the skin of a large animal, perhaps a bear or deer. Held in place by a hood that covered her head, it hung low, half way down her short legs with the dead animal's tail dangling on the floor. All around us stood the dark, wooden houses with their beautifully carved doors, many with ibex and markhor horns hanging over the entrance. On the mosque's roof some girls with grubby faces and shaven heads played a game similar to ring-a-ring-a-roses. Their shrieks and laughter rose up to greet us but then they were called inside and we were left alone with silence.

Silence. Real silence. Not a breath of wind, or the bleating of a goat. Even the drumming of the river, that had of late been an almost constant sound rumbling in our ears, was but a distant memory. From up here, high on the mountain, the river stood still: a discarded silver ribbon disappearing into Kund's dark belly.

'If Afghanistan was at peace,' said Ismael wistfully, 'I could organise tours, treks, to these places. The tourists would love to see this, I think.' Mohammed Nebi passed me a large bronze hookah packed with fresh tobacco. I lit it, inhaled and let the thick cloud of smoke disappear into the saffron sky. Ismael was right. I suddenly felt unbelievably lucky. To be sitting here, on top of this mysterious valley, having spent the afternoon in the garden of Indra, made me swell with contentment once again. It was the ultimate joy that travel can bring, as it had on the train at Marwar Junction, crossing the snow-covered Shandor Pass or swimming in Lake Mundol. To be somewhere totally unfamiliar, experiencing a world so different from my own, that just for a while I was living a wholly new and contrasting life.

The unmistakable sound of gunfire rang out down the valley. Two rounds, then a third. Pulled from my reverie, I sat up straight and looked at Ismael and Mohammed Nebi. They were turning around, trying to decide from where the noise came. Was it from over the bridge, on the far side of the valley, or from the other end of the high village? The echoing mountains made it hard to tell. Whichever was the case, it was hardly an unusual noise and on the flat rooftop for a moment no one moved or said a word. Then there was a fourth shot. This time I saw the earth on the roof below leap crazily into dust, and then again and again, climbing higher towards us as two more bullets struck. A seventh shot thudded and whined as it ricocheted off a rock just below us.

'Gord's holy trousers, I should make for cover if I was you!'

Suddenly everyone was on their feet, piling frantically towards the open doorway of the guest room. Mohammed Nebi crouched behind me, shielding me as I moved. He was my host, if I were to die while under his protection, the shame on his name would be immense. I could see the door beckoning safety, watched as Ismael disappeared within. But for some reason it didn't seem to get any closer. I could hear my heart, my lungs. I watched my feet and legs move as though running under water. And then I was there, crashing through the entrance and on to the floor. The shooter was no marksman and as we all crouched safely behind the stone wall, the noise of the firing drifted away and quiet was restored. Perhaps he was just trying to frighten us. If that was his aim he had succeeded. It was the first time in my life I'd been shot at, and it didn't feel good.

After a while darkness fell, carrying any lingering danger away. Even so Mohammed Nebi ordered three more of his men, armed with Kalashnikovs, into the room to guard Ismael and me for the night and left another with a powerful radio sitting on a ridge above the other end of the village. Bringing the receiver into the room,

Mohammed Nebi sat down with the hookah. He packed it and smoked to calm his nerves.

'What is the problem here?' I asked, having taken a toke myself – it made me feel pleasantly light-headed. 'Why all the men this afternoon in the orchard, the guns . . . that shooting?'

'There is problem with family from village on the far side.' Mohammed Nebi pointed towards the other end of the high village. I had asked him earlier if I could take a walk there but he had not let me, saying it was too dangerous. This explained why. He sat in silence, looking pensively at the carpet before him. I thought that was going to be the only explanation I would receive but after a minute of silence he continued. 'It has to do with woman,' he said slowly. I was not surprised. In small communities, where political, tribal, and religious differences are minimal, the local feuds normally revolve around either land, livestock or women.

'There was girl from Pul-i-Wama who my son want to marry. The son of man from the other end of the village up here also want to marry her. My son he won the girl and they married last season.' Nearly all the weddings in Nuristan, I had been told, take place in October when the young men come home from the aylaks. 'But this year they kill my son, shoot him while he was walking up the path, so two month ago we kill their son . . . We shoot him on path also.' There was little emotion in his voice. He sat cross-legged, leaning against the wall, his bearded face lit orange by the lamp. He could have been talking about taking his goat to market.

'Do you think that's what the shooting was about?' I asked.

He shrugged. 'It's possible. They are dangerous people. The blood feud is supposed to be finished – they kill one, we kill one – but with them I don't know. They have tried to shoot me before, that is why I always travel with guards. Maybe they try again or maybe tonight they know you here and try to shoot you. For Nuristani, the best way to shame our enemy is to kill our enemy's guest.' He looked at me dead-pan. 'It is nothing personal.'

The radio crackled and our eyes all turned towards it. He moved and adjusted the volume to hear better but then the static died away again and we were left once more with silence.

———◆———

Another mid-June day borrowed from late November. The giant limes did little to break the scything wind. It tore down from the north-east, across the even earth and into the small wooden hut at the corner of the pick-your-own strawberry field. I leaned back on the creaking chair, placed chin on fist, looked beyond the water dripping on to the punnets of fruit and watched old Mrs Arnold shuffling up the lane. You simply wouldn't believe what happened yesterday ... All her stories started that way.

I should've closed up. Gone home. Put the sign up: Rain Stopped Picking. But there'll always be someone daft enough to drop by — more often than not, Mrs Arnold. I don't think she even likes strawberries. She never looks at the ones she buys. No, she doesn't want strawberries at all, she wants to talk.

I stood up and cheerily approached the counter. For today was different. Today, I didn't mind the monotony of the rain or the chill of the wind or even being a captive audience for tales of grandchildren, gas bills, bladders, bunions and bowels. Even the knowledge that I was spending my days back on Dad's farm, working the same fields I'd grown up in, couldn't dampen my spirits. It still didn't seem quite real but a big decision had been made. Every time I thought about it I felt energy and anticipation start to flood my system. What should have been a depressing, claustrophobic Lincolnshire sky was instead a horizon daring me forward. I knew to many I would be running away but I didn't care. I'd had enough grief, I needed a mission, a challenge that would force the demons away. Besides, what would I be running away from? A multitude of meaningless jobs? A broken past? Since El Salvador I hadn't lived, I'd simply survived. Inside, I knew it was time to go away and chase some dreams again.

'Afternoon, Mrs A.'

'Oh, hello duck.' She always called me that. 'Miserable day.'

I looked over to where my motor bike stood dripping beneath a tree. 'Not for me Mrs A. I've been making plans. Plans to travel to Africa.'

'Ooh,' she said, pausing for a moment and peering up at me with curiosity. 'Well, you simply wouldn't believe what happened yesterday ... '

Over the next four days I spent a great deal of time at the house of our face-scarred guide, Abdullah Khan, beside the river in Pul-i-Wama. He was a kind man, underneath his disagreeable looks. For hours, Ismael and I sat on his rooftop smoking his hookah, talking. Abdullah Khan had never heard of Alexander either, although, purely to please, for a while made out that he had. Like everyone else he subscribed wholeheartedly to the Quorresh theory, and proudly repeated the story I first heard from Sher Gul. He was also a musician and played a strange instrument he called a waj. Made out of walnut wood it resembled a cross between a harp and a guitar with a calf-hide cover and four deer-gut strings. But the tuning was different from anything I knew and the music, though deep and resonant, to my ears lacked melody.

One day while we were sitting in Abdullah Khan's guest room a friend of his turned up wearing a worn and faded Washington Red Skins jacket. Having introduced himself, the first thing he told me was that he and his wife had had thirteen children, nine boys and four girls, of which the first twelve had died before they'd reached the age of two. Shocked, I asked him why? But he just shrugged. 'They cry in the night,' he said, masking his face with an indifference he obviously didn't feel, 'and morning time they're gone.' Only the last born had survived; he was now twenty-two and visiting a doctor in Peshawar. I wondered if something as simple as boiling their drinking water would have saved his family.

After repeated requests, Abdullah Khan eventually agreed to show me beyond his roof and guest room to the living quarters of his home, where his wife spent her time. I had still not seen a female face in the province, much less a dwelling's inner sanctum and I was interested to do so. He told me to wait, which I did for more than an hour. When I was finally ushered down from the roof and shown inside, I was disappointed, though not surprised, to see that the room had been almost completely cleaned and now contained next to nothing. Everything had been bundled into a small side room where Abdullah Khan told me they slept. There was a hearth in the centre of the floor and a few cooking implements hanging from the wall and two of the grotesque inflated goats' skins. And standing in the corner holding Abdullah Khan's young son's hand was his wife, swathed in a golden burqa. Feeling very uncomfortable, I left quickly.

John had told me of a female American aid worker who had tried to penetrate Nuristan the previous year. Even though she'd had a local guide and dressed appropriately she had only managed to make it as far as Gusulak – where John had been to inspect the clinic on the border with Kunar – before being forced to retreat at gun point. In the pagan past women were free to choose their own husbands, divorce them if they so desired and had a major say in village affairs. No longer. In Islamic Nuristan, like much of Afghanistan, women's rights are limited.

The day before we were due to leave, the porters mutinied again. They had earned themselves some money and, having had a week to think about it, didn't much relish the prospect of heading back into the wilder reaches of a land that had left them tired and sore and covered in bites. From Wama they could travel home easily to Darr-i-Noor. For them the journey was over. We tried, somewhat half-heartedly, to persuade them to stay, but realising quickly we were engaged in a fruitless task, we gave up and let them go. In fact, after a moment's reflection, John was pleased. Even though we still had some 200 kilometres to go, he felt confident we could hire new porters along the way. From the start he'd considered them a nuisance, immature and devious – wholly at odds with his opinion of what a real porter should be – and the resentment caused by the confrontations on the first days of the journey had never really died. Besides, as he pointed out, without them the group would be smaller – John, Haji, Ismael, Masood and me – and therefore easier to organise and less of a burden on our hosts' hospitality. I wasn't quite so sure. Without confirmed porters, lugging a twenty-kilo rucksack became a distinct possibility. Though I did feel rested and fit I was still very aware of the fact that we had two more passes to cross. Having paid them they shook our hands and, much excited about returning home, quickly left.

It was amusing to watch Nia Matullah trying desperately to find someone else who could help us on our way. At first he assured us he had a donkey man, and would meet us early the next morning to strike the deal. At midday we found him skulking in his shop where he told us that the young boy who sings the azam at the mosque up in Wama had fallen from a roof, broken his arm and gashed his face and he had had to help bring the boy down. He assured us again that he would have the man by two. At three he informed us that the donkey man couldn't find his donkey, it was lost in the high pastures. At four when the donkey had been found, the man's wife had been stung by a scorpion. It was like watching a schoolboy thinking of excuses for not having done his homework. But finally, in a desperate bid to be shot of us, he persuaded a friend of his to take us with his two donkeys back past Kusht – the home of our friend King Lear with his magnificent toilet throne – to Paski, the first village in the Parun Valley. A price of two lakh was agreed upon; 100,000 afghanis – about $7 – for each donkey. He agreed to meet us just after dawn.

12 Valley of Peace

'They was all turning up the land in the valley as quiet as bees and much prettier.'

It was dark by the time we arrived in Kusht. Abdul Kharliq, the donkey driver, who had agreed to meet us at the clinic in Wama at six o'clock for an early start had failed to show. At noon, we found him, deep in benign conversation with two old men at the village mosque. 'You can't hurry an Afghan,' Haji had said, placatingly. 'You might as well shoot bullets at the djinns. Here everything happens at God's speed.' Abdul Kharliq had then declared it was time for lunch.

The donkeys – bizarrely named Afghanistan and Pakistan – were also very slow, much slower than the porters, but at least they didn't make such a noise, or argue, or stop to have their photo taken, or get on John's nerves, or beg pills for body pain. They were also a great deal more pleasant to look at. Once the two beasts were loaded and on the road the journey had gone well, albeit at a more leisurely pace.

As we struggled with the donkeys up the steep incline to the village, King Lear beckoned us into his home with the same grave expression he had employed a week earlier while informing us about the grisly state of his bowels. John's pills having rectified that problem, his anxiety today was of a different nature.

'Three more dead!' he exclaimed, shaking his head in a desperate manner, enjoying himself no end. 'How many more will die before those grey-beards in Barg-e-Metal reach a conclusion? Allah ou' Akbar!' He threw up his hands. 'But this is a bad situation.' He showed us into his guest room where we found the village mullah, sitting crossed-legged with a face as vexed as his friend's.

'Rockets, here in Kusht ... ' mumbled the mullah, disconsolately, pushing his prayer beads quickly through his hand, 'Insh'Allah. Insh'Allah.'

In this melodramatic style our two lugubrious hosts went on to explain that for years, as long ago as anyone could remember, way back into Kafir times, Kusht had been at war with Kamdesh, a village on the other side of the mountains. The cause of the conflict was a water channel. According to our hosts, it had been constructed by the people of Kusht from a river that flowed through their land. But on its way to irrigate some far off crops the channel cut a course through land belonging to the people of Kamdesh. The Kamdeshis simply diverted the water during that phase of its journey to their own fields, claiming the water as their own, and leaving nothing for the land belonging to Kusht. Over the centuries this disagreement had led to many deaths. In the old days, the fighting had been with swords, bows and arrows and later jezails, the famous Afghan musket, but Kalashnikovs, grenades and landmines were now the order of the day. The three people Lear had referred to had been killed in a rocket attack on Kusht the previous day. A jurga of village elders, similar to the one Ismael's father had been a part of twenty years earlier, was in session in Barg-e-Metal. They had sat for fifty days but so far had reached no conclusion.

Bandol, Pushol, Kantiwar upper and lower, Wama and now Kusht and Kamdesh, did every village in Nuristan have a murderous quarrel? Leaning back against the wall I did a quick calculation. On the journey so far, I'd heard about twelve recent killings and enough violent hostilities, and threats of such, to fill another book.

With the exception of the odd article of clothing, a small number of carved doors and pillars and the wine troughs in the Garden of Indra, I had been heavily disappointed not to discover any physical links to the Kafir past. We'd seen no effigies above the graves of the dead, been offered no wine and seen none of the silver chalices in which the drink used to be served. The ancient shrines had been knocked down, and the temples had been destroyed. Added to that we'd been told that the last important party – or feast of merit, as they were known, when a man would gain credit with his village by feeding them as grand a meal as possible – had taken place in the early seventies; most of the traditional, lattice-work stools had been succeeded by the Afghan custom of sitting on the floor; and we were still to witness a woman's face. Even the legends of their ancestry had been all but wiped out and replaced by a mullah's tale. Like recent converts the world over, the people of Nuristan have zealously taken to their new found faith, and in the process have annihilated almost every remnant of their pagan past. But for all that, murder, it would seem, is still very often the order of the day. Families still fight families, villages fight villages and valleys fight valleys. They continue to steal each other's goats, seduce each other's women and kill each other as a consequence.

Through a mixture of luck, cunning and daring-do, Peachey and Danny had come to the area and united the warring tribes. Rallying the fighting men under a single banner they'd formed their combined army, created their revenue, policies and laws. They'd forged a peace and become true rulers. If they were to tumble from the skies once again, more than a hundred years later, the task confronting them would be exactly the same. This part of Kafiristan is now Nuristan and the infidels have been enlightened. But beyond religion, little of their ways seem to have changed.

The next day, leaving Wama to the south and the Kantiwar Valley to the west, we journeyed east again and then north into a new landscape. Until now we had walked mainly through the narrow V-shaped valleys with steep walls and precarious paths, where the sun's rays reached for just a few hours a day. Now the cliffs withdrew, taking with them the forests of pine and holly oak, leaving a flat valley floor punctuated by groves of white poplar and silver birch. We were moving into the wide U-shaped valley of Parun.

With the increase in the level land came a rise in agriculture. Beside the water meadows where cattle grazed lay large fields. Crops of tall wheat, maize and millet grew, ripening fast in the summer sun. High and isolated, the Parun experiences long, harsh winters and is often blanketed in deep snow for seven months of the year. With such a short growing season men and children help the women work the land, weeding and irrigating, mending channels and cutting hay. But even out here, under the warm sun, purdah was sacrosanct. At the first sight of strangers, women pulled their veils further over their faces and those close to the path turned their heads to the ground. Even girls as young as three or four wore a head scarf. The men who passed us carried no guns and smiled and shook our hands in a most friendly manner, every time insisting on a full Afghan welcome. At one place we passed some shepherds from Badakshan, the province to the north, herding their sheep to the markets of Peshawar and at another we crossed paths with a band of mullahs. Dressed in white cloaks and white turbans, they formed a travelling religious education centre, taking the word of their creed to this isolated corner.

At three, all along the valley, men and women stopped their work, laid out a rug, shawl or hessian sack beside the crops, turned towards the west and crouched in prayer. We stopped by a hazelnut tree so Haji, Ismael, Masood and Abdul Kharliq could join in. I watched the sun falling towards the speckled cliffs, sending shafts of golden light into their faces.

In the early evening we arrived in Paski. The village was in two sections, one on the flat land between the track and the river and the other behind, climbing in the usual manner on the valley side. We had a letter of introduction to a Paski village elder, but when Ismael inquired where he lived we were told that he had been hit by a Taliban rocket in Kabul. His family were still in mourning so could not offer hospitality so we were directed to a small Red Cross clinic where the doctor was pleased to entertain us. While feeding us well on chicken and rice, in a room lit by electricity, the doctor explained something of how the Parun Valley worked. It was very different from the constant antagonism of the rest of the region.

There are only six villages in the Parun Valley with a total population of approximately 5000 so the valley's strength did not lie in numbers. They had good land, as we had already seen, which, used efficiently, could produce ample food. But the valley's wealth had a rarer source than fertile land. What the inhabitants seemed to have worked out was that through co-operation and unity – seemingly the very antithesis of the Nuristani way – they could achieve far more than as individuals. For example, six years earlier, the village elders of Paski had decided they wanted electricity. By going to each house and requesting two goats and a cow they had raised the money needed to build a macro hydroelectric installation, giving the whole village light. 'Bring light to the land of light,' as the doctor poetically put it. The exercise was repeated at each of the other villages. When Dewa, a smaller village up the valley could not raise enough money, the others helped them out. With the power they could stay later in the fields, knowing they would still have light to cook by. They could run a threshing machine: two more goats each and one was purchased. The same co-operative principle applied at harvest time, when they helped each other in the fields, or when a bridge needed building or repairing or trees had to be cleared. In short, the whole valley was responsible for the welfare of each village and each village for the welfare of each individual.

With everyone having an interest in the valley as a whole there was no crime. The last person to be shot was a luckless woman who happened to be hit in the throat by a descending bullet fired into the air by an exuberant youth at a wedding celebration. The last murder had happened twenty years before – no small miracle in this country. They found the man and shot him.

Throughout history, the people of the Parun have been thought of as different by other Nuristanis. Having little aptitude or interest in war or violence, in the past they were derided as weak and spineless, not part of the true Kafir's barbarous society and were often interned as slaves. Though they, like all other Nuristanis I asked, maintain that they are descended from the people of Quorresh, they are considered by many as outsiders, belonging even to a different race.

'They are not of the Quorresh,' Abdul Kharliq had said at lunch, with more than a little hint of contempt. 'They are from the armies of Sikander.' My heart had jumped at the mention of Alexander, the acceleration of blood making my skin positively tingle. It had been the first time I had heard his name spoken by a Nuristani. Everyone I had asked from Bandul to Wama had claimed ignorance of the Macedonian warrior. Suddenly it had seemed the trail was alive again and I'd badgered Abdul Kharliq for more information. But much to my disappointment he'd been unable to back up his claim with any substance and the enigma had remained unbroken. All he could manage was to reiterate that their language was different and they were different.

Five different languages are spoken in Nuristan, and these also have various dialects, but all have their roots in the indo-aryan tongues that came to the subcontinent with the migrations from Central Asia between the fourth and second millennia BC. All, that is, except for the language of the Parun, which has had linguistic anthropologists baffled for years. In the forties and fifties the great Norwegian linguist Georg Morgenstierne studied the Parun language at length and though lost as to its original root did discover some interesting points, the most curious of which was that it was extremely tied geographically. A simple morning greeting – 'Good morning, how are you' – could convey exactly where the speaker had come from. It might explain, for example, that he had crossed the river, rounded the spur and was on his way to the village. If he had come from a side valley and had never crossed the river or rounded the spur, the greeting would be uttered differently. This extraordinary situation means that if two people from the Parun Valley meet each other elsewhere, say in Jalalabad, they cannot use their own language. It has no meaning whatsoever without the geographical landmarks; they would have to speak Dari or Pashtu, as they did with us. Rather bizarrely Morgenstierne also deduced that, given the strange and hesitant, almost stammering, way the people speak, one of their leaders must have had a very bad stutter which everyone had copied. Lending a mite of credence to Abdul Kharliq's theory that they were descended from Alexander, Morgenstierne also discovered that the Parun word for a three legged table is tripos, the same as the ancient Greeks'.

Having been to the house of Mir Alam to offer our condolences and prayers, the next morning we pushed on up the valley towards Istevi, which lies a day's walk below the Paprok Pass. The closer we came to the village the fewer men there seemed to be. Once more, in the fields only small children and black cloaked women bobbed beside the crops. As we entered the village, we discovered why. Even in the valley of peace it seems there can be wars.

Gathered on a flatish maidan on the river's right bank just below the village was a large group of angry men. Some were mounted on rough-looking horses with long dark manes and wild tails while others stood or squatted on their haunches, talking in groups. All were armed, some with Kalashnikovs, others with shotguns or older rifles of British and Russian origin. They had belts of ammunition draped over their waistcoats and carried their patoos like knapsacks on their backs. A few women hurried between them handing out what appeared to be bread wrapped in cloth. The occasional burst of gunfire ripped through the valley as one of the party released his anger, others cried and thrust their guns towards the evening sky. The faces were grim, all cast in granite. And these were the Nuristanis that didn't like war!

Abdul Kharliq stopped an old man who spoke Pashtu. A small group of Gujurs – a tribe of nomadic herders – had apparently raided one of the aylaks in the night and stolen a hundred head of cattle. The cattle belonged to only four men, yet a raiding party of about eighty had gathered to reap justice. It was the valley working in harmony but, this time, in search of grisly retribution.

As we watched the men preparing for war it was hard to see anything very different between them and their neighbours. They looked every bit as menacing as any Nuristani I'd seen.

Suddenly the muezzin's screeching voice, charged into a metallic rasp by four grey tannoys strategically placed around the village, came piercing down the valley. Though we could not decipher his blood curdling yells, the gist of what he was saying was easy enough to follow. 'God is great, God the merciful . . . hurry up, go get your guns and kill the Gujur dogs!'

A youth with one milk eye led us under an arch, past the mosque, where two pack horses were being loaded with provisions – eighty men would take some feeding in the high hills – and up a carved tree trunk to a guest room. We put our bags down and stood on the roof.

The sun was already well hidden behind the cliff, casting the valley floor in deep shadow. All at once, on some invisible command, the group moved forward up the valley and into the face of a chill breeze that blew down from the north.

As I watched them go, I had a mad momentary urge to rush down to join them, to be part of their band, a believer in their crusade. As it was, I wandered back inside, dropped wearily to the cushioned floor and lit a cigarette.

'They came last night,' said Mohammed Khan, the village elder to whom our letter from the doctor had been addressed. He looked washed out, as lank and pale as a winter leek. A pallid face with red-rimmed eyes and a thin grey beard. Shaking his hand had been like clutching a bag of dried bones. Strangely, on his jacket a locust clung like a broach. 'Six, maybe seven Gujur men. In this aylak there were only three people, two youths and a boy. The others had come down to help with the crops. They shot the dogs, held the boys and took the animals away.' He spoke resignedly. It was obviously something he had witnessed many times before. 'The two youths have followed them, the boy came back to tell us.'

'Which way will they go?' asked John.

'They will head over Paprok but stick to the high ground away from the village of Kamdesh and try to reach Pakistan where they can sell the animals. They're almost a day ahead of us, but they are herding a hundred cattle which will slow them down . . . We will see.'

Later, when I left the room to brush my teeth in the irrigation channel, another horse was being loaded up in the courtyard by the wooden mosque. A man with a ruddy face, hard and pensive, and an ancient rifle slung across his shoulder tightened the ropes around the animal's girth while another held its head. The bridle was old and coarse, the flat saddle made of felt. A boarded window creaked in the wind and, flickering like a gaslight, a large, dim bulb above bathed the scene in a surreal glow. Noticing me watching, the man with the gun turned from the horse. His eyes were cold and contemptuous: I felt my stomach turn. He held my gaze for a moment then bowed his head, touched his heart and offered the usual pleasantries. And there, in that simple gesture, seemed to lie the heart of the paradox that had characterised my journey through this land of light.

Because of the Nuristani's homicidal reputation, their cruel looks and penchant for armaments, I'd carried with me a deep sense of fear and trepidation throughout the trip. At times – under the Karik Pass, in Wama or Kantiwar, when real danger had hissed and spat – the feeling had been intense. But in a lesser form I had felt it from the beginning, making it impossible ever truly to relax. But now I wondered in how much jeopardy had our lives really been? Had anyone actually intended us harm; to kill or take us hostage? To Victorians, possibly thanks in part to the Kipling tale, this land had been a synonym for suicide: a place so wild and savage that only a lunatic pair of renegades would ever dare to enter. And, as I had witnessed, the locals were assuredly no strangers to thieving and killing. But the fact remained that with barely a quarter of our journey left to go, still only one Westerner had lost his life to violence in the province.

As I returned the greeting and watched the horseman ride away into the night, it occurred to me that it was this very fear, this tension that made Nuristan tick: the knife-edge balance between honour and vengeance, good and evil, between goats and Kalashnikovs. The tribesmen, I sensed, thrived on the omnipresent danger and risk their remote homeland seemed to offer. As it had been for their ancestors, it was their way. And yet now, for me, there was something lacking. It felt as though somewhere between the puritanical indoctrination of Islam and the political machinations of the surrounding civil war, Nuristan had lost its soul. The original pagan spirit of Peachey and Danny's Kafiristan had been squeezed out. Only the violence and menace remained, juxtaposed with the country's physical beauty. There was still plenty of challenge to be found, but not enough of the rewards I was looking for. Peachey and Danny's quest had partly been to find a land where they could fit in and feel more settled. I suddenly realised what was missing for me here: should I stay a thousand years, this place could never feel like home.

We hung around the following day, said goodbye to Abdul Kharliq and his donkeys and sorted out new porters and guides to take us over the pass for the final phase of the Nuristan journey. From Gama, the first village on the other side, we were splitting up. John had decided to go north to Garam Chasma where his friend was living just over the Pakistan border, while I was heading east to the valleys of the Kalash. As all the young men were off with the raiding party, securing help was not easy but in the end we found two men who agreed to accompany us for a reasonable rate. One, an opium-addict from Badakshan – who, being short and scruffy with a boil on his nose, reminded us both of Baldrick from the TV show *Blackadder* – would go with John and Haji on their journey. The other, a local man called Sayeed Karim, agreed to bring the only horse left in Istevi and take Ismael, Masood and me on to the village of Paprok, a little further down the valley. That afternoon while washing in the river I smelt in the breeze the first, unmistakable chill of autumn.

———◆———

We were all drunk, even Samuel, and he swore blind he never touched a drop. With the border closed there was little else to do. Empty beer bottles cluttered the table, cigarette butts littered the dusty floor. By a grass hut a tethered goat yawned and an old dog slept beneath a baobab tree. Under the mellowing African sky, the air was peaceful and still. Finding a half-full bottle, I took another gulp.

'You 'ave dis good beer in In-gland?' slurred another of the customs men, slouching on my left.

'That would be impossible,' I replied diplomatically.

He grinned and slipped backwards, falling against a tree. The other men laughed and drank more beer.

By some strange quirk of fate, I had arrived at the Nigerian border on the morning they'd decided to count their population. While an army of officials – 500,000 I was told – scoured the country for a thumb-print of every human soul, all land borders, airports and seaports were closed. For a day, a week? No one knew how long because the process had never been attempted before. And no one cared; least of all me. The border would open eventually and I'd continue on my way. Time held little relevance for me now.

'An what es et dat you do?' asked Isa, a friendly immigration officer. 'What es your occupation?' I thought this question might be coming up soon and it was one to watch. Travelling was considered relatively harmless by officials, but documenting the experience, as I was doing, was considered highly suspicious. By now, however, I was buzzing on an alcohol high and feeling at one with my new friends. So far we'd talked of everything from Gary Lineker's troubled toes to the state of political unrest in their country. I felt sorely tempted to share my plans to write a book about this incredible African journey. I wanted to explain my feelings of kinship with Jack Kerouac, rolling along the road, how I felt like Jupiter on his travels and that far from running away from a troubled past I

knew now that I was charging head-long towards a bright new future; at the end of this journey there wouldn't be only sparkling sea, there would be salvation. Luckily, this moment of madness passed. They were still Nigerian government officials, whatever state our heads were in.

'Right now I'm not doing anything in particular,' I said feeling a warm and contented glow within. 'I'm taking a break from life back home, seeing the world.' I threw out my hands expansively. 'A free spirit, like the wind, riding my iron horse to God knows where.'

'Well, you would be,' said Isa, 'but for dis close border.' And everyone burst out laughing again.

———◆———

Following the multiple tracks of the Parun's small army, we climbed up the valley. As we sat on a stone hut having lunch, four armed men approached. They were the advance guard to the raiding party returning home. They had found the tracks of the Gujurs but had not spotted the men. They expected the Gujurs would reach Pakistan safely, and make a great deal of money – one bullock would be worth US$100 at least. Or perhaps they would lose them to another bunch of renegades as they passed through Kamdesh territory. Either way they were lost to the Parun.

As we climbed the steep shale path, clouds moved across the sky blotting out the sun and threatening rain. A few large drops fell with a splosh on to the rocks but thankfully it held off – rain on the pass would not be much fun, for us or the eighty odd men ahead – and the higher we climbed the clearer the sky became. Once again I noticed John's expression lighten as we moved up the valley to the quieter lands beyond the world of humans.

The aylak with its low stone shacks hidden in the lee of the rocky cliff was deserted. The raiding party had taken a different route. Above the tree-line there was no wood but we made a fire out of dung from one of the small stone corrals and baked maize bread over a thin slab of slate. Sayeed Karim whipped up the dough, throwing it from hand to hand like a Napoli pizza maker. It tasted delicious.

When the meal was over, Haji, Ismael and Masood crouched on the far side of the fire with Sayeed Karim and Baldrick, making a hookah out of a lump of mud and a Bic biro. John and I sat in profound peace on the other side of the hearth, the black sky above us shimmering with a million stars.

'You probably think it's strange,' said John quietly, gazing into the fire, 'that I don't make friends of the Afghans.' Surprised by the personal nature of his tone, I sat up. 'I used to,' he said. 'I used to be all pally-pally with them, treat them equally, make friends, but every time they shafted me. Just when you think you can really trust someone, just as you get close, they turn round and rip you off. It's happened time and again and I end up having to sack and make enemics out of them and that doesn't pay.' He picked up a stick and poked the glowing embers. 'Trouble is, you're here with money and stuff they want – they've had a hard life, a life with nothing, it's understandable – but in the end that's all you are to them. The closer a friend they think you are the more they'll try to take. It's better to keep your distance, that way you can achieve more.'

John's experience could not be challenged. He was one of the longest-serving aid workers in the country and was greatly respected. But as I looked across the fire to where Ismael, Haji and Masood were laughing, trying desperately to make their strange hookah work, I felt enormous affection for them and deemed myself lucky that I wasn't soured by such past experiences. With the journey nearing its end, John, the closed book, was opening up.

'You grow up quick in this country,' he said, reflectively. 'I mean, in this line of work. It's a bloody strange way to spend your early twenties, that's for sure. While my friends from school and university were out in their BMWs on the King's Road chasing girls, I was running aid convoys over active front lines.' He spoke without conceit. 'I've been out here so long it's now England that feels strange. Try going to a dinner party back home and have a conversation about someone's, I don't know . . . a new Le Creuset set or conservatory extension, curtain material, it's kind of hard when you've just returned from a place where people are blowing each other to pieces.' Looking wistfully into the fire, he sighed. 'I used to find it very hard.'

The boys let out a little cheer as Haji exhaled a lungful of thick smoke. Ismael took the lighter and bent down to try out the strange device.

'It doesn't bother me so much now,' John continued. 'I have a small but strong core of old friends back home and there's always the Afghan connection.' He was at a crossroads, he said, trying to decide whether or not he should carry on in Afghanistan, in aid at all, or whether the time had come for him to pack up his patoo and shalwar kameez, shave off his beard and move into a business of some kind. Part of the reason he'd wanted to come to the mountains was to think these things through in the environment he liked the most.

'But whatever the hardship, the problems,' he said after a long silence, 'I think I've been very lucky. To have been able to spend five, nearly six years in a beautiful and fascinating country, paid a decent wage, with the contacts and logistics of a large organisation behind me. Like everything in life there are good sides and bad. England is sometimes hard, and who knows what might have happened if I'd not taken that job with the Norwegians, but joined the army as planned. But it's no good looking back with regret. I'm sure we can all do that. Look where I'm sitting now.' He smiled and pointed towards the stars. 'No, I've been very lucky indeed.'

I rummaged through my bag and pulled out a cigar Jeremy had given me back in Delhi. 'I've been saving this,' I said to John. 'You might as well light it.' I knew how much he enjoyed them. 'It'll be our last chance, at least in the peace of the mountains.' I unwrapped the cigar, and handed it to him. His face glowed.

'Ah, a cigar in the hills, what pleasure.'

The pass, though the highest of them all at almost 5000 metres, was crossed without mishap. It had been used extensively by muja-hadeen supply convoys during the war with the Russians and was littered with the white rib cages of horses defeated by the heavy armaments and medical stocks they carried. Just over the pass on a ridge of shale, Haji found a torn rocket launcher manual. There were old match boxes, rusty horse shoes and spent bullet cases. He told us the Russians dropped many butterfly mines on to the pass, but with a life span of little more than a year they would all have long since expired. The way down was steep but easy to define.

We stopped at the small village of Gama, where the valley split into two. We had a letter of introduction to a most disagreeable man whose first look almost turned us to stone. He was not, it seemed, best pleased at the thought of the hospitality he was obliged to provide. His name was Mustafa Khan and he looked, in a rather moth-eaten way, like Henry VIII. As it happened, he had also had six wives. Two had died and one he had divorced, but unlike the British monarch, he was able as a Muslim to keep the last three at the same time. He had broken his left arm falling from a horse some years before and it had been set at an extraordinary angle. Twisted almost 180 degrees, the palm of the hand hung down facing away from his leg.

We hadn't been there long when Sayeed Karim announced that he would not go on to the village of Paprok, a further ten kilometres down the valley, as originally planned. Unless I paid him double he would turn round now. This was strange and disappointing behaviour from a man of the Parun, one who had but a day before been uttering expressions like 'Beloved guests, it is my honour, my duty. With me there is no problem.' I found out later that Sayeed Karim was in fact not of the Parun, he had simply married into them. He was actually a Gujur, so perhaps his demands were not so out of character. Haji and John both tried to change his mind, reminding him about his honour and duty, but it was all to no avail. He sat smiling as outside the darkness gathered, knowing I would have either to use him or pay him off. I was all the more annoyed because I liked him.

Eventually, Mustafa Khan said that he had a horse and would be happy to take Ismael, Masood and myself to Paprok in the morning. It was only a two-hour walk he said, so I thanked him and agreed to let Sayeed Karim go. As it was only a short journey, if Mustafa Khan changed his mind by morning or demanded a ridiculous rate, we could always walk it ourselves. Although now I was beginning to feel weakened by weeks of limited food, I was confident I could carry a rucksack that far if I had to. I paid Sayeed Karim three-quarters of the sum originally agreed.

That night at dinner Mustafa Khan tried to push us into a theological debate: the Bible versus the Koran. As neither John nor I knew a great deal about either it was a sticky wicket to be playing on. In Afghanistan, to be a Christian, ahl-i-kitab – a person of the book – is OK, you've just missed the plot. But to be seen as an atheist, well, you might as well crap in the krut.

'It says in the Bible,' Mustafa Khan announced with all the assurance of a Mormon preacher, 'that Jesus sleep with prostitute.'

Before I could get tripped up in this infernal debate, John, cool as you like, interjected, 'In our culture, there are three things it is considered rude to discuss.'

Mustafa Khan looked at him. 'And what are they?'

'Politics, religion, and women.' John smiled.

But Mustafa Khan just looked at the floor, his face clouded with confusion and shook his head. 'What else is there left to talk about?'

Early the next morning we packed our bags and prepared to leave. This time it was John's Badakshi porter, Baldrick, who refused to go on without a pay rise. Having seen Sayeed Karim get away with this ploy, he thought he'd try it on too. But John explained that if he did the job well he would get a bonus with which he could buy opium and soon the deal was back on. At nine o'clock, three hours late, Mustafa Khan finally appeared. He said he wanted a thousand rupees – £20 – for the journey. It was laughable. I calmly picked up the rucksack and walked out into the bright morning sun.

In the lee of the low cliff, beside the bubbling stream we said farewell. John and I hugged in the Afghan way. Brief and rigid, it didn't hold much passion. A Peachey to my Daniel? Not quite. But we'd rubbed along, we hadn't rowed and on a journey like ours that actually said a great deal. From the sticky start he'd proved a decent companion, a capable group leader; a great deal better, I imagine, than Uncle George might have proved. Had the route of the trip been up to me we'd probably have just nipped straight up the Bashgul Valley and fled for Pakistan and the Kalash at the first opportunity. If it hadn't been for John's insistence on doing something 'a bit special', a phrase that at the time had given me cause for considerable concern, I would probably never have seen Bandol, swum in Lake Mundol, climbed up to Wama or walked through the Parun Valley, and now it was almost over I was thankful to him and told him so. He just smiled. John was at heart a quiet man, perhaps from having spent so much of his adult life alone and in this wild land. He kept his thoughts to himself.

What motivated him – the persistent spirit that had pushed him forwards, both on our journey and through his unusual life – I'd never discovered, much less understood. I just hoped that if there had been a riddle, he'd solved it now.

It seemed ironic that it was not in John but in Haji, an Afghan freedom fighter and a profound Muslim, truly a man from the other end of the world, that I had found someone I was sure was a real friend. The hug I shared with him was long and genuine. He stood back, clasping my shoulders and in a rare moment of solemnity said, 'Jon Bibly Sahib, I pray one day you find Allah.' Then he smiled broadly, his clear eyes shining. 'Or, OK, pretty wife.' We laughed and I watched them go.

Theirs would be the harder journey, five days over two more passes, but they were all fit and strong and were now carrying little. On reaching the Pakistan border Haji would return to Jalalabad and then Darr-i-Noor to resume his harsh life with the wife and children he so adored; Baldrick – I never did know his real name – would travel on to his home town of Faisalabad, no doubt loaded down with a goodly stash of opium to see him through the cold winter months; and John, after a brief stay in Garum Chasma, would return to Peshawar to continue his life, whatever direction it took.

As for me, as I watched my friends start up the trail, I was suddenly swept by a wave of anxiety and doubt. I was nearly at my final destination, at the edge of my fairytale land: Kafiristan. After all, this was really what I had been dreaming about for over a decade, what if it didn't live up to my expectations? What if, like so often, reality was no match for fantasy? And anyway, what was I hoping to find there? I hadn't really asked myself this question before – the sheer romance and challenge of the journey had seemed enough of an answer at the time – but apprehension now dwarfed my anticipation: what *did* I expect to discover? The lost pagan land of my dreams? Myself? A descendant of Alexander the Great clutching a battered copy of *The Man Who Would Be King*?

But when the three of them had disappeared from view beyond a distant ridge, I turned and looked back at Ismael and Masood, the remnants of my group, savoured a long, deep breath and all at once felt foolishly happy. My moment of doubt passed as quickly as it had come. Ismael, like Haji a real friend, and the unerringly reliable Masood stood watching me, and noticing my contented expression, smiled too. Our journey would not be so hard. In Paprok we would find a porter or two to help take us round to the Bashgul Valley and up to Barg-e-Metal. There we'd rest for a day before attacking the last pass. And really, what a moment that would be, to stand 4650 metres up on the infamous Durrant Line – the invisible border, drawn by my countrymen all those years ago – and look down into one of the ancient valleys of the Kalash. This was, quite simply, the moment I'd been longing for and I'd be damned if I wasn't going to make the most of every second. For over that pass, not in Afghanistan but back in Pakistan, I knew I'd finally find the place where my old friends had once been kings.

A rucksack on my back, I lifted my stick and in flamboyant style pointed down the valley. 'Come on, boys,' I said, with a grin. 'We have a journey to make . . . a journey to Kafiristan.'

PART FOUR
To the Land of the Unbelievers

13 Under a Pagan Moon

'For Gord's sake leave the women alone.'

An extraordinary noise made me pull up short. Standing alone, I peered surreptitiously around the wizened trunk of a huge tree, which shaded the path from the late-summer sun. At first I couldn't see where the strange sound had come from. Before me was an orchard and beyond that the river and an arid cliff. I could see no people at all.

There it was again, floating like birdsong on the tranquil air. Remaining hidden, I followed the sound's trajectory to the base of a tree. A young woman in a long black dress, her neck adorned with a multitude of red and yellow beaded necklaces and her wrists by jangling bracelets, sat rocking back and forth with obvious delight. On her head a beaded band rested like a crown. I stared, captivated. Her peels of laughter were one of the most beautiful sounds I'd ever heard.

To get a better view, I moved quickly and quietly to the other side of the tree trunk. From here I could see the outline of her friend. Older, maybe in her early twenties, her cheeks were also burning with merriment. She seemed to be telling a story. Reaching the conclusion, she slapped her hand against the other's leg, threw her head back – making her colourful head-dress tumble down her back – and fell forward on to the other. Their giggling was so infectious, I found that I was smiling too.

In Nuristan, Islamic traditions had run deep and though the burqa was rare, the women had made a determined – and successful – effort to avoid letting their faces be seen. The last time I had cast my eyes on such a lovely image as these laughing young women had been when passing the singing Passia girl in the fields above Dawlat Shah, before we'd crossed the Karik Pass. Since then

I had not so much as caught a glimpse of a young woman's face, never mind heard her voice or laughter. For more than five weeks I had not heard a combustion engine, touched an inch of asphalt or seen a vehicle move – all of which had given me a great deal of satisfaction – but until that moment it hadn't really occurred to me that all those days had passed without my seeing something as natural as the spectacle that now appeared before me. And now that it did, I couldn't take my eyes from it. Like Mowgli at the water hole I was mesmerised, staring with wonder at the soft fair skin, the high cheek bones, the glistening eyes, full-lipped mouths and the lengthy dark plaits. The nose of one was too long and forehead of the other too shallow for them to be considered classically beautiful but to my deprived eyes the image they made was wondrous.

'Aye, tis like I said,' whispered Danny in my ear, *'boil 'em once or twice in hot water and they'll come out like chicken and ham.'*

Suddenly, a young girl shrieked. Swinging skilfully from a low branch above the women she landed on her feet and pointed at me. Only six or seven years old she didn't appear angry, just surprised. She wasn't the only one. Watching the women, I'd failed to notice the child in the tree above and, lulled by the laughter, had allowed myself to be drawn into the open. Now, standing by the wall, where the tree afforded only marginal cover, I had been caught red-handed . . . a voyeur! In Nuristan, committing such a crime would have led to a sorry conclusion. Greatly embarrassed, I turned my face away.

'Hay baya,' called the woman who'd first caught my attention. She beckoned with her hand. 'Kawa pariz?'

I didn't understand the words but the gesture needed little translation. Smiling, she was indicating that I should join them. Confusion smothered me. The idea, after living for weeks under strict Islamic code, seemed preposterous. It felt wrong to be looking at them, never mind sitting with them. I studied the ground.

'Baya, baya.' This time it was her friend who called and I looked up again. She had moved from under the tree and I could see her voluminous black dress, held tight around the middle by a thick cotton sash and trimmed with colourful embroidery. With her right hand she repositioned her head-dress, which I now noticed fell in a long tail down her back, and then placed both hands on her hips; it was a stance that said, 'Come on, we won't bite.' When she waved again, I placed my bag on the wall and climbed over to the other side.

The journey from Gama with Ismael and Masood had gone as smoothly as could be expected. The Nuristanis we'd hired as porters had played their usual trick of travelling half way, then throwing down the bags and refusing to move another inch until their wages were doubled. But by then although scrawny and thin, resembling the local poultry, we were also fit and strong. Feeling mighty brave, we told them where to go and carried our possessions ourselves. At Barg-e-Metal Masood left us to return to Jalalabad, taking with him half the remaining kit, including my gun. Ismael and I attacked the last pass alone. It wasn't the cleverest move and though we found the aylaks, where we stayed the night, early the next morning we couldn't find the pass. Climbing ridge after ridge only to be confronted by a precipice or false summit we wasted at least two hours – and bags of precious energy – before Ismael eventually hit upon the right path and led me safely across the border back into Pakistan.

For hours we walked together down the mountain path, along the river, under the pines and across the high meadows but just above the first habitation Ismael asked me to wait while he went on alone. As an Afghan refugee he didn't want to be stopped by border police crossing the frontier illegally. With a feringhee he'd have been much more visible and if caught possibly sent back. So we'd hugged a fond farewell and I'd watched as he disappeared along the path. He wasn't so interested in his Kalash cousins. A few days before we'd set out on the journey he'd fallen in love. He was keen to return to Peshawar to see his intended bride. In the event there were no police, the border was unguarded.

'Tsatruma baya?' said the older of the two women when I reached her. With a puzzled expression, I glanced from one woman to the other. I sat beside them on the grass beneath the tree, stretched out my tired legs and put my hands behind me. They smiled.

'Nuristan?' the younger one asked.

'Balé,' I answered positively, nodding my head encouragingly. 'Nuristan . . . Barg-e-Metal.'

'Nuristani assussa?' Now it was her turn to appear baffled. Her eyes creased together as she frowned. Through her right nostril was a hole for a nose ring filled with a tiny twig. Around her eyes were a swirling mass of dots painted with some kind of dye.

'Nai, nai,' I said, laughing. 'Ingrizi Inglestan.'

'Ah,' she nodded and grinned. 'No Mussilman?'

'No Mussilman.'

She pointed at herself. 'Ma nam Bagi Gul.' She then gestured to her friend and said 'Shahidah.' The little girl was back up the tree, crawling along a branch above us. Bagi Gul mimed a baby being cradled in her arms, pointed at Shahidah and then to the tree. 'Sherra,' she said.

At that moment Sherra shook the tree and it began raining fruit. Luscious apricots bounced on the ground beside us. We scooped them up where we sat and started to munch happily. Juicy and sweet, the rich tangy flavour made my taste buds sing.

The afternoon sun was just starting to dip behind the high ridge to the south of the river, throwing a broad block of shadow across the orchard up towards our tree. I could smell the warmth in the grass and the wild flowers. As I leaned over to reach another apricot, a different odour filled my nostrils: that of Bagi Gul. Mild and pleasant, it was a cosy fragrance, like a mellow cheese or warm milk. I breathed in deeply.

'Ta nam khia?' Bagi Gul pointed at me.

'Jonny,' I replied.

'Jooo-ni,' she said slowly, looking into her lap as though working something out. Then she smiled and clapped her hands. 'Jonny Talib.' And again they broke out laughing.

Denied access to the joke, I leaned back against the tree and smiled to myself. If this was Kafiristan, I liked it a lot. I began to feel myself unwind. We sat beneath the tree for an hour, miming, joking, eating fruit and watching the shadows lengthen. Then, sensing a deep fatigue creeping up my limbs, wishing the journey to be finally over, I asked Bagi Gul the way to the house of Saifullah Jan.

Saifullah Jan was a name I had been given back in Peshawar as a contact for when I finally reached the valley. As the only highly-educated member of Kalash society, he fought for their rights with the regional and national governments and was therefore well-known and greatly respected. He spoke excellent English and apparently liked his wine. I'd been told he'd be able to put me up. The contact was useful. When I'd checked in Barg-e-Metal who I might speak to among the Kalash my host had said, somewhat ironically, 'Those dirty Kafirs, they're miserable idolaters. Do not stay with them.'

Bagi Gul stood up and indicated that she would take me. Leaving Shahidah and Sherra, we walked back across the grass field and climbed over the wall. Having picked up my bag, we started down the track.

Saved from conversion to Islam by the fact that their land fell on the eastern side of the Durrant Line, in the British sphere of influence rather than the Afghan Amir's, the Kalash are the last of the pagans living in the Hindu Kush. Inhabiting three narrow valleys of Bumburet, Birir and Rumbor — where I now was — this hardy tribe has been largely forgotten by the outside world. Like the people of the Parun, the Kalash were despised as being weak and submissive by their Kafir cousins across the border — before the British happened along they were often interned as slaves and forced into hard labour by the tyrannical Muslim rulers of Chitral — and often found themselves victims of the Kafirs' thieving raids. But the polytheistic religion of the Kalash has much in common with their neighbour's old beliefs. Like the Afghan Kafirs of yesteryear, the Kalash worship a profusion of ancestral gods, hold religious festivals, drink wine and — though these practices have largely been forgotten here too — are still known to judge a man by the size of the parties he gives and place effigies over the graves of their dead. Their language comes from the same Indo-Aryan root and they almost certainly originate from the same ancestry. They too sit on stools rather than the floor and are often fair in complexion. In fact the only thing they don't seem to share with the Afghan Kafirs — and, so it had seemed, today's Nuristanis — is the desire to kill anything with a pulse. It is said that the Kalash of old were fighters but with the spread of Islam through the region they were forced to retreat further and further up into the hills until they settled here. Exchanging their bows and arrows for goats and the plough they became a passive race, existing off the land. Though the presence of Allah still chips away at their culture, the Kalash are the last to carry the torch for the old ways of Kafiristan.

The tranquil afternoon was turning into a balmy evening. On the cramped terraces women still worked. Some stopped as we passed and shouted jokes to Bagi Gul, who giggled at the obvious innuendoes. But not all were amused. As we rounded one corner an old woman, holding the branch of a thorn tree down low for her goat to eat, yelled at us. Her harsh face told me it was not a compliment.

But Bagi Gul just laughed. 'Nai, nai,' she answered the wizened old woman, 'Ingrizi, Ingrizi – English, English.' She then turned to me, pulled on my beard and shook my head. 'Mussilman,' she exclaimed, with false anger. With two fingers she mimicked the use of scissors. In Afghanistan a beard had been essential if I was to fit in. Not any more it seemed. Still, in a way I was pleased; a month in the mountains had finished off my disguise to a treat. Now it seemed I was the real thing.

Passing under a copse of large trees tangled with snakelike vines, we entered the village of Balanguru. As in Nuristan, houses made of flat stones and spliced beams were stacked in a jumbled confusion up the hillside, packed densely by the confines of the narrow valley. By a water channel below a small mill women scrubbed their headgear and washed their dresses. Many of the robes hung dripping from branches like wet flags. Around a dusty yard, young girls played tag. Some boys with catapults around their necks, one with an Imran Khan sticker on his chest, blew condoms into balloons while others herded three red calves up towards the orchard. A group of men stood smoking. Bagi Gul introduced me to one of them. He was a tall man called Gul Naip Shah; like my sadhu friend back in the Punjab, he had no nose, just an extended hole in the front of his face. He said he would take me to Saifullah's house and, Bagi Gul turned and left. I wondered if I'd see her again.

A minute later Gul Naip Shah led me round a corner and, with a very strange smile, pointed to an open-sided veranda above what I took to be a stable. I climbed the notched tree trunk and looked into the room. At the far end was a hearth glowing bright with burning embers. Before it, squatted a woman baking bread. Hanging from the walls were tatty hessian sacks, two plastic bags, a huge wooden fork, two iron griddles and a hurricane lamp. Above the fire a bunch of dry holly dangled. Closer to the entrance two men, one old, the other somewhere in his forties, and a teenage boy sat on low stools around a central table. All wore dour-coloured shalwar kameez, and two the flat Chitrali cap. They looked up.

'Saifullah Jan?' I asked expectantly, my eyes darting from one face to the next.

'I am Saifullah,' said the man without a hat. He had a round face with straight fair hair and deep green eyes. Though portly, he was a handsome man. 'You must be the Tsatruma ...' He smiled teasingly. 'The man from Nuristan.'

I laughed nervously, a little bemused. 'Yes, well I have just come from there. My name is Jonny. How did you know that?'

'We heard there was a foreigner coming from there. We didn't believe it. Nuristan is a dangerous land. But now I see it's true. Come.' He pulled out another stool made of wood and latticed goat hide. 'You are the first person to enter our valley this way for many years,' said Saifullah. 'It is a long walk and the Gangalwat Pass is not an easy one. But you made it and you are welcome here.' He said something to his wife who turned and smiled then flipped over the bread. 'You want coffee or wine?'

What a choice – neither had passed my lips for a long time. Still, there was no question which I would take. 'Wine ... if that's OK.'

'Of course.' He turned towards a door that led to the dark sleeping area while I made myself comfortable. 'Gulistan,' he shouted. 'Da, da.'

'Gulistan. What a beautiful name,' I said earnestly. 'Land of the Flowers?'

'I think you would say Rose Garden.'

It was a title that certainly fitted its owner. A moment later the most glorious little girl appeared. With long blonde hair tied in traditional plaits she had cartoon eyes as large as Bambi's. Too wide at the collar for her waif-like frame, her dress fell from both shoulders revealing creamy skin, paler than my own. She had a delicate chin, a sweet up-turned nose and mulberry marks on both cheeks. At first her expression was hard but as her father grabbed her affectionately around the waist, it burst like a flower into a enchanting grin. Saifullah took the old Teacher's whisky bottle she was carrying, pulled out the corn-cob cork and poured some of the murky yellow liquid it contained into two glasses.

I took a sip. It was sharp and acidic and in any other circumstances quite undrinkable. Now it was delicious. I drank the rest of the glass quickly and Saifullah filled it up.

'Nuristani man,' said the old man, appearing to notice me for the first time. Thick grey eyebrows drooped at the ends, mirroring the line of his moustache, above which jutted a wide hooked nose. Watery eyes and sunken cheeks descended to a narrow jaw out of which sprouted tufts of white stubble. Though thin and lined, it was one of the most amiable faces I'd ever seen. What he said wasn't amiable at all: 'You killing man. Three year ago Nuristani, they take me one hundred goat. Now I only sixty. They, you, stealing man.'

I sat back, unsure how to respond.

Then he laughed warmly, revealing toothless gums and placed a hand on my knee. 'Me joking man, me Khazi Kusht Nawaz,' he chuckled. 'I pulling legs. You Ingrizi. Me Kalasha. Talking man, funny man . . . keep the stories in the head.' He tapped his hat and grinned broadly again. 'Me *siiiinging* man.'

'The Khazi is the guardian of the legends,' said Saifullah. 'With his songs and his stories he reminds us all who we are and where we came from. He is one of the last true Khazis we have left.'

The Khazi nodded enthusiastically and started to prove what Saifullah had said by launching into an old song. From outside floated the rich murmur of a passing flute.

'You have arrived at a good time.' Saifullah offered me a cigarette, which I accepted and lit. 'Tomorrow the festival of Uchau begins. The men return from the high pastures with all the cheese and butter to last their families the winter.' He took a sip of his wine. 'Big festival. Night dancing.'

'Uchau,' repeated the Khazi. 'Singing, singing.'

Saifullah's wife, Washlim Gul, handed me a thick chapati, fresh from the fire. Hungrily, I broke it and ate a large piece. Packed with crushed walnuts and melted goat's cheese, it was delicious and I made as much clear by moaning loudly.

'Jaou,' said the Khazi, indicating what the bread was called, and helped himself to a piece. Pushing it to the back of his mouth he found a good tooth and we both munched happily.

The shadows finally won the day and the room became dark. Saifullah and Yassir, his son, talked quietly, the Khazi sang, Washlim Gul tended to supper and Gulistan beat the nose of a goat that had somehow managed to enter the room in the hope of stealing potatoes. I sat back against the outer wall of the raised veranda and looked beyond the lower village, the trees and mountains to the distant sky. Hot bread, a glass of wine, a festival of dancing and singing to look forward to, all in a place I'd dreamed about for years. To say that I was content would be to sell the emotion and the moment horribly short. There would be no more staggering through wild rivers or scaling high passes, no more deals to be made with conniving porters or petulant commanders and at last the threat of murder had gone. The spectre of living in a lawless land, never knowing what might be waiting round the next corner, had weighed heavily on me. Now I could relax, really relax, without a worry of any kind.

But it wasn't just the fading anxiety that made me feel so calm. When travelling you are forced to adapt, constantly to change your ways in order to blend in and get on. During the course of this journey I'd discovered that this is as true with those of your own nationality as it is with people from a different race and creed. But as I sat there on my little stool, drinking my wine, eating my bread, surrounded by my new-found Kalash friends, I realised that at that moment I wasn't changed at all. I was myself, completely myself – as though I were sitting with Jeremy back in Delhi or my oldest friends in a London pub. As the pale moon entered stage left from behind a far-off cliff, I quietly began to sing.

There was great excitement in the forest. Young boys, youths and men, all in new or clean shalwar kameez with feathers in their caps and flowers in their waistcoats, charged up the path. Some carried bags full of chapatis that the women had been baking since dawn.

Others held sprigs of green juniper or clusters of holly. With Yassir, I hurried along in their midst.

Bursting from the trees, we came to the river. We clambered over boulders to where the main torrent ran and with a crowd of a hundred stood impatiently staring towards a ridge above the far bank.

It was a glorious morning with the air still and cool, as crisp and refreshing as the crystal water babbling before us. How pleasant it was to feel the sun's rays caressing my face. Once awake, I'd wasted no time in taking Bagi Gul's advice. Washlim Gul had lent me some scissors, a razor and a mirror and surrounded by Gulistan and a group of her friends I'd said hello again to my face.

Almost at once, the first herdsman returning from the summer pastures was spotted walking, practically jogging, along the mountain track. Someone near the front raised an arm and shrieked to us all. The gentle murmur exploded into a roar. People threw up their hands and waved their caps. Soon another man rounded the corner and then another and another and within a minute there was a column of men hurrying towards the water. On their backs they carried conical baskets laden with the precious cheese: their staple diet for the long winter months. As rough as the men were, they resembled a victorious army returning with their booty.

The leader, Din Mohammed, reached the swirling torrent and stopped. At its broadest point the river was only five or six metres wide and the only way across was to stagger through the freezing water. The herdsman looked puzzled. Adulation and honour were his for the taking and yet ... He glanced to the crowd who beckoned him on. Worriedly, he pulled up his trousers and started to walk out from the last boulder into the current. Despite the cold, sweat glistened on his brow. His bandy legs bent beneath the strain as the thundering torrent reached his thighs. Trying desperately to find a footing, he held on to the last rock. It was obvious he'd never make it.

Luckily, Jam Sher Khan, a tall strong man with sideburns that ran into a thick moustache, realised this and shouted him back. Looking around, Jam Sher Khan's eyes struck upon a handy plank. Calling to three others, he ran off to collect the wooden beam and within minutes the herdsmen were marching safely across. As Din Mohammed touched our bank a great cheer rang out. Patted on the shoulders and head, he pushed proudly through the crowd like the captain of a victorious team on his way to collect the FA Cup.

'Come,' said Yassir. He had his sister's fair hair and father's green eyes. He attended school in Chitral and also spoke English. 'It is time to go to temple. Temple of Sajigor.' We clambered over the boulders again and headed back towards the forest.

The religion of the Kalash is complex and unique, deriving from an ancient form of Hinduism. They worship Khodai, the omnipotent creator, and a profusion of lesser gods and ancestral spirits, including Mahandeo, the guardian of crops; Dezalik, goddess of birth; Jestak, goddess of the family; and Sajigor, god of the flocks. Often the gods have to be appeased by sacrificing a cow, a goat or even a few chapatis at one of the many temples and shrines dotted around the valley and festivals are used to ask the gods to look kindly upon the people in the months to come or to give thanks for the past season. Shamans talk to the gods, fortune tellers predict what's in store.

Venerating the goat as the greatest gift of the gods, the Kalash religion juxtaposes a 'pure' land in the high pastures with an impure domain in the villages. Only men can herd the goats into these sacred lands as women are considered less pure. They can worship only at certain temples, must wash in the river below the men and during menstruation are confined to a special house called the bashali. But unlike their Muslim neighbours, Kalash women – like their Afghan Kafir cousins of the past – have substantial leverage in local activities as well as much greater personal freedom. They can choose their husband and leave him when they like – so long as the new suitor pays twice the dowry the original paid. Yassir told me of one girl who, at fourteen, had already had two husbands and was moving on to the third. Once children are born women rarely change husbands. In Kalash society children belong to the men.

These different customs have offended Muslims living in the same valleys. Claiming that they were immoral, in the 1950s they forced whole villages to convert. Thanks to government legislation such conversions were stamped out and though in the 1970s there were only a little over 2000 Kalash, the population is growing and now numbers well over 4000.

In a clearing of holly oaks, an area the size of a tennis court had long ago been levelled out and paved with flat stones. At one end was a metre-high wall out of which crude carvings climbed. On a bench against the wall sat the village elders and in front of them squatted the male crowd. A part of the temple floor was cleared and covered in old patoos. One by one, the returning herdsmen dropped their baskets and laid out their cheese. Then all at once the talking stopped and an entranced silence reigned.

Next to the Khazi sat an old man with hennaed hair. Over his shoulders was draped a coat of gold brocade and from his hat there reached a long white feather. He stood up, holding a flaming stick. 'This Baraman,' Yassir whispered urgently into my ear. 'He religious head of all Kalash.' Moving slowly, Baraman made his way through the crowd towards a tall holly oak. Amongst its branches hung twisted horns and from beyond the glade sighed the trembling river.

Just off the edge of the temple floor, Baraman bent and lit a small fire. In an instant a billowing cloud of bluish smoke rose from the juniper needles. Caught by the sunlight that slanted through the trees, it spread in brilliant columns. Still no one spoke: a sense of expectation hung like a spell. All faces, young and old, were drawn to the flames as though in a trance. Then a young lad jumped to his feet and dragged a docile goat forward.

Having gathered the animal, the old priest pushed its head into the scented vapour. 'Sooch, sooch,' he cried, asking Sajigor, god of the flocks, to purify the sacrificial beast. 'Sooch, sooch – be pure, be pure.' The animal bayed and struggled, trying to free itself, but Baraman held it firm. Again he forced its head forward, mumbling prayers thanking Khodai for the summer's dairy harvest. We all sat riveted. Another man emerged from the crowd. Having received the goat from the old priest, he flipped it on to its side. Holding it down, he quickly slit its throat.

At once the silence burst into happy chatter. Boys leaped up, handed out chapatis and large chunks of fresh cheese. And once

Baraman had sprinkled the fire with the animal's blood, we ate sitting cross-legged in the dappled shade.

Back in the village, there was a buzz of expectation. Women sat in animated groups, gossiping, eating their cheese and cooking fresh bread. Many now wore a larger head-dress on top of the usual headband. The head-dresses, made out of thick cotton and covered in cowry shells, buttons, old coins, beads and bells, reached half way down the women's backs. Some had tall feathers of varied colours poking out of them, making the owners appear like Indian squaws, others had giant pom-poms. Many of the women had not seen their men for more than two months. When they spotted them gambolling merrily down the track, they let out a shriek of pleasure and jumped from the roofs to greet them. As they disappeared into their homes, the others laughed and made jokes.

In the dusty village square, in preparation for the dancing, young girls squashed mulberries and with the juice drew designs on each other's faces: circles on the cheeks, dots around the eyes and little crosses on the forehead and chin. Others simply took biros and scribbled all over each other. Gulistan's hands, arms and cheeks were covered in bright red ink. I watched for a moment as she drew a watch on the wrist of a friend.

After a lunch of jaou and dhal, I was suddenly overcome with fatigue. The two-day, eighty-kilometre hike from Barg-e-Metal to Balanguru – climbing 3000 metres to the head of the pass, dropping 3000 down the other side – had taken its toll, as had the whole journey. I was thin, hadn't eaten a proper meal or had a full night's sleep in weeks. I pulled the charpoy on to the roof outside the room I'd been given by Saifullah, lay down and slept.

The Khazi woke me at dusk.

'Sleeping man,' he said, 'we go dancing, singing, drinking.'

I pulled myself up to sit on the edge of the rope bed and rubbed my eyes. Cut off by the cliffs and trees, what was left of the sky was already dark and studded with stars. I could hear the beating of drums from a promontory somewhere high above. It reverberated eerily through the valley like distant thunder. The Khazi handed me a bottle of wine. Pulling the corn-cob out with my teeth, I took a large gulp. A broad grin ploughed his weathered face.

'Is good, da?' he said. 'We drink. Is our culture.'

I looked at the label. The bottle had once held vinegar. Far from convinced that the original liquid had been replaced, I took another draw and agreed earnestly. 'Proosht Khazi,' I said, using the Kalash word for 'all's fine'. 'Where I come from, believe me, it's our culture too.'

He sat on the floor beside the charpoy, stretching his right leg out before him. Five years ago, the Khazi explained, he'd woken one morning to find his leg bent double at the knee. Unable to move it back down, he was powerless to walk. When he realised it wasn't going to heal of its own accord, he sold many of his precious goats to raise the required funds and travelled to Peshawar to have an operation. But much to his consternation – it had cost him sixty animals – the operation had not been a total success. They simply released whatever it was that was jamming it one way and fixed it solid the other. Now his leg was as straight and rigid as a steel pole. Still, he could at least walk. Or could, if he didn't trip over the giant boots given to him by an American anthropologist. He wasn't in the least bit bothered by the fact that they were four sizes too large. The same man had taught him his strange English. I passed him the bottle of wine but he refused.

'You drinking man. Tonight me singing.' Using the charpoy as a lever, he pulled himself up.

'Khazi, you're always singing man.'

He chuckled, 'You always sleeping. Me no sleeping, only singing.' And he hobbled off the roof.

The haunting drums grew louder as we made our way up the mountain path. A procession of women and young girls walked before us, lighting the way with sticks of flaming juniper. Tiny bells jangled on their head-dresses and their black gowns billowed about them. Merrily they laughed and sang. Coming from the hillsides, along the water channels and through the trees, other groups lit their routes with the orange flames, moving like constellations in the darkness. Far off up the track a flute rang out. We crossed the river and started to climb up a steep bank out of the village into the forest. The wine was coursing through my scant frame, replenishing my energy. I took another gulp.

Soon we came to the clearing in the trees. Around a roaring fire, circles of wild dancers whirled and spun. Two youths battered a lolloping rhythm on goatskin drums hanging from their necks. By the climbing flames old men with faces as gnarled and craggy as the surrounding cliffs cheered and cried; the Khazi moved up and stood beside them. In his long braided coat, Baraman stood pointing his stick across the fire and singing in a tremulous voice. As he did so old women pushed forward and stuffed rupees into his hat.

'Baraman sing the story of Daginai,' came a voice at my shoulder. I turned to see Yassir's face glowing orange before the flames. 'This famous song is always sing now when men return from high pastures.'

'Shabash!' cried the elders suddenly, as the old priest's voice rose and fell. 'Shabash, shabash! – Bravo, bravo!' They hit the fire with their sticks and a spasm of sparks flew like tracers into the night.

'Daginai, he fall in love with wife sister,' Yassir shouted into my ear. 'When he go to high pastures he send signal with smoke to lover and she send signal back.' I offered him the wine which he took. 'But one day the wife she find out and kill her sister. With no more signal, Daginai return to valley very sad and sing to all of loss of love.' Yassir took a gulp and handed back the bottle. 'He then go to her grave, lie with her and push dagger through his heart.'

I stood back to allow some dancers past. Out on the edges of the glade, groups of boys and young men wrapped in patoos against the chilling air huddled together smoking hashish and telling jokes. Some chased girls around trees, down towards the river and into the darkness. Others staged mock fights amongst themselves. Then the drummers began to pick up the beat. The lines of dancers peeled away into groups of threes and fours to spin like tops, the women replying to Baraman's musical legend in perfectly harmonious trance-like wails. Looking at the fire, the dancing women, the drummers, the Khazi and the village elders, my mind flashed back to Marwar Junction and my filmic reverie on the train. At the time I'd consigned it to the realm of fantasy and wild imaginings. But now it had come to pass. It seemed I'd found my Shangri-La.

With a sudden clatter, the drumming ceased and all stood still. Silence spread. Glancing toward the inky darkness, I saw the full moon rising right on cue. A chill wind licked the trees, the river rumbled and the fire burned. Moving aside, Baraman passed his stick to the Khazi. Staring vacantly into the flames he began to sing his pagan song. Low in pitch, trembling with passion, drifting like a spirit over the fire, across the earth and through the pines, came the voice of ancient tales. I turned to Yassir for a translation of the story but he was nowhere to be seen. I looked back. An old woman rested her chin on the Khazi's shoulder. Glistening tears filled her eyes and tumbled down her wizened cheeks. Men, boys, women and girls stuffed notes into the Khazi's cap. He pointed the stick further out over the roaring fire, rubbed his bristled chin and then closed his eyes.

'Shabash!' cried the old men and again the drums began to beat. Slow at first, soon they tore into a frenzied rhythm: da-de-de, da-de-de, da-de-de-da, repeating over and over, faster and faster. People leaped and danced and jumped and sang. I turned again, looking for Yassir, but was at once swept up into the mêlée. Circling the fire in the festive throng, I was first spun one way and then the other. An orange face appeared before me. The long nose and wild eyes I recognised as Bagi Gul's. Her smiling mouth was wide and sensual. Intoxicated by more than the wine I leaned forward. Wailing voices filled my ears, the dark face held my vision.

'Jonny Talib,' I heard her say. And then in an instant she was gone.

———— ◆ ————

The girl sitting beside me glanced up nervously. For a moment the dynamo failed and the train roared into darkness. With a clatter the light returned, blasting the carriage with its neon glow. She edged as far away as her seat would allow, clearly supposing she was being accosted by a subway lunatic. What to say? How to approach? This was a moment I'd fantasised about ever since I'd started writing. And now it was happening. I could hardly contain myself and grinned idiotically. For goodness sake Jonny, try to be cool.

'No, um, excuse me,' I blurted, 'I'm sorry to bother you. I was just wondering if you were enjoying your book?'

'My book?' She turned to the cover then back to me. Obviously still convinced I was about to roll my eyes and dribble, hand her a Scientology pamphlet, or at least try to get her phone number, she replied cautiously: 'It's OK. Quite good actually.' She was about twenty-five I guessed, definitely attractive in a chiselled, remote kind of way, with fair hair and blue-grey eyes. This probably wasn't the first time strange men had started talking to her on the Underground.

'How far have you got.' I could see she was on chapter fourteen. 'Reached Angola yet?'

'No. In the Congo, Brazzaville. Why, have you read it?'

'You might say that.' I held out my hand. 'May I?'

She looked at me and seemed to weigh up the moment before slipping a marker between the pages and passing me the book. Turning sideways to face her, I opened the cover to reveal the photograph on the inside front and held it up next to me. At first she narrowed her eyes quizzically. Then the connection was made.

'Ha!' she exclaimed, her expression transforming in an instant; she seemed genuinely impressed. 'My God, you're the author. Wow, first one I've met.'

I closed the book and handed it back. I looked down at my hands, not sure quite how to continue. 'Well, I am kind of. That's to say, I did write it. Apparently, according to some writers' guild or association or some such thing, you have to have written two books to be technically considered an author. The first can be a one-off so to speak. So far that's my only one.'

'So what are you doing now?' she asked. 'Writing another?'

'No, no,' I shrugged. 'You know, just this and that.' The truth was, having written my book, out of necessity, I'd gone back to dispatch riding, van driving, decorating.

She dropped her head on to one side and gazed vacantly into the carriage. 'I should love to be a writer, must be the best job in the world.' I nodded agreement and then joined her gaze. The African journey had taught me many things about myself, others, the world in general and through it I'd managed to break free from the shackles of grief. But had it shown me who I really was? Now I wondered. Was I a writer or was I simply a traveller who lucked out with a published book? I was happy, I felt content, fulfilled even, but I also sensed that once again something important was missing. This time it seemed unlikely a new Melanie would happen along to fill the void. This time I knew it would be up to me. 'Yes,' I said, turning to my reader, 'you're right. What a great job it would be.' With a sudden shudder the tube began to slow down as it entered a station. 'Oh.' She looked through the grimy window. 'This is my stop.' She held the *book out to me again. 'I know it's a bit embarrassing but would you mind signing it for me?'*

'Embarrassing? Are you joking?' I took out my pen and having asked her name, on the first page scrawled my name and brief dedication. 'To Sarah, from the writer to the reader, with thanks.'

14 End Game

*'Dravot was King, and a handsome man he looked
with a gold crown upon his head.'*

'Jonny Talib!' There was a rap at the door. Recognising the voice
of Gulistan, I sat up. Shaking my head, I pulled my legs from
beneath the torn cotton quilt and stretched. The shafts of sunlight
that pierced the room in blocks of solid gold told me it was late. If
the sun had climbed above the eastern cliffs it had to be well past
nine. It also meant the rain had stopped. 'Jonny Tal*eee*b!' she called
again.

'Yes, yes.' I stood up, disturbing particles of dust that danced
crazily through the beams. Since Bagi Gul had rechristened me a
month ago, most of the kids had followed suit. If Taliban meant
'seekers of truth', I'd concluded that Jonny Talib must mean 'Jonny
the Seeker', which I'd pondered was not a million miles from the
truth. Pulling on a jumper, I opened the door.

Standing before me, Gulistan was bursting with some important
news. She grabbed my arm and shook it. 'Rad-*eeo*, rad-*eeo*.'
Shrieking something about Afghanistan she darted past me into the
room.

Slightly bemused, I left her to find my radio and walked out on to
the flat roof of the house below. The sharp autumn morning
stretched away beyond the village through the turning trees and
marbled hills to distant sparkling mountains. The previous week the
weather had been dismal, with a continuous drizzle falling in the
valley and snow burying the peaks high above; the passes to
Nuristan would soon be closed, winter was on its way. On the table,
a pot of tea steamed gently next to a fresh loaf of jaou. I breathed in
deeply, stretched and then sat on the stool and poured myself a cup.

'Taliban, they take Kabul.' From below, I heard Yassir's voice. A moment later his face appeared as he clambered up the notched tree trunk and climbed on to the roof. 'Yes, yesterday. General Masood, he leave without fight and Taliban move in. First they take Jalalabad, then Kabul.'

Gulistan came bounding out of the room carrying my short-wave radio. Having taken a mouthful of jaou, I turned the radio on and twiddled the frequency dial.

At first there was nothing but fuzz. Deep in the valley, surrounded as we were by the giant mountains, reception was usually bad. During the month I'd been in Balanguru, I'd barely gleaned a whisper out of the world service. With the clear sky, I hoped today might be different. Within a few minutes, I'd tracked down London and, although the reporter's voice had to fight its way through thick static, soon after I caught the word Afghanistan . . . 'Taliban militia who seized con . . . Kabul yesterday . . . in what appears to . . . relatively bloodless take-over. Earlier in . . . week the radical Islamic movement march . . . Jalalabad, south Kunar and Laghman provinces where heavy fighting was re . . . and arri . . . capital only hours after General Masood and the government of President Rabanni had fled to the north.' Though I had a hard time deciphering the crackling voice, the report went on to explain that the Taliban's Pythonesque 'Ministry of Good and Abstaining from Bad' had been busy issuing decrees banning women from work, closing all girls' schools, forcing people into the mosques at gun point, making it law that men grew beards. They had banned kite flying, chess and football.

So the Taliban militia had finally won Kabul. The 200 fanatical students who had burst from the religious schools of south-western Pakistan two years earlier had raised an army and claimed the ultimate prize. Now controlling over two thirds of the country and, most importantly, its vital heart, it surely wouldn't be long until the rest would fall into their grasp. For Rabbani and Masood it appeared the end of the game. But then again, this is Afghanistan and who can say what might happen. The war has been going on for seventeen years, it may well continue for seventeen more. One thing, however, did seem certain: we'd got through the country just in time. With the Taliban in charge, things could have proved very different indeed.

'These people are crazy,' said Saifullah later that evening as a group of us sat on the veranda of his home. He spoke without malice, it was a statement of fact. 'They call us dirty Kafirs with no religion, no God. These people use theirs for their own end. Power is all they want. At least we are true to our ways.'

He poured me a glass of wine and then passed the bottle to Jam Sher Khan who was sitting behind us at the low table with a giant of a man called Gul Zaman: he must have stood seven foot tall and was as broad as a tree trunk. 'For many generations,' said Saifullah, 'we have been ridiculed by the Muslim. When I go to school in Chitral they make fun, make me sleep in stable with goats where they say I belong. Years before, they make us wear feather in cap so they know who we are. Before that we are slaves. Now I have many good Muslim friends, people who understand we are not so different, but some cannot see.' He thought for a moment. 'Live and let live, that is good. These Taliban . . . ' Unable to find the right expression, he simply shook his head.

'And see,' exclaimed the Khazi, who sat beside me. He was pointing down towards the path where a man and a horse walked in the gloom. 'Looking now. See how they take all.' Two large sacks of walnuts were secured to the animal's back. 'Oh my brother,' cried the Khazi mockingly, 'take fruit, take trees, take shalwar kameez.' He pulled at his grimy collar and laughed mirthlessly. Not all, it seemed, was rosy in my Shangri-La.

'They have been taking our walnuts for years,' said Saifullah, resignedly. 'Long ago many Kalash give away the rights to the fruit from their trees. They were uneducated, they did not know what they were doing. Someone offer them some beads, a cloth cap, a few rupees and they take, signing away the fruit for ever.' Nearly half the valley's crop was taken each year by the people of Ayun, the Muslim town that stands at the entrance to the valley, not to eat but to sell in the Chitral bazaar. And following the construction of a jeep track that lead to just below the village of Balanguru, outsiders had stripped whole areas of the ancient woodland, exporting the produce for their own gain. Saifullah had taken these people to court and, miraculously, won the first two stages of his fight. He had only to prevail in the supreme court in Islamabad to regain what the Kalash maintain as rightfully theirs.

But taking such action had also brought Saifullah enemies and three times they had tried to kill him. In the worst attack a hand-grenade was lobbed through the chimney into a room he and some friends were occupying. The explosion injured Saifullah and killed his brother.

'What many Muslims don't understand,' explained Saifullah, lighting a cigarette, 'is that our religion is not so different from theirs. Though we worship in a different way, we still pray – to Khodai or Allah, it is the same. To them we are Kafirs – unbelievers – and our land is Kafiristan. But really there is no such place, there never has been, and if there are Kafirs you will not find them here.' He took a drag and blew the smoke out thoughtfully. 'We believe in god, same as them, same as you.' He smiled and leaned back. 'Perhaps we are dirty but no more so than other herdsmen and farmers. And we *are* uneducated but what does this mean?' He laughed loudly and took a sip of his wine. 'They say we are pagan, pure pagan, and maybe we are . . . but as you have seen we are not without honour.'

Yassir, Gulistan and three other children emerged from the dark room beside us and moved in close around the fire. Their grimy faces shone bright before the glowing embers.

'And we have been here looong time,' said the Khazi, shaking his head in a reflective manner. 'Looong time. Before Mussilman.' He rubbed his chin and smiled. 'We come with Sikander many time ago; before, before.'

I sat bolt upright at the mention of Alexander's name. For days now, I'd been urging the Khazi to tell me some of the legends of the Kalash: where they came from and who they were. My hunger for the tale was about to be satisfied for now the Khazi began to talk. But not in English. Warming to the theme he'd followed many times before, he slipped back into the vernacular so the children could understand. Saifullah translated his moving words very quietly into my ear.

'Many, many years ago,' said the Khazi, pulling wistfully at the tufts of grey hair that sprouted from under his chin, 'maybe 500 generations back, when the land shook and all the goats were wild, Sikander Julkhan marched his great armies east. Fighting, fighting as they went, they conquered all the land before them. Kings fell in battles and their countries became Sikander's. But Sikander was not a bad man. He did not kill all, murder, rape and torture. He left the people saying, "If you are good and take my rule no one will die." '

I looked around the darkened veranda. We were all leaning forward on our stools. All, including Gul Zaman and Jam Sher Khan, who must have heard the story a hundred times before, sat and stared at the Khazi, hanging on his every word. Besides his voice and Saifullah's quiet murmur, the only sounds were the crackling fire and the distant, whispering river.

'Then he came to the land of Tsyam.' Here the Khazi stopped, closed his eyes and turned his face towards the smoky ceiling. 'Tsyam was our homeland. Here Sikander left a small army with his General Sulak Shah. He told Sulak Shah to rule for him while he continued on his way. Over the Khyber Sikander went with his armies and they entered Hindustan.

'But Sikander Julkhan never returned, never came back to the land of Tsyam.' He shook his head sorrowfully and looked at the floor.

'After a time, Sulak Shah and his four sons started moving to the north with their wives. First they lived far away in Gilgit,' the Khazi gestured with his hand beyond the raised veranda and into the night. 'Then they moved to Chitral. Here they lived and ruled a great nation. Eight kings for eight generations. The king was a big man, a fighting man called Shumalik and he called the country Kalashdesh.'

One by one, he looked at all of us. Finally his eyes came to rest on Yassir, his face troubled. 'But then came the Mussilman. With a big army they beat our king and took Chitral. We moved to Ayun but still they came, made us slaves, converted us to the ways of Allah and killed many. The Mussilmen took Ayun and we moved further up the valleys to Bomburet, Birir and here to Rumbor where we have lived ever since.' The Khazi's mouth slipped into a loose smile, his watery eyes looking vacantly before him. He then filled the silence with a haunting song. I recognised it at once as the musical tale he'd sung at the festival. In the quiet, the low tremulous notes reverberated around the room like a living force.

My mouth had dropped open. Entranced by the lyrical storytelling, I realised I'd been holding my breath. I leaned back and looked out from the open veranda into the night, and exhaled a silent sigh. It was the tale I'd been waiting and longing to hear. I knew anthropologists had argued that there were tribes living in these mountains long before the great Macedonian warrior passed by and that by mixing with the women of the region his soldiers had only added their genes and customs to an already established culture. But I didn't care. The people of the Kalash believed that they were descendants of Alexander's army and that was enough for me. Another part of my wild fantasy – another thread of Kipling's inspiring story – had been fulfilled. And now, at last, it seemed everything was in place. Surrounded by the rugged mountains of the Hindu Kush, I was sitting on a stool, drinking wine, surrounded by pagans – whose faces were indeed as pale as any Englishman's – who claimed their ancestry from Alexander the Great. I glanced up at the stars and smiled.

Above the high horizon, thick grey clouds sat on the Afghan frontier like an invading army waiting to advance. When winter did come it would do so quickly and everything had to be ready. In the fields people worked. With scythes swishing through the brittle sheaths, women cut the last of the maize. They collected walnuts and gathered firewood and straw that they carried home. Men ploughed the stubble with oxen, stripped the grapes from the vines and squashed the fruit with bare feet in hollowed-out tree trunks before leaving the juice to ferment in wooden urns. Each family had its own vines, just as each family had their own goats, fruit trees, corn fields and grazing grounds up in the high pastures. Boys and girls helped where they could, often high in the branches of a walnut tree or caring for a baby resting beneath.

With the Khazi off in his fields higher up the valley, Saifullah away working on his court cases and Yassir at school in Chitral, I had little to do but wander the mountain paths. From the high water channel above Balanguru, the Rumbor Valley cascaded in a giant sweep of rich autumn colours: dun, ochre, rust and gold merging through the dying foliage with fading greens, browns, yellows and reds. Beneath the drowsy sun, distant cries and laughter echoed and delicious scents abounded. With the sky blue, the shortening days in my Shangri-La remained idyllic. But as I watched the white hand of winter move silently down from the high mountains across the tundra and into the trees I knew it would soon be time for me to leave.

Returning one afternoon as the tumbling sun filled the valley with an intense orange glow, I was set upon by Yassir. Very excited, he rushed up and took hold of my arm.

'Jonny Talib!' he exclaimed, agitated. 'You must come. All the elders are with the tum puchawao.'

I was surprised by his forcefulness. 'The what, Yassir?'

'The tum puchawao...' He turned and pointed towards a house at the top of the village. 'The bow shaker.'

'Oh,' I said, following him from the square, 'well that explains everything.'

'No, no,' he said, as we disappeared into the warren of homes. 'Shyeen Gul, she go to Chitral to have baby – you remember? But she have problem again. Baby no coming so they cut.' He stopped beside a water trough and with his index finger made a line across the bottom of his belly.

'A caesarean,' I said.

'They cut baby out and tie her back.' He turned and continued to climb through the labyrinth of narrow alleyways, ducking under overhanging roofs now packed with firewood and golden straw, clambering over walls and fences, being careful not to tread on the drying fruit. 'Yesterday they bring her back, but jeep ride no good for woman with big cut. Now she very weak, baby too.' I didn't doubt it. Two, maybe three, hours in the back of a beaten up, stiff-suspensioned Willis jeep, crunching through pot-holes, up and down, around hair-pin bends, all the while half choking on powder-fine dust. It didn't bear thinking about. Still, what did all this have to do with the 'bow shaker'?

'Bow shaker, fortune teller,' said Yassir, as we reached the water channel at the top of the village. 'Shyeen Gul husband he worried that wife and child die so he ask the bow shaker future. Maybe gods angry. If so, the bow shaker will know, tell shaman and shaman will talk to gods ... find out what must be done. If gods no angry, all OK.'

Inside the room it was warm and quiet. Six old men stood around the central fire, watching another sitting forward on a frail charpoy. He wore a fawn waistcoat and tatty grey shalwar kameez with a red cotton scarf tied about his neck. With a huge walrus moustache, lined face and pale skin, in the dim light he appeared to have hopped from the pages of a Dickens novel. With his elbows resting on his knees, he held between his fingers and thumbs strands of goats-hair yarn below which swung a twig of willow bent into a bow. The bow shaker's opinion could be sought on many matters, Yassir explained, including health, marriage, the weather or a long journey, though little was as important as the situation confronting him now: a woman and child's life hung in the balance. All the elders, especially the husband, were concentrating hard, staring at the swaying bow. A tall man with forearms as thick as my thighs stood just inside the door. Naturally worried, his seasoned face was set grave and hard. All were willing the bow to be still.

But it would not rest. Instead of coming to a halt beneath his hands – indicating all was fine – the arc of the bow grow wider and wider, swinging wildly from side to side, almost up to the horizontal. The bow shaker gazed immobile before him but among the others a murmur arose. One man threw some pine needles on to the fire and another began to whimper softly, eyes closed and appeared to go into a trance.

'This the shaman, Zandullah Khan,' whispered Yassir. 'Gods are angry. He will talk to them and find out what must be done to save wife and child.' Zandullah Khan was a short man with cropped grey hair and whiskers sprouting from his ears. He wore a torn tweed jacket and wellington boots. The others stood back to give him room as he swayed to and fro chanting softly.

Suddenly he stopped and opened his eyes. They were rheumy, wide and red. There was a distance about him, as if he was stoned or perhaps possessed. He then muttered something in the vague direction of the husband, who was standing, expression unchanged, waiting for instructions.

'He say Khost Akbar must go to orchard and get his cow,' said Yassir with an air of excitement. 'Gods very angry, no goat but cow. Khost Akbar have only one. He must bring here and kill . . . sacrifice to Khodai.'

'Will that make everything better?' I asked, unable to keep the scepticism out of my voice.

'Of course.' Yassir regarded me as though I were simple.

Everyone left the warm room and filed out on to the roof. The late sun was turning the far-off peaks to a rosy pink but the valley was lost in gloom. The air was cool, transforming my breath into translucent mist. I stamped my feet and blew warm air into my hands. Jam Sher Khan made a small fire near the edge of the roof and around it the shaman quietly swayed.

It didn't take long for the word to spread. Soon a small crowd of grubby boys had gathered to watch the preparations from the wall above the bow shaker's house. Other men arrived but no women or girls. Still, it was an event that would be shared by all – once the beast had been killed and butchered the cooked meat would be distributed throughout the village.

When Khost Akbar returned, he did not look happy. His cow was a beauty. Rusty red, the colour of autumn leaves, it was a fine well-covered animal, young, with two small horns twisting out of an elegant head. Leading it on to the roof with a rough rope halter, unconsciously he placed a hand behind its ears and stroked it gently. The shaman started to spin, lurching in so many directions the elders had to stand by the edge of the roof to prevent him falling off. As he swung his arms and moved his feet, his old face turned to the shrouded sky. He moaned, as though in pain.

Khost Akbar handed the rope to Jam Sher Khan who led the beast to the centre of the roof. With a deft trip he flicked the unsuspecting animal on to its side. Two other man then held it down while Jam Sher Khan took out his knife. All eyes where glued to the doomed creature. Holding the soft fold of flesh beneath the cow's neck Jam Sher Khan cut in a quick sawing motion. The animals eyes bulged in their sockets, tongue popped from its mouth and with one shuddering spasm its life disappeared; it was over in the blink of an eye.

Blood from the headless carcass was collected in a metal bowl and sprinkled over the fire while the shaman chanted. A moment later the cow's torpid head was picked up by its horns like a bizarre hunting trophy and placed amongst the flames. The shaman fell silent and slumped to his knees. The boys began to whisper, then laugh and fire their catapults into the trees. Khost Akbar picked up his halter. As with the goat at the temple of Sajigor, the smouldering head was covered in juniper needles and a bluish smoke began to rise. The acidic odour of burning hair was hidden by the scent of the pine.

In the fading light, Yassir led me back down the hillside between the congested housing.

'You want to see Shyeen Gul and baby?' he asked, setting a brisk pace before me. 'Come on, I show you.'

'Is it all right?' I asked, a little surprised. If the woman was so seriously ill that her husband's only cow had had to be sacrificed I doubted she'd be over keen on having me visit.

'Of course,' came his confident reply. 'She live just near to you.'

We passed the front door of the room I'd been staying in and climbed on to the adjacent roof. A wicker basket full of walnuts was propped against the wall beside the entrance, where a girl sat with a myna bird resting on her shoulder. One by one she was breaking the walnut shells between two rocks and retrieving the nuts. We pushed opened the door and stepped inside.

The room was dark and it took my eyes a few seconds to adjust. Covering the fire was a large griddle resting on a circle of stones. Around it sat two young women. One held a young boy whose face was coated in a burnt goat-horn paste to protect his skin from the elements, the other was baking bread. On the black walls hung sprigs of holly, chains of threaded nuts and wooden farming implements. Shoved against them were four charpoys, all empty except for one. Through the gloom I could see the pretty face of another young woman. Maybe twenty, she had wide dark eyes and clear skin with a strong jaw and pale lips. A handful of freckles peppered her nose; she closely resembled a friend back home. Lying on her back, resting her head sideways on a pillow, she appeared tired but in no pain. She smiled warmly. Next to her bed was a tiny cot. In it I assumed was the baby.

'Ishpata, baya,' said the women with the boy, welcoming me with the term for brother. She indicated that we should sit down. Though I recognised her, I didn't know her name and Yassir introduced us saying she and the one making bread were Shyeen Gul's sisters, Mina Bibi and Syta Gul.

'They kill the cow?' asked Syta Gul nonchalantly, turning the thin chapati with a finger and fork.

Yassir nodded.

'Proosht,' she said, 'then Khodai will be happy, all will be fine.'

Less convinced by the powers of animal sacrifice, I asked Shyeen Gul how she was feeling.

'Proosht, baya,' she said with an effort as something caught inside her. She stiffened slightly against the rising pain and then relaxed again. 'Fine brother,' she repeated, 'everything is fine.'

'Is this the baby?' I asked, leaning forward to look into the crib. I could see nothing in the shadows but a bundle of woollen rags.

Shyeen Gul nodded weakly. Letting go of the young boy who waddled past us bare-bottomed towards the door, Mina Bibi stood up, walked to the crib and hauled out the pile of woolly fabrics. She turned and plonked it in my lap.

Greatly surprised, I laughed anxiously and clasped the bundle tensely. Looking around I realised all the faces were watching me, smiling. I felt the warmth exuding from the swaddled mass and peered down amongst the cloth. Still carefully cradling the child with my left arm and hand, I pulled back a piece of clean white muslin and saw the most precious image. Unsqueezed and tugged by the rigours of childbirth, the tiny sleeping face made about as perfect a sight as eyes could see. I turned slightly to catch more of the firelight. The infant's nose, chin, cheeks all seemed flawless; her mouth was wide, the same shape as her mother's; she was sucking sweetly on her lower lip. I could tell she was a girl for on her head rested a tiny brocade cap and around her neck there already hung some beads.

'Oh,' I said smiling like a simpleton, 'she's beautiful, Shyeen Gul, really so beautiful.' I rocked her gently as Yassir peered in over my shoulder.

'What's her name?' I asked, glancing up towards Shyeen Gul. At a couple of weeks old, I assumed that she had one. But Shyeen Gul just smiled slightly and shrugged.

'No name,' said Syta Gul pouring more of the maize flour mixture on to the griddle. With a sudden jolt she looked up, 'You name her,' she exclaimed.

'Me?' I asked in patent disbelief. 'Me, really?' I looked at Shyeen Gul, who nodded encouragingly.

'Yes,' she whispered. 'You name her.'

I turned my eyes down towards the heavenly image, stared at the delicate face and without a moment's hesitation said: 'Melanie.' I looked up at their faces one by one. 'Melanie Bibi,' I said.

'Proosht, proosht, baya!' cried Mina Bibi excitedly. 'Very good!' Clapping her hands, she turned to Shyeen Gul and repeated the name 'Mel-arr-ni Bibi. Hey, very beautiful.' And to my amazement Shyeen Gul nodded vigorously and tried to laugh. Finding the effort too great, she contented herself by easing slightly higher in the bed and joining the others in the room trying out the new name.

Grinning broadly, I glanced again at the innocent little bundle in my lap and suddenly I was struck by what I had done. For the first time, maybe the only time, I had named a child; given it something it would carry for the rest of its life. When Mina Bibi had asked me to name her I'd reacted instinctively, not thinking at all. The enormity of the request, the privilege, the responsibility, suddenly crashed over me.

Overcome with concern I blurted out, 'No sisters, it doesn't have to be Melanie.' Hurriedly I tried to think of other favourite girls names. 'Sarah,' I declared, 'Sarah Bibi, or Isabel, Isabel Gul.' I scrambled hard for more, 'Rachel or Tara. Yes, Tara Bibi, in Hindi that means little star.' I pointed though the door towards the sky but I could see that they were unimpressed. All three of the women shook their heads in unison and happily repeated, 'Mel-arr-ni Bibi.'

'Do you really like it?' I asked Shyeen Gul.

She nodded again, 'Shisho'yak, baya. It's beautiful, brother.'

I looked back down at the little face. Ah well, I thought, perhaps it was meant to be.

It had been seven years, almost to the day, since I'd held my Melanie in my arms; the length of time I'd been told it would take truly to come to terms with her death. Holding this new life, I sensed I had. I knew the child's chances of survival were slim, regardless of her weak mother and difficult birth. Throughout these valleys the child mortality rate is staggeringly high with as many as forty per cent not celebrating their fifth birthday. The first year was usually the hardest and winter was just around the corner. Cradling the child on my lap, I removed the leather cord from around my neck and let the twisted lace unwind in my hand. The elephant god

Ganish twirled in dance against orange firelight. It was the protective amulet Jeremy had given to me in Delhi what felt like a lifetime ago. While wearing it I'd come to no harm, perhaps it would now safeguard Melanie Bibi. I kissed the charm and, carefully lifting her head, slipped it around her neck and fastened it tight. She wriggled, yawned and opened her eyes. Like my Melanie's, they were blue.

Staring into the window of this new-born soul a deep contentment washed over me; and with it came understanding. As Saifullah had explained, there is no Kafiristan, there never has been. It was only ever a name carried in the minds of outsiders. Yet to me Kafiristan did exist – as a flame in the hearts of men looking for their dreams. To the Kalash, and the Afghan Kafirs of yesteryear, theirs was not a land of either 'unbelievers' or 'light', it was simply home. And the intoxicating, completely unexpected truth was that sitting in that beautiful place, accepted as a member of the family by those who lived there, sharing their life and drinking in their hardships as well as joy, it felt like home to me also. I'd found my Kafiristan. I didn't need to be crowned a King.

Mina Bibi stood up again and, having wiped her hands down the side of her dress, held out her arms. Giving the infant a kiss on the cheek, I passed her back. And with that, let Melanie go.

'Coco Ingrizi,' Mina Bibi said, holding the baby up and nuzzling her face. 'That's your English uncle.' I smiled, not needing Yassir's translation. I now had a pagan niece in the Hindu Kush. Mina Bibi handed her over to Shyeen Gul who pulled her close, placing her face against her warm breast.

As we walked outside I felt frosty air caress me. The first of winter's lonely snowflakes were starting to fall.

A triangle of light poured through the window, soaking the wooden floor in a pool of silver. Turning on my torch, I squinted at the clock; it had just gone five. I lay back, pulled the covers tight around my chin and stared outside. Between the empty branches of the mulberry tree, riding high above the cliffs, a waning moon was shining.

'The Khazi never sleeps,' Saifullah had told me the previous evening, as we drank a last bottle of wine. 'You'll find him up before dawn, squatting beneath his fields.' I'd said goodbye to everyone else. There was only the Khazi left.

Already half dressed against the night's chill I threw back the quilt and stood up. Quickly pulling on the rest of my clothes, my boots and cap, I grabbed my small canvas bag and noiselessly slipped the bolt on the door. Outside, the sky was clear and the air raw. Smothered in a deep frost, the village sparkled and glowed. Stepping gingerly across the roof, I clambered down the tree trunk and was away into the stillness. At the top of the village I turned right along the water channel, taking the path towards Kalasha-gram.

Very soon I was high up on the side of the valley. The path was clear, easy to make out: moonlight reflected off its icy rim, firing the slate to a gleaming marble. Where foliage or rocks cast the route in shadow, I used my torch to light the way.

Before long, I noticed a small group of terraced fields ascending in a staircase on my left towards some trees. The maize had been cut but clusters of straw were still piled on the stubble, looking like wigwams in the ghostly glow. Then my eyes were drawn by the image I had come to find. Sitting on a rock, on the edge of the path, one knee pulled beneath his chin, his bad leg outstretched before him, was Khazi Khost Nawaz, silhouetted against the sky like a scrawny buzzard scanning the plains. As usual, he was singing softly. Frozen vapour drifted from his mouth like smoke.

'Khazi,' I called out in a low voice, 'I have come to say goodbye.'

If he was startled, he didn't show it. He turned towards me, his old face lost in the shadows and clapped his hands together. Shuffling down from the wall, he hobbled along the path to greet me. 'Today I go,' I said, almost in a whisper. 'Today I leave.'

'No goodbye,' replied the Khazi, putting his arms around my waist and hugging me tightly. 'Kalasha no word, goodbye. You coming man again.' I knew he was right and it made me feel better. Though I've seldom returned to the far-off places where my wandering feet have led me, I knew with absolute certainty I'd return to the Rumbor Valley one day. We moved back to his ledge and sat down.

'I've brought you a present,' I said and from my bag pulled out the Ryan Giggs T-shirt which he'd earlier admired. Holding it up, I turned my torch on to the picture of Manchester United's number eleven in full flight.

'Ah, this running man!' exclaimed the Khazi happily, taking it from me.

'Best damn running man there is,' I said, and watched as he stripped off his jacket and slipped the cotton shirt over his grimy kameez. He sat back, looking proud. I laughed mischievously at the image he made: anthropologists must love me. He placed his hand on my shoulder and grinned simply.

"'Shake hands with the man, Peachey," came a familiar voice. "We're going now. We've urgent private affairs in the South, at Marwar Junction."' And as I heard Danny's familiar growl once again, I realised I had others besides the Khazi with whom to make my farewells.

I owed an enormous debt to Peachey Carnehan and Daniel Dravot. Their exploits were my introduction to the world of literature and later, rising from the pages as fellow travellers, they'd guided me through their kingdom. They had brought me here and shown me all this, and for that I was eternally grateful. Their spirit would always remain burning brightly in my chest.

Compared to Peachey and Danny's departure from this land, mine would be easy. A jeep would carry me to Chitral in a couple of hours, the following day I'd reach Peshawar and the day after that I'd be back in India where another kind of challenge would begin: from mountains and valleys to the blank page. As for Kipling's friends, the fates demanded a far crueller price. From a rope bridge they made old Danny tumble, *'turning round and round, twenty thousand miles, for he took half an hour to fall 'till he struck the water'.* And poor Peachey they crucified. But Peachey didn't die. And so amazed were they that they sent him home, carrying Danny's head in a horsehair bag. Oh yes, Daniel Dravot died in Kafiristan, but in his time he had been the King, with a golden crown upon his head. He'd lived his destiny, become a god even, and while he'd ruled his pagan land, he had been truly happy.

Looking vaguely into the darkened valley, where the river twisted like a shimmering serpent, the Khazi coughed once and started to sing again.

'Khazi,' I stopped him, 'what is this song you sing? What's . . . ?'

'This b*eeeg* song. Is story I like.' As he said it, he shook his head.

'Is about man, King-man, many many time ago.' He thought for a moment, pulling at his chin. 'One day Kafir they come from over pass, take wife-Queeen, and take goooat.' It was hard to tell which he considered the greater crime. 'All say to King, no go, them Kafir man, bad killing man. But King sad and want wife back. "No cheeeldren I have," he say, "this my wife, it cannot be. She my love." So he go. He go with friend, beeeg friend, who help him find the way. They climb to pass, cross the pass and walking down to find wife-Queen.'

He took hold of my arm and whispered conspiratorially. 'For week no coming back. They all think King dead, and friend dead too. They say both is bad, should never go. For two week is same-same but then they cooome back.' He clapped his hands together. 'Back ooover pass. No killing and they haaave Queeen.' He stopped for a moment and smiled broadly, 'And take they goats!' Happily the Khazi slapped his bad leg and waved a determined finger. 'Ooone hundred goat, Kafüür Afghani goat!' Then he roared with laughter that must have been audible from one end of the valley to the other.

'Shabash!' I cried, remembering the old men by the fire.

'Aye aye, shabash, shabash,' chuckled the Khazi, then he sighed quietly. 'Khazi singing man. Is good song.'

'What was the name of the King?' I asked, hoping I might already know the answer. Above the cliffs the eastern sky was brightening. If I was to make the jeep I had to get going.

'This King he name is Shumalik.'

'Oh,' I said a little downcast. 'Not Jonny Talib.'

'Choni Talib!' exclaimed the Khazi with a look of astonishment. 'No, no!' He took hold of my hands and stared intently into my eyes, as though about to teach me an important lesson. His wizened old face was creased and furrowed. 'Choni Talib, was King's friend.'

I gave the Khazi a long hug, then jumped down from the little ridge and walked off along the water channel. The birds were singing, smoke rising and from the darkness the valley took shape. I smiled to myself. Gord's holy trousers, and all along I'd thought myself the King.

Epilogue

'And that is where the matter rests.'

And so the dolphins have moved on and soon I'll have to join them. The other travellers also migrated with the end of the mango season. The palm-leaf bars are being taken down and the guest houses are closing. Out on the horizon, far out to sea, pregnant clouds are massing; in a week they'll charge, so the fishermen say, and who am I to doubt them? It's a relief – India is in need of a wash. Beyond the paddies and the banyan trees the small town hides deep in rubbish. Paan and oil stains mark the roads and the open drains lie stagnant. The beach looks tired, too. Seaweed, coconut husks, driftwood, plastic bags, fruit peel, even the remains of a giant turtle, decorate the coastline in a necklace of debris. It's fine for the crows but little else. When the monsoon finally breaks it will be a blessing and the bleached earth will sigh. It's been good spending the winter down here, but now it's time to move on, start heading north again, like the dolphins.

After my journey I didn't go home. I'd always dreamed of living for a while on an endless beach with a calm, clear sea to swim in and warm, soft sand to walk along at night. So I rented a hut on the very edge of India, under the palms and among the dunes, with a dazzling view across the Arabian Sea: what better place could there possibly be to sit for a while and remember?

On a shelf above my desk rests the battered copy of *The Man Who Would Be King*. Facing forwards, the worn cover stares down at me, still daring inspiration. Inside, spread across the opening page, Melanie's words remain. The reader and the traveller did combine and now it seems they've borne a writer. But have they? To be honest, I'm still not sure. Trouble is, I never felt very much like a musician even when I was paid to be one. Does a second book really prove I'm an author any more than I was ever a stunt horse rider, a photographer, a strawberry farmer, waiter, crook or courier? But, you know what, it really doesn't matter. For I realise now that that's just me, a man who lives by many stars. I'm simply not a person destined to travel life along a single path; as it was for Peachey and Danny, for me variety holds the key.

When I was twenty-one – all wide-eyed and drooling at the world – I read my first ever book. In that tale two brave men had a distant dream to rise up from their frustrated lives and make their mark; to take fate by the scruff of the neck and march it along a different path. Against all the odds, they succeeded. When I read that story a seed was sown within me, an idea that whatever I wanted I could achieve, all I had to do was take a chance and try. So I tried. I set out on a quest, a journey to find that same land and then to write a book. And now it's done. Inside, a dreamer's heart has always beaten; now there's a man who's seen those dreams come true. So am I writer? I look from my battered copy of Kipling's book, to my computer and out to the blue horizon and smile to myself. Daniel Dravot was a King, if only for a few months, and yes, today I am a writer.

Acknowledgments

Before I sign off with some lengthy acknowledgments, let me just add a couple of points I have learnt since finishing this book. Not long after I returned from India I met John Hayward for lunch in London and he told me a curious tale. I don't wish to add gratuitous colour to a story already told but according to him it seems as though the danger we'd felt in Kantiwar, while being guests-cum-captives of Haji Gafor, wasn't fired simply by over-active imaginations... it had been very real. Some weeks after John had gone back to work he'd met Amir Shah Masood while on an aid delivery mission in Northern Afghanistan. On telling the Lion of the Panjsher that we'd just been to Nuristan, Masood swiftly replied, 'You are lucky men, you and your friend. You nearly didn't return.' He then went on to explain that the radio communication between Haji Gafor in Kabul and his brother, Abdul Rashid, in Kantiwar – regarding what should be done with us – had, just as we had feared, been of a highly alarming nature. So much so in fact that Masood, who at the time was monitoring the conversation close by in the Panjsher Valley, had ordered a troop of his finest mujehadeen warriors to stand by, ready to board a helicopter gunship to swoop in and liberate us should we get the thumbs down from Gafor. As it happened, Ismael's connections saved the day and no such 'Ramboesque' rescue mission was necessary. But it does go to illustrate that not all our fears were groundless.

You may also be interested to learn that John decided to stay in the Aid world and is still working in Kabul, and Melanie Bibi survived her first long winter. And so on with the thanks...

This journey, this book, would not have been possible had it not been for the help, guidance, generous hospitality and encouragement of countless people. You have read my tale and know the names of some of these people: my gratitude to them is unbounded. But there are others, who, for whatever reason, have not made it into the story and my debt to them is equally great. Organising the logistics for the trip – especially where Afghanistan was concerned – required many favours from all kinds of people, expatriate Westerners and locals alike. Most had no idea who I was and all were extremely busy with far more pressing matters than my crazy jaunt. Still, when I went seeking information, advice, bureaucratic assistance, transport, accommodation, lessons in local etiquette etc., every one of the people listed below gave all that they could to help me on my way, and for that I will always be grateful.

First, in India I should like to thank my great friend Jeremy Sheldon for putting up with me in Delhi, also Andrew Studd, Gill Hall, Louis Halmkan and Clive Tucker for showing similar hospitality when Jeremy wasn't around. A big thank you to Philip Hurst for all his help and advice and to Rosemary King, Amanda Bowen, Tim McGirk, Ian Hughes and all the Acharya family. Thanks also to Nell Paton for making a cold and rainy weekend in Kullu much more enjoyable than it might otherwise have been.

In Pakistan I should like to thank Kass Reitvelt, Henrietta Miers – especially sorry you became a victim of the editor's sword! – Helen Poulsen, Karen Waite and Nicol Barton, at Learning For Life, Peter Jouvenal, Robert 'Mac' McCray, Ewen McLeod, Megan Douthwaite, James Blount, Mufty, Shuja Rehman, Col. Khushwaqt ul Mulk, Maj. Khushahmed ul Mulk and Dr Yusef Nuristani, whose assistance was invaluable.

In Afghanistan I should like to say a huge thanks to Andrew Graham and Jill Harrison – without the enormous amount of help they provided, the journey through Nuristan would have been very much harder to organise. Thank you also to Nick Danziger, Mette Sophia Eliseussen, Ross Everson, Carla Grissann, Thomas Gurtner, Christian Marie, Mark Lavine, Alex Lyon, Tanya Power-Stevens, Dr Labib and Marzia Mullzada at the Karte Sye Hospital, all at ACTED, Solidarité, ERU, MERLIN, Halo Trust & the ICRC. The work the employees of these organisations do is truly humbling. And of course great thanks to John Hayward. His help and experience made the whole thing possible.

On the beach I should like to thank Rob Arnold, Juliet Brawn, Felix Costello, Delia Curro, Simon Dyson, Pete Hillman, Phil 'Fraser' Jones, Jamie Whittington, and all at Johncy's for keeping me sane while I bashed away at the keys.

And back home in England I should like to thank Nicola Akroyd, Desmond Balmer, Dimple Bath, Mark and Carol Beattie, my brother Chris, Mina Bond, Lucy Clifton, Guy Denning, Kate Ellis, David Goodale, Miranda Haines, Jared Harris, Rachel Jervis, Dr Schyller Jones, Guy Joseph, Ann Llewellyn, Beverly Martin, Rhiannon McLennan, David Newell, Paul and Jo Ross, Zoe Scurfield, Robert Tasher, Lindsay Treanor, Nic Van der Sman, Jim White, Caterpillar Boots – for giving me the toughest and most comfortable walking gear imaginable – and the Royal Geographical Society. A very big thank you to Jennet Walton and Robert Sutton, who have both offered a great deal of advice. And once again a very special thank you to my parents.

I should also like to express my gratitude to my agent, Mark Lucas, to Tom Weldon – formerly of William Heinemann – who gave me the chance to make this journey and write this book, to Katie James and to my brilliant editor, Victoria Hipps.

There is, however, one person to whom I feel extremely indebted. While his own life was frantic, Andy Hobsbawm took the time to read my original manuscript, work out where and how it could be improved, and then, with patience and skill, draw out of me what was needed. He is the best friend anyone could have.

Finally I should like to acknowledge two more great friends, Phillip Mulleneux and Michael Martin. Their smiling faces I shall always miss greatly.

Apologies for inevitable omissions.

Running with the Moon

A Boy's Own Adventure:
Riding a Motorbike through Africa

Jonny Bealby

'Epic' *Daily Mail*

Jonny Bealby was devasted when his fiancée, Melanie, died unexpectedly while
they were travelling in Kashmir. Two years later and still heartbroken
and utterly disillusioned, he took on the challenge of a lifetime. Setting off
with only his motorbike for company, he began a daring and dangerous
journey around the African continent in a desperate attempt to unearth
some meaning in his life.

A true love story, *Running with the Moon* is a tale of great adventure and courage.

'Bealby handles this tragic tale with endearing honesty and
tenderness. It is the romantic's naivety, not to mention his
irrepressible energy, optimism and courage, which... charm the reader'
Daily Telegraph

'Touching and honest'
Traveller

'An intriguing and... poignant record of one man's journey'
Impact

arrow books

Silk Dreams, Troubled Road

Love and War on the Old Silk Road: On Horseback through
Central Asia

Jonny Bealby

The first time I met Rachel I knew I was in trouble.

Whilst in Islamabad investigating the possibilities of setting up an
adventure travel company, Jonny Bealby met the woman of his
dreams. Not only that, but Rachel was the person with whom he
could *live out* his dream – to travel the Old Silk Road on horseback.
On his return to Pakistan that Christmas, however, Jonny was faced
with those dreadful words: 'I've met somebody else.'

With his heart set on the journey, as well as the possibility of a TV
deal, Jonny set out to find a Quixotic stranger as his companion. In no
time he found Sarah – attractive, warm and funny – the perfect
candidate for a possible romance. Unfortunately, though, during their
search for the Heavenly Horses that would carry them across the
Mountains of Heaven, their fledgling friendship was beset by problems
of communication, inexperience and the difficulty of adapting to
radically different cultures and surroundings.

Not only a stimulating travelogue, Jonny and Sarah's adventure is an
intriguing and heart-warming illustration of human relationships as
they are tested to their limits.

'An absolute page turner... I found myself firing through the
"travelling" passages so that I could get to the latest camp-fire
dust-up... Wonderful descriptions of the Mountains of Heaven
and the ancient city of Samarkand' – *Wanderlust*

'Reads like a cross between Rick Mears' *Extreme Survival* and
Streetmate. An incredible adventure' – *OK! Magazine*

arrow books

Buy *Arrow*

Order further *Arrow* titles from your local
bookshop, or have them delivered direct to
your door by Bookpost

☐ Running with the Moon	0099436655	£7.99
☐ For a Pagan Song	0099436736	£7.99
☐ Silk Dreams, Troubled Road	0099414694	£7.99
☐ The Luck Factor	0099443244	£7.99
☐ My Losing Season	0099468328	£7.99
☐ I didn't Get Where I am Today	009942164X	£7.99

FREE POST AND PACKING
Overseas customers allow £2 per paperback

PHONE: 01624 677237

POST: Random House Books
c/o Bookpost, PO Box 29, Douglas,
Isle of Man IM99 1BQ

FAX: 01624 670923

EMAIL: bookshop@enterprise.net

Cheques (payable to Bookpost) and credit
cards accepted

Prices and availability subject to change without notice
Allow 28 days for delivery
When placing your order, please state if you do not wish to
receive any additional information

www.randomhouse.co.uk